MIND, SELF AND INTERIORITY

Mind, Self and Interiority

THOMAS DUDDY

Avebury

Aldershot • Brookfield USA • Hong Kong • Singapore • Sydney

Published by
Avebury
Ashgate Publishing Limited
Gower House
Croft Road
Aldershot
Hants GU11 3HR
England

Ashgate Publishing Company
Old Post Road
Brookfield
Vermont 05036
USA

British Library Cataloguing in Publication Data

Duddy, Thomas
Mind, Self and Interiority
I. Title
126

ISBN 1 85972 153 2

Library of Congress Catalog Card Number: 95-79271

Printed in Great Britain by Ipswich Book Co. Ltd., Ipswich, Suffolk.

Contents

Acknowledgements

The author and publishers are grateful to Elsevier Science Ltd for permission to include in Chapter 1 substantial sections of an article entitled 'Privacy, self-knowledge, and the inner eye: the Cartesian project revisited' which is due to be published in a forthcoming issue of *History of European Ideas*.

Preface

What is genuinely mysterious is how something made of particles, and which can be looked into with suitable tools and instruments, can have an inside not at all accessible to such tools and instruments, how it can have an inside in a sense quite different from that in which having an inside is also something it shares, if not with particles properly so-called, then at least with things composed of particles.

Alastair Hannay, 1990, p. 183

Introduction

Contemporary philosophers are engaged in a radical revision of the concepts of mind, consciousness, subjectivity, self, self-knowledge, and self-identity. This revisionist approach began with the philosophical behaviourists who denied the existence of souls, minds, and inner selves; the Wittgensteinians followed suit by seriously questioning the ways in which we think about introspection, self-knowledge and inner mental processes; the functionalists, more recently, have denied the existence of a unitary, autonomous self; the eliminative materialists have relegated all mental concepts to the status of an outmoded folk theory which should be replaced by the concepts of the neurosciences; reductionists like Derek Parfit have set out to subvert our belief in self-unity and personal identity; and various post-Freudian, post-structuralist European philosophers have argued that the self is socially constituted, that the ego is illusory or imaginary, an effect of pre-linguistic childhood experience and interpersonal relations. In other words, contemporary philosophers and other thinkers seem no longer to accept that minds, selves, or even persons really exist.

What unites many contemporary philosophers and theorists from other disciplines is their determination to purge philosophy, psychology, and even common sense, of the conceptual legacies of Cartesianism. The philosophy of Descartes, because of its insistence on a dualism of mind and body, is perceived to be the main source of erroneous beliefs about fundamental aspects of human consciousness and identity. Descartes' texts are read as canonical sources of solipsism, introspectionism, scepticism about other minds, and various indefensible notions about privacy, self-knowledge, and personal identity. To defend the concepts of privacy, interiority, subjectivity, self or self-unity, even with due deference to the claims of materialism, is to risk dismissal as a closet Cartesian dualist. This is precisely the risk that I take in the following chapters, the aim of which is to challenge the anti-Cartesian bias of contemporary philosophy of mind, and to show in particular that this bias has inhibited

1

progress towards adequately complex concepts of mind and self. More affirmatively, the book will attempt a reappraisal and reclamation of the concepts of self, subjectivity, and interiority with a view to defending them against not only standard critiques by behaviourists, Wittgensteinians, materialists, eliminativists, and functionalists, but also against the influential critiques offered by European 'theorists of the subject' such as Lacan and Foucault.

The aim is not to defend Descartes on the grounds that his views are correct but on the grounds that too much has been imputed to him, with the result that too many concepts have been found objectionable because they have been interpreted as Cartesian. It will be argued that Wittgensteinians, behaviourists, functionalists, materialists and other anti-Cartesians have been particularly mistaken in assuming that the ideas of self, introspection and 'the inner life' are necessarily or typically Cartesian concepts. It will be suggested that certain conceptions of a subjective mental or inner life are in fact defensible without recourse to a problematic Cartesian dualism; and that what we need is a radically post-Cartesian philosophy of subjectivity which will advocate not a duality of mind and body but a duality of the inner and the outer, of the subjective and the objective, of the first- and third-person perspectives.

The main claim of Chapters 1 and 2 is that many of the arguments marshalled by the behaviourists and Wittgensteinians against introspectionism and against the notion of a private language are more effectively directed at an empiricist epistemology than at a Cartesian psychology. I hope to show that once we appreciate the peculiar methodological nature of the Cartesian project, it makes little sense to regard Descartes as an introspectionist or to regard the Cogito as an incorrigible datum of introspection. Once we realize that introspection and privacy are not the hopelessly Cartesian concepts they are made out to be, we should be able to place them in a new light and consider them for inclusion in a post-Cartesian philosophy of mind.

Among the points made in Chapter 3 and Chapter 4 are (a) that the distinction between the mental and the physical, so often regarded as the original sin of Cartesianism, has been found unavoidable even by contemporary materialists; (b) that the difficulties faced by philosophers of mind have not been created by Cartesianism alone but by the persistence in the language of our era of this fundamental conceptual distinction; (c) that the distinction between the mental and the physical has ethical as much as metaphysical implications in that it enables us to make an important and morally significant distinction between first- and third-person perspectives; (d) that certain conceptions of privacy and introspection are not inconsistent with materialism, and (e) that the only version of materialism which can effectively replace dualism is one which can give an adequately subtle, complex, non-reductionist account of people's 'inner life' consciousness.

2

In Chapter 5 various attempts by functionalists and advocates of Artificial Intelligence to give a reductionist account of the so-called Cartesian ego are found wanting, and are seen to be based on a misconception of the concept of a unified self. I will be suggesting that the concept of a unified or even unitary self is not necessarily unacceptable to materialism. In other words, the concept of a unitary self is not so hopelessly Cartesian as to be philosophically indefensible, and is not at all inconsistent with the belief that the self is fundamentally complex and protean in nature. Nor does the acceptance of such a concept of the self commit us to anything like the idea of a self or soul in the originally Cartesian sense of an independently existing entity. The claim that the self is in some sense indivisible is defended but on strictly non-Cartesian grounds.

Chapter 6 was written in response to the attempt by philosophers, psychoanalysts, and cultural theorists to reduce subjectivity to a 'deep' effect or function of language and cultural practices. While it is acknowledged that this approach is sometimes profound and enlightening it is also argued that it does not seriously challenge the basic, minimalist notion of the first-person subject which is the legacy of Cartesianism. It is suggested that Lacan's claim that the ego is imaginary is based on an over-reaction to, and a misunderstanding of, the Cartesian project, and that Foucault's discovery of 'technologies of the self' does not show that selves are wholly constituted by linguistic or social practices.

It is acknowledged in Chapter 7, the concluding chapter, that Parfit's recent attempt to reinstate a 'bundle theory' of the self has been a significantly serious challenge to the notion of a Cartesian or any other kind of ego. But it is nonetheless claimed that the closer Parfit comes to a complete analysis of the self or person the more objectionable his thesis becomes, especially in the light of Sidney Shoemaker's important 'argument from empirical properties'. The notion of a divided or fragmented self is found to be incoherent, although it is suggested at the same time that this does not rule out the possibility that the self is thoroughly complex and can undergo radical changes. The final section of the chapter deals very critically with the claim made by some literary theorists that modernist literature supports the case of the reductionists in presenting us with images of a fragmented, multiple, discontinuous self.

In short, this book is a critique of the indiscriminate anti-Cartesianism of contemporary philosophy of mind. It is, in particular, a detailed querying of the wisdom of a materialist or reductionist approach which would eliminate the concepts of mind, self and interiority in the name of the elimination of the Cartesian ontology.

1 The case against privacy

It seems undeniable that each of us enjoys a private mental life which is inaccessible to public scrutiny. We like to think of our mental lives - our unexpressed thoughts and feelings - as being profoundly 'innermost', and we suspect that if we were compelled to publicize all our thoughts and feelings we would have a seriously impaired sense of self. If we were subjected to a deeply intrusive technology of surveillance which monitored all our thoughts and psychological states it is arguable that we might fail to acquire a sense of self at all. We imagine that such a technology would be soul-destroying in the measure that it would render impossible the kind of privacy that we associate with having an inner life or even a 'self'. But do we assume too much here? Do we assume too readily that this interior privacy which we cherish so much is an intrinsically valuable feature of our individual natures or identities? Do we even assume too readily that there is in fact such a feature?

It is a remarkable achievement of contemporary philosophy, at least since the publication of Wittgenstein's *Philosophical Investigations*, that it has rendered the concept of privacy highly problematic. Wittgenstein's remarks on mental processes and his rejection of the idea of a 'private language' have been interpreted as an attack not only on the sort of mind-body dualism usually associated with Descartes but also on certain conceptions of privacy, introspection, and self-knowledge which are assumed to originate with Cartesian dualism. Even philosophers who could not be characterized as Wittgensteinians now cheerfully accept that Cartesian dualism generates profoundly unacceptable conceptions of mind, self, and interiority, and that Wittgenstein has done us all a valuable service by rejecting not only Cartesian dualism but also the related and subtler evils of Cartesian privacy, Cartesian self-knowledge, and Cartesian introspectionism. It was Descartes, after all, who argued in favour of a dualism of self and body - who argued that, while it was possible to doubt the existence of the physical world, including his own body, it was not possible to doubt his own existence as a thinking thing, and who argued at the same time that nothing was better known to him than his own mind or self.

In the view of many contemporary philosophers, especially those influenced by Wittgenstein, this sort of Cartesian reasoning leads to what P.M.S. Hacker (1975) has called 'epistemic privacy', i.e., the belief that each thinker's mental states can be known only to himself and cannot be known at all by others. A corollary of such epistemic privacy is scepticism about other minds: if mental states can be known only by the person who has them, it follows that one cannot know anything of the mental states of others. One cannot know what mental states others are having at any particular time, or that they have mental states like mine, or even that they have mental states at all - in which case one could not even properly refer to 'others', since the term implies not merely other beings but other beings with minds like one's own. Is such solipsism the price of privacy? If we accept Wittgenstein's arguments against epistemic privacy, must we surrender our 'intuitive' belief in the existence of an inner mental life? Is our sense of self illusory, the legacy of an objectionable Cartesian dualism? To avoid being solipsists or sceptics about other minds must we rid ourselves of a particular picture we have of ourselves? Must we agree with Anthony Kenny (1989) when he says that 'the self' is a piece of philosopher's nonsense brought about by a grammatical error, a misunderstanding of the reflexive pronoun? To answer these questions we must look more closely at how the Wittgensteinian critique of privacy - and of 'the self' and self-knowledge - came about, and at how it has come to be directed at dualistic conceptions of the person.

The private language argument

In his *Philosophical Investigations*, Wittgenstein explores, questions, and casts aspersions on the notion of a self-taught language that others could not learn or understand, a language so private that it would have not only a private use but also a private semantics. In a much-interpreted passage he writes:

> A human being can encourage himself, give himself orders, obey, blame and punish himself; he can ask himself a question and answer it. We could even imagine human beings who spoke only in monologue; who accompanied their activities by talking to themselves. - An explorer who watched them and listened to their talk might succeed in translating their language into ours. (This would enable him to predict these people's actions correctly, for he also hears them making resolutions and decisions.)

5

But could we also imagine a language in which a person could write down or give vocal expression to his inner experiences - his feelings, moods, and the rest - for his private use? Well, can't we do so in our ordinary language? - But that is not what I mean. The individual words of this language are to refer to what can only be known to the person speaking; to his immediate private sensations. So another person cannot understand the language. (1963, §243)

In these paragraphs Wittgenstein is obviously emphasizing the public nature of all language, including the language of a hypothetical community of individuals who talk to themselves, i.e., soliloquists or monologuists. Even though the soliloquists make a private use of language, their language is public and in principle intelligible to others who care to watch their behaviour and listen to their talk. The soliloquists are human beings, after all, who engage in various public and recognizably human activities and practices into which their private uses of language are interwoven. This common human behaviour constitutes 'the system of reference by means of which we interpret an unknown language' (§206). The soliloquists are not even alien to us in their capacity as soliloquists since we already know what it is like to talk to oneself, or to leave notes for oneself, or to keep a personal diary. We possess, in other words, the concept of a private use of language. A private use of language, however, does not mean that the language itself is essentially private, or that it is privately learnt and privately self-taught. It is private only in the sense that it is not used to address others directly or at all. It is still available to others who might wish to translate it, to learn its grammar and vocabulary, and it is in that sense a public language after all. In the case of the community of soliloquists we are presented with a visible community making a private use of language in a public context, and in such a way that the rules of the language are going to be determinable in principle. As Hacker points out, the soliloquist has a language which is as rule-governed as ours, 'and even if he is quite solitary, his language, though not shared, is sharable' (1975, p. 221). The sort of private language which is ruled out is one which is not teachable to, or learnable by, anyone other than the individual who uses it. The private linguist would be someone who uses words in such a way that no-one else can understand them. Such a language-user could not exist, it is suggested, since the concept of a human language is the concept of a public, rule-governed human activity which is by its very nature teachable to, or learnable by, others.

At this point, however, the private language argument already begins to become contentious, with philosophers taking different positions on its significance and implications. There is disagreement also on the role which the argument plays in Wittgenstein's own later philosophy, and even on what Wittgenstein means by the term 'privately', especially as it is used in the following section:

6

And hence also 'obeying a rule' is a practice. And to *think* one is obeying a rule is not to obey a rule. Hence it is not possible to obey a rule 'privately': otherwise thinking one was obeying a rule would be the same as obeying it. (§202)

Colin McGinn interprets 'privately' to mean 'inwardly', i.e., taking place within the sphere of consciousness, 'in logical independence of behaviour' (1984, p. 47). This interpretation seems consistent with the specific version of the private language argument expressed in §243 since it allows for the conceivability of the solitary but public rule-follower while ruling out the possibility of someone following a rule in his own head. Someone who purports to follow a rule privately and inwardly, or who purports to make the right connection between a symbol and a certain sensation (for, say, the purposes of keeping a very private diary which only he will understand) can concentrate as hard as he likes on a certain sensation every time he writes the chosen symbol, yet no criterion of *correctness* can be applied in such a case. In such a case, whatever is going to *seem* right to the private linguist *is* right. And that, as Wittgenstein says, 'only means that here we can't talk about "right"' (§258). It is only in the context of a public language involving external checks and appeals to public criteria that the practice of obeying or following rules, including rules for the correct use of sensation-words, makes any clear sense. The notion of a private, self-taught, inwardly-referring language which consisted of private acts of naming, private acts of definition, private acts of checking and correcting - in other words, private instances of rule-following - is an entirely obscure if not incoherent one.

Saul Kripke (1982) takes a rather different view. He wishes to emphasize the importance of the concept of agreement within a community of rule-followers. Agreement among the members of a community is a precondition of there being rules at all. Unless there is continued agreement in applying a rule in new cases, the rule will have no meaning. Unless there is agreement in the interpretation of signs and rules, certain marks and sentences will not continue to function as signs and rules. It is not rule-following as such which is fundamental to the establishment of meaning but the practice *by a community* of following a rule. This practice must be a community practice since following a rule implies the possibility of success or failure in interpreting and applying a rule, of making right or wrong moves with regard to the rule. This in turn implies that there exists a community of proficient rule-interpreters who are justified in drawing attention to failures and successes, in checking and correcting learners and novices and anyone else who is wont to make mistakes. The learner is a learner of practices, a rule-follower who is always, as Kripke puts it, 'interacting with a wider community' (p. 89). This suggests that the community's practices constitute the 'justification conditions' for determining whether learners are following some rule or not, or following the correct rule or not. The learner does not have the authority to make this determination herself, to lay down her own justification conditions. This is the point of Wittgenstein's saying that to *think* one is obeying a rule is not to obey a rule. If it is not possible to obey a rule privately, then thinking one was obeying a rule is not the same thing as obeying it. For Kripke, obeying a rule privately means something like obeying a rule in isolation from a community. It does not just mean obeying a rule in one's head or inwardly, as it does for McGinn. The private language argument does, of course, apply to the sort of case identified by McGinn but this is only a special case of the more general point which Wittgenstein has been making about the nature of language, community practices, and rule-following. What Wittgenstein is doing in §243 is simply 'going over the ground again in this special case, marshalling new specific considerations appropriate to it' (1982, p. 3).

But is this right? McGinn insists that the community interpretation is not borne out by a study of the relevant passages in the *Investigations*. Wittgenstein describes rule-following as a practice, but does not say that it is or must be a social practice. Elsewhere he uses words like 'custom' and 'use' but again does not qualify them with 'social' or 'community'. In McGinn's view, he meant only to say that rules must be followed on more than one occasion. Rules must have a regular or repeated use:

> And this is part of Wittgenstein's general thesis that meaning is use: a sign has meaning only in virtue of being (repeatedly) used in a certain way. *This thesis does not in itself carry any suggestion that meaning is inconceivable in social isolation.* (1984, pp. 78-9)

In a very thorough critique of Kripke, G.P. Baker and P.M.S. Hacker also reject the 'community' interpretation. In their view, Wittgenstein's remark that following a rule is a practice has nothing directly to do with social practices. It is meant to emphasize another fact altogether, i.e., the fact that rule-following is an activity, 'a normative regularity of conduct which exhibits one's *Auffassung* of a rule, manifests how one understands a rule' (Baker & Hacker, 1984, p. 16.). Following a rule is a practice in the sense that it is a regular action of a particular kind. It may be - and usually is - a social practice also, but the point of the argument is not to establish this but to show that rule-following, especially in language-learning and language-use, is 'a kind of customary behaviour, a form of *action*, not of thought' (p. 21). The important point is that the foundations of language are not to be grounded in inner acts or private experiences, but in 'normative regularities of conduct'. As with McGinn's interpretation, the position taken by Baker and Hacker seems to accommodate both §243 and §202. It allows for the possibility of a community of soliloquists, each following his own rules, his own practices, whereas Kripke's account does not seem to allow for such a community. If Kripke is right, the

8

soliloquists of §243 cannot be said to follow rules because they are following them privately, and so cannot be coherently said to possess a language at all, since a language is a communally-instituted, communally-sustained, rule-governed practice.

Rather than attempt to resolve the differences between the Kripke faction and the McGinn or Baker and Hacker faction, we should try to state the general implications of the private language argument as non-controversially as possible. We can safely say (i) that the argument denies the possibility of a private language involving internally private acts of sensation-naming or internally private acts of identification and re-identification of internal states; (ii) that it is only in the context of a public language involving external checks and appeals to public criteria that it makes sense to talk such practices as the applying of criteria and standards, or the following of rules, including rules for the correct use of sensation-words; (iii) that the language of sensations - and of 'inner' states generally - cannot be considered a private language in the sense of a language that one learns to apply entirely by oneself to one's own internal states; and (iv) that the language of sensations is learnt, like all other language uses, in the sorts of public contexts and frameworks - 'forms of life' - in which rules are obeyed and in which mistakes can be made and corrected.

This claim - or set of claims - seems to be a reasonable one. It is simply reminding us of the fact that language is essentially public, something learnable and teachable in public contexts.[1] Some interpreters and supporters of Wittgenstein's philosophy have claimed, however, that the private language argument is also an attack on the notion of a private object. They have gone so far as to say that if the language of sensations requires a public framework - is learnt and used in public contexts only - then there is really no sense in talking about private experiences or private aspects of experience. Private experiences or mental states can have no role to play in public language-games. Our sense of having private inner lives is illusory if it leads us to assume that there is something inherently or intrinsically private or subjective about our experiences - about such things as the feelings that accompany our memories of some indescribable or incommunicable (we think) childhood dream. The reason that some Wittgensteinians take this extreme view is that they interpret Wittgenstein as an opponent of dualistic conceptions of the person. The ultimate significance for them of the private language argument consists in its ruling out solipsism ('I can be certain only of my own mind, my own existence') and all those forms of mind-body or self-body dualism on which solipsism is predicated. They assume that there is a close conceptual link between the notion of an immaterial mind and the notion of privacy since only dualists could believe in the existence of a private self or mind which is contingently and problematically related to the public body and its behaviour. But is it the case that there is a conceptual link between dualism and privacy? Is it the case that Descartes, for example, is committed to solipsism, to scepticism about other minds, to the idea of a private

9

language,? Is it the case, conversely, that the concept of an inner, private mental life is indefensible except in terms of a solipsistic Cartesian dualism? The aim of the following sections will be to show that the answer to all these questions is 'no'.

Privacy as the mark of the mental

Anthony Kenny (1966; 1989) has been an influential proponent of the view that Wittgenstein's later philosophy is an attack on what he calls 'Cartesian privacy'. According to Kenny, Descartes' innovation in the philosophy of mind was the substitution of privacy for rationality as 'the mark of the mental' (1966, p. 360).[2] This substitution came about, he suggests, as a result of Descartes' attempting to define the specifically human in terms of consciousness alone. For an earlier philosopher like Thomas Aquinas human beings are distinguished from other animals by virtue of such things as their capacity to understand geometry or their ability to entertain a desire for wealth. The contrast between human and non-human is stated in terms of species-specific functions or faculties rather than in terms of an absolute dualism of consciousness and matter. According to the Thomistic conception, the human self - whose identity becomes a profound issue at death - is not at all reducible to a disembodied mind or intellect. It is the possession of intellect understood in a distinctively functional sense, not the possession of consciousness or awareness understood in a dualistic sense, which distinguishes the living human individual from other things. The typical activities of intellect include understanding, judging, and willing but not sensation or even mental imaging. The activities of intellect are conceivable without the medium of the body but sensation, emotion, and imaging are regarded as inconceivable without a bodily medium in which they can be realized. Disembodied spirits or intellects (which are in a sense not wholly human) do not experience sensations or emotions, and have the capacity neither to imagine nor to remember. Pain - so often discussed as the paradigmatic mental state of modern philosophy of mind - is something necessarily physical in Thomistic psychology, since it can only be experienced in and through the body. For Descartes, by contrast, pain is something purely mental, viz. a *cogitatio* or 'thought', and cannot exist without the mind in which it occurs: 'By the word thought I understand all that of which we are conscious as operating in us. And that is why not alone understanding, willing, imagining, but also feeling, are here the same thing as thought' (AT VIII, 7; CSM I, 222).[3]

When Kenny claims that Descartes substituted privacy for rationality as the mark of the mental, he has in mind the privacy of these Cartesian mental states or 'thoughts'. Cartesian mental states, on this interpretation, are supposed to be private to their owner or subject in the sense that while others can only infer

10

their existence, their owner or subject cannot be unaware of their existence or nature. A Cartesian mind is defined, it seems, by its capacity to have privileged access to, and indubitable knowledge of, its own contents or operations, rather than as that faculty which reasons or contemplates or which animates and 'informs' the body. The definitive mark of the mental thus ceases to be public and becomes bound up with privacy and subjectivity instead, making it natural to think of the mind as being an especially hidden and private realm. Whereas the rationality of an Aristotelian or Thomistic 'rational animal' can be assessed according to public criteria, the phenomenally private mental experiences of a Cartesian thinker cannot. A rational animal's understanding of geometry, for example, is not a specially private activity, since a teacher of geometry may be able to show him that he is quite mistaken about a theorem which he claimed to understand. He has no special authority to pronounce on the presence or absence of understanding in his own case. In matters such as the understanding of geometry one's own sincere statement is not the last possible word. On the other hand, in the case of a Cartesian thinker it appears that no one else can be in a better position than himself to know what sensations or otherwise private thoughts he is having.

It seems that there is a privacy, an interiority, an inscrutability about minds, understood in the Cartesian sense, which renders the contents of such minds inaccessible and uncheckable. Even one's private 'understanding' of a geometrical theorem will remain unassailable and incorrigible as long as it is not made public. To have a Cartesian mind is to have a subjectively inner private life which is not reducible to public, objective, behavioural states of affairs, and which is not accessible, even indirectly, to observation by others. This 'Cartesian' view opens up such a chasm between inner self and outer behaviour that it creates a scandalous problem about other minds. How can I know what others are thinking or feeling - or even know that they think or feel at all - if there are no necessary or natural links between inner process and outer behaviour? How can we even have a language of mental states, of sensations? If sensations and other mental states are so peculiarly 'inner', so private to the person who has them, how can we teach, or be taught, the names of sensations or other psychological states? If I cannot know what psychological states a language-learner is undergoing - if the learner's behaviour is not a natural expression and an adequate criterion of her internal states - then surely I cannot know if the learner ever gets her sensation-words right. If the learner makes a mistake in applying words to objects in the world she can be corrected by others until she gets it right. But in the event of her having purely 'private', inaccessible sensations I would have no opportunity to check and correct and thereby teach the proper use of the appropriate sensation-words. The learner would have to teach herself the use of these words. But how can the learner give herself such private lessons? How can she be a learner and at the same time check that she is getting it right, that the sensation which she now calls pain is the same sensation which she yesterday called pain. It seems that we are allowing for the conceivability of private meanings, private rules of use - namely, a private language. We are allowing for the possibility of a language in which words are intelligible only to their private user and 'refer to what can only be known to the person speaking, to his immediate private sensation' (Wittgenstein, 1963, §243). But we can begin to allow such a possibility only as long as we ignore the implications of what we are claiming. We are ignoring the fact that the meanings of words are, as a rule, settled upon and learnt in public, i.e., in communal, social, interpersonal contexts. We are ignoring the fact that *bona fide* language-learners (and language-users) are always corrigible, i.e., they are always open to being corrected in their uses of words. The learner is a learner of practices, a rule-follower who is always, as Kripke would have it, interacting with a wider community - a community of potential 'teachers' or correctors.

It is Kenny's view that Wittgenstein's private language argument is directed effectively against the egocentric, solipsistic notion of privacy that is implicit in Descartes' texts, that Wittgenstein's private language argument is indeed best understood as a critique of Cartesian dualism and of the solipsism it entails. He expressly sets the Cogito argument and the private language argument in opposition to each other, arguing that 'the referents of the words of Wittgenstein's private language correspond to Descartes' *cogitationes* ' (1966, p. 361). The comparison of the two arguments, viz., the Cogito and private language arguments, is neatly facilitated by the fact that Wittgenstein took the same example - pain - to illustrate his thesis that Descartes had taken to explain the notion of clear and distinct ideas. Given Descartes' dualism of mind and body, the Cartesian *cogitatio* corresponds in the case of pain, for example, to a private sensation disconnected from bodily expression. This leaves Descartes open, it appears, to the charge that he is a solipsist and, implicitly, a believer in private languages. If the mind 'stands in need of no material thing' in the course of enjoying its thoughts, then the language in which it 'articulates' those *cogitationes* must be a private language.

The purportedly Cartesian concept of privacy and self-knowledge is then believed to raise the hypothetical problem of how sensations and other internal states can be named or identified in one's own case. Since sensations can only be known privately, it follows *ex hypothesi* that they can only be named privately, which seems to assume the conceivability of a private language with private rules and a private learning procedure. But since the very notion of a private language, involving private rules and private acts of identification and re-identification, is considered more or less absurd, it follows that there must be something terribly wrong with the original 'Cartesian' assumption that one can only know one's own sensations and that these cannot be known by others. It follows also that there is something very wrong with any philosophy which seeks to define the mental in terms of a very special sort of privacy.

12

But this belief that Descartes is a semantic solipsist, a would-be defender of privacy and private languages, is not as well-founded as its advocates assume. The aim of the following sections is to show that there are no necessary conceptual links between Cartesian dualism and the privacy or incorrigibility thesis; that it is a mistake to 'Cartesianize' privacy in the way that some Wittgensteinians have done; and that the concept of privacy is in fact defensible without recourse to a Cartesian dualism.

The epistemology of person-perception

The private language charge against Descartes would have validity if Descartes had arrived at the Cogito by simply contrasting the certainty of his knowledge of his own thoughts and sensations with the uncertainty of his knowledge of other people's thoughts and sensations. But this is not how Descartes proceeded. He is not more doubtful of his knowledge of other people's sensations than he is of the existence of God or of the existence of material bodies. Indeed, he does not even list other minds and their contents among the things of which we may doubt. We may be tempted here to say that other minds are included under the catch-all of 'the things which may be brought within the sphere of the doubtful' but we should resist this temptation. There is for Descartes no specific problem about other minds, nor about knowing that others are conscious, or in pain, or undergoing any other sensation. Once he has eliminated the possibility of a universal methodic doubt through his discovery of the Cogito, *and* exorcised the spectre of a malignant demon by proving the existence of a non-deceitful God, *and* established that he possesses the God-given means of arriving at the truth, he has no difficulty in recognizing certain 'teachings of nature'. It cannot be doubted, he argues, that in each of the teachings of nature there is some truth. Nature teaches him, for example, that he has a body whose needs are indicated by sensations of pain, hunger, and thirst. These sensations also teach him the 'general lesson' that he is not only lodged in his body as a pilot in a vessel but that he is 'very closely joined, and, as it were, intermingled with it,' such that he seems to compose with it one unit or whole (AT VII, 81; CSM II, 56).

Among the teachings of nature which Descartes might have acknowledged in this context, had he been able to foresee modern criticisms, is that the language of private sensations is 'very closely joined' with outward criteria, with the public expressions of sensations. To make such an acknowledgement would not undermine the substance of Descartes' position but should be quite consistent with it. He could not, of course, make this claim unproblematically. There would remain a serious problem about the nature of the interaction or intermingling of mind and body. How, for example, does body intermingle with mind to produce, say, sensation in one instance, action in another? But

13

despite the difficulties which such a standard question creates for Descartes it is not part of his project to deny that mind and body do in fact interact. If a modern Cartesian were convinced of the merits of Wittgenstein's observations on the conceptual or 'grammatical' relations between inner states, outward criteria and psychological language she would not be embracing an anathema, but rather taking on board a modish variation on the problem of interaction or intermingling. Since Cartesian dualism posits the interaction of mind and body, the distinction between inner process and outward criteria simply translates, within the Cartesian methodological project, into a problem of how the (mental) inner and the (bodily) outer are related. The fact that the 'how' of mind-body intermingling is not adequately explained by the Cartesian dualist does not mean that the dualist is not really an interactionist or interminglist after all - it only means that she is not giving a very good account of what interaction or intermingling is supposed to be. Similarly, the fact that the Cartesian may not be able to offer a good account of the relationship between inner processes and bodily behaviour does not mean that she cannot accept the outwardly criterial status of behaviour in the ascription of psychological language.

The passage in Descartes' texts which can be most revealingly re-interpreted to show that the private language argument is not effectively directed against Descartes is the famous hats-and-coats passage from the Second Meditation. In the course of an argument concerning the nature of perception Descartes makes the point that

> when I look out of the window and see men crossing the square, as I just happen to have done, I normally say that I see the men themselves, just as I say that I see the wax. Yet do I see any more than hats and coats which could conceal automatons? I *judge* that they are men. And so something which I thought I was seeing with my eyes is in fact grasped solely by the faculty of judgement which is in my mind. (AT VII, 32; CSM II, 21)

This passage might seem to suggest that while we have certain knowledge of our own minds or selves, we have only a questionable inferential knowledge of other persons. But if we examine the context of the passage, we see that it is used merely to illustrate a distinction which Descartes has been making between sensory perception and intellectual judgement. He wants to show that knowledge of not only one's mind but also of bodies (such as pieces of wax) is not the achievement of the senses but of the mind or intellect alone. His argument is that a piece of wax is perceived by virtue of the intellect or faculty of judgement, and not by virtue of the senses. The perception of wax 'is a case not of vision or touch or imagination - nor has it ever been, despite previous appearances - but of purely mental scrutiny' (AT VII, 31; CSM II, 21). In other words, in the rationalist Cartesian epistemology, sensory awareness is at most a necessary condition for the acquisition of knowledge of sensible objects

- it is not a sufficient one. Even our knowledge of bodies or material objects is essentially the work of intellect, not of the senses alone, despite the fact that bodies appear to be purely objects of sense. There is, then, no knowledge short of mental scrutiny or intellectual 'grasping'. Things, whether persons or bodies, are not perceived when they are merely sensed but only when they are fully and finally grasped by the intellect. When Descartes uses the term 'perception' he is not using it in the way that an empiricist might use it but in the special rationalist sense of an act of insightful intellectual apprehending or cognizing.[4]

In the Cartesian epistemology, then, perception and judgement cannot be taken to involve the making of inductive or analogical inferences. To perceive in the Cartesian sense is to acquire an intuitive or demonstrable insight into a nature or substance, regardless of whether the nature in question is that of a piece of wax or of a hatted and coated figure in the street. To make an inference from sensible appearance to inner nature would involve placing an empiricistic faith in the senses and in appearances. One of Descartes' *Postulata,* after all, is that his readers should realize how feeble are the reasons that have led them to trust their senses, 'and and how uncertain are all the judgements that they built up on the basis of the senses' (AT VII, 162; CSM II, 115). Descartes' reason for dwelling on the perception of a piece of wax in the hats-and-coats passage is to emphasize that the true perception or cognition of the piece of wax is not an act of sense but an intuition of the mind, an act of understanding. Since this is how all objects are adequately perceived or understood in the Cartesian epistemology it follows that the true perception of human beings will also involve an intuition of the mind, not just an act of sight, touch, or imagination. This Cartesian proposal to regard intellectual apprehension rather than sense-experience as the source of certain knowledge should be sufficient to counter the claim that in Descartes' philosophy other minds or other people's mental states are unknowable. Human beings are at least as intelligible as pieces of wax, and they too are intelligible 'by the faculty of judgement' rather than by the activity of the senses. If one interprets the hats-and-coats passage to mean that Descartes makes an inductive or abstractive leap from figures (a sense datum) to persons (an inference), then one is reading him as an empiricist. But Descartes is not an empiricist. It is *in spite of* what is seen that he perceives/judges other people to be moving about in the street. The senses by themselves are so conceptually uninformative, as it were, that they reveal nothing about the essential natures of things, regardless of whether these things be persons or pieces of wax.

Descartes may, of course, be quite wrong in arguing along these lines, and it may be quite unclear how the senses are involved in the cognitive process, but the point is that there is no evidence in the most pertinent texts to conclusively support the claim that the private language argument has a direct bearing on the Cartesian philosophy of mind. The assumption that Descartes has a particular problem about other minds is mistaken. There is no reason why a Cartesian, on the basis of texts already examined, should not agree with Wittgenstein's dictum that 'the human body is the best picture of the human soul' (1963, p. 178), since this dictum is consistent with the idea that the soul is embodied. Indeed this dictum could be taken as a fitting conclusion to the hats-and-coats passage. Nor is there any reason why Descartes should not agree with Wittgenstein's remark about his hypothetical companion, 'My attitude towards him is an attitude towards a soul. I am not of the *opinion* that he has a soul' (p. 178).

Descartes without introspection

Still, it may be claimed that though Descartes does not explicitly admit a problem about other minds he ought to have done. It is, after all, in the Second Meditation that he declares that there is nothing which is easier for him to know than his mind (AT VII, 34; CSM II, 23). Does not this sort of thinking lead him in the direction of solipsism, of scepticism about minds other than his own? Not if we fully acknowledge the nature of the Cartesian project. The fact that Descartes understands his mind to be more *easily* known than anything else does not mean that other things cannot also be known with certainty. In the Cartesian narrative which leads doubtfully up to the Cogito and then leads away from it recuperatively, there is an increasing acceptance of more and more 'truths' about the mind, about God, and about material things. The fact that some truths, previously doubted, are admitted systematically, if belatedly, to the new canon does not make them any less important. It means only that they are not self-evidently true in the logical manner of the axiomatic truths from which they are derived. The 'ease' with which one knows oneself is analogous to the ease with which one intuits or apprehends self-evident axioms in some deductive system of truths. In the Cartesian system the priority which axiomatically intuited truths like the Cogito have over subsequently derived truths does not mean that these derived truths cannot also be known with certainty. Derived truths are arrived at systematically - and, as it were, with difficulty - but this does not diminish the degree of certainty with which they can be known. If it did, then the whole basis of the methodic Cartesian epistemology would collapse. It is in this methodological sense of 'ease' and 'difficulty' that we should understand Descartes' claim that there is nothing which it is easier for him to know than his mind. His claim should not be understood in terms of introspective intimacy or directness of acquaintance with his inner self. Even when he reiterates in the *Principles* that we know our minds better than our bodies, it is not introspective knowledge of the nature of mind which is referred to but to confirmation of its existence, in the sense that every act of perception of a body, even where it is mistaken, is at the same time

16

a self-evident confirmation of the fact of one's own consciousness and existence as a perceiver. A particular thought, perception or judgement may be false, 'but it cannot be that, when I make this judgement, my mind which is making the judgement does not exist' (AT VII, 9; CSM I, 196). This is just another way of invoking or reiterating the logic of the Cogito, of saying that while one can always entertain doubts about the existence of a particular body, one cannot entertain doubts about the existence of the doubt-filled mind itself. The point is once again a logical or methodological one which has nothing to do with the sort of immediate and serendipitous data that might be generated by an introspectively cognitive inner sense.[5]

An inner-sense account of self-knowledge is unavailable, then, to a systematic foundationalist and rationalist like Descartes who denies the cognitive superiority of sense-experience, regardless of whether such experience is directed inwards or outwards. After mentioning instances of experience which undermined his faith in the senses, Descartes writes:

> And this applied not just to the external senses but to the internal senses as well. For what can be more internal than pain? And yet I had heard that those who had had a leg or an arm amputated sometimes still seemed to feel pain intermittently in the missing part of the body. So even in my own case it was apparently not quite certain that a particular limb was hurting, even if I felt pain in it. (AT VII, 77; CSM II, 53)

Clearly, Descartes has no use for the kind of introspective inner sense that is central to empiricist theories of self-knowledge such as Locke's.[6] His occasional references to the activity of an 'inner eye' does not, any more than his reference to an internal sense, justify an introspectionist interpretation of the Cogito or the Sum res cogitans. One such reference occurs in the Sixth Meditation, in the course of his distinguishing between understanding and imagination, when he claims that he can understand what a chiliagon is without imagining it. Even when he imagines a simpler figure, such as a pentagon, he finds that this act of imagining 'requires a peculiar effort of mind which is not required for understanding' (AT VII, 73; CSM II, 51). This power of imagining is not, he decides, a necessary constituent of the essence of his mind since if he lacked it he would remain the thinking thing which he knows himself to be - i.e., he would continue to possess the capacity to understand.

He seems to confuse the issue in the next paragraph by saying that when the mind understands, 'it in some way turns towards itself and inspects one of the ideas which are within it' (AT VII, 73; CSM II, 51). But the phrase 'in some way' (*quodammodo; en quelque façon*) should alert us to the fact that, for Descartes, this turning towards itself of the mind does not - cannot - take the form of a literally inner seeing of mental objects or concepts. The 'inner eye' reference may be read as a graphic or figurative way of emphasizing the natural ease and completeness with which the mind or intellect is natively disposed to transfer its attention from imaginable objects to unimaginable concepts, i.e., to concepts which do not lend themselves to being visualized, pictured, imagined, or otherwise introspected. The notion of introspection which remains in this account is a long way from anything that might be enjoyed by, say, a Lockean introspector of internal, imagistic ideas.

Descartes must be expected to offer, in the measure that he remains true to his rationalism, a distinctively non-introspectionist account of how self-knowledge is possible. Such an account is in fact already present in his philosophy, in the form of a theory of intuition and deduction, and a theory of innate ideas. Intuition and deduction are, we are told in the *Rules*, the only actions of the intellect by means of which we can arrive at knowledge, including self-knowledge. Intuition is 'the indubitable conception of a clear and attentive mind which proceeds solely from the light of reason' (AT X. 368; CSM I, 14), while deduction is 'the inference of something as following necessarily from some other propositions which are known with certainty' (AT X, 368; CSM I, 15). The Cogito and the Sum res cogitans are exemplary fruits of these two actions of intuition and inference. If our concern is with concept-formation rather than with propositional knowledge, then the Cartesian rationalist will resort to innatism. It is not necessary to go into detail on the usefulness of innatism as a theory of concept-formation, or even to attempt to abstract a coherent version of innatism from Descartes' texts, in order to be able to say that the Cartesian theory can be taken to cover not only ideas of the 'external' world but also ideas of the 'internal' world. In the Third Meditation, for example, he argues that the idea of God is innate in him, 'just as the idea of myself is innate in me' (AT VII, 51; CSM II, 35). In other words, intuition, deduction, and an innatist theory of ideas - and, of course, the theory of clear and distinct perception - will play the sort of role in Descartes' epistemology of self-knowledge that is played in empiricist epistemologies by the concept of introspection. Descartes, in short, is not an introspectionist because he is not an empiricist.[7]

Descartes is engaged primarily in the search for foundational certainties, and should not be mistaken for a latter-day 'qualia freak' or phenomenologist of subjectivity. Consciousness is of interest to Descartes, the discourser on method, only to the extent that it provides him with the founding propositions of his system, viz., the Cogito and the Sum res cogitans. He does not regard consciousness as a ghost in the machine to be studied introspectively but rather as the source of the primary propositional 'givens' in his burgeoning system of certain propositions. The self and consciousness are important only because they constitute privileged points of departure in a systematic struggle against the methodic doubt, not because they are things whose contents can be infallibly introspected. The Cogito is best understood, then, as the conclusive outcome of a process of purportedly universal sceptical reasoning, and not as the record of an act of introspection. It is not an item of psychological, empirical self-

18

knowledge at all, not the outcome of a sensational close encounter with one's self, not a report from the realms of privacy and introspection. Its indubitability makes sense only in the peculiar context of a methodic doubt concerning our knowledge of the existence and essential natures of things. What matters to the Cartesian is the unique logical relation that obtains between the existence of a *cogitatio* and the existence of a methodically doubting *res cogitans* - a relation which only becomes significant in the foundational stages of a system which begins with hyperbolic doubt and aspires to hyperbolic certainty. Such statements as 'I am in pain' or 'I am thinking' have no particular significance if they are offered merely as incidental data, as first-person reports, as items of psychological information. The Cogito itself - especially the Cogito - loses its logical force and point if uttered outside the context of the methodic doubt. (The word 'even' should be deleted from the following statement by Kripke: 'According to Descartes, the one entity of whose existence I may be certain, even in the midst of doubts of the existence of the external world, is myself' (1984, p. 121)). The indubitability of a *cogitatio* does not become an issue until the process of methodic scepticism has begun; and to discuss indubitability apart from such an exceptional process should be as meaningless to a Cartesian as it is to, say, a Wittgensteinian.

Descartes without self-knowledge

Peter Geach reports that in one of his lectures Wittgenstein mentioned Lytton Strachey's imaginative description of Queen Victoria's dying thoughts: 'He expressly repudiated the view that such a description is meaningless because "unverifiable"; it has meaning, he said, but only through its connexion with a wider, public, "language-game" of describing people's thoughts' (1957, p. 3). What is repudiated by Wittgenstein is the idea that our first-person thoughts or utterances are in any sense cognitive, or constitute a form of knowledge, viz., knowledge of the self. He objects to the expression 'I know I am in pain', and tries to limit the use of the term 'know' to cases where uncertainty and doubt are possible: 'It cannot be said of me at all (except perhaps as a joke) that I know I am in pain. What is it supposed to mean - except perhaps that I am in pain' (1963, §246). It would certainly not be appropriate to ask someone how he knows he is in pain, or whether he is certain he is in pain. There is not, it is claimed, a genuine use of the verb 'to know' which could be understood as an expression of certainty in conjunction with first-person present-tense sensation statements. Wittgenstein's point is a typically 'grammatical' one, having to do with the logic or grammar of knowledge-claims:

I can know what someone else is thinking, not what I am thinking. It is correct to say 'I know what you are thinking', and wrong to say 'I know

19

what I am thinking'. (A whole cloud of philosophy condensed into a drop of grammar.) (p. 222)

It is philosopher's nonsense to say such things as 'I know what I am thinking' or 'I know I am in pain' since one normally says 'I know' only in situations where one can also express uncertainty or doubt, or in situations where one can 'find out'. Since there is no question of being uncertain, or believing, suspecting, or finding out that one is in pain, then neither can there be a question of knowing that one is in pain. The expression 'I know' means 'I do not doubt' where doubt is possible; or it may mean 'I am certain' where uncertainty is possible. Whereas it makes sense to say about other people that they doubt whether one is in pain, it does not make sense for one to say it of oneself. The same grammar applies to 'learn'. One cannot be said to learn of one's sensations - one just has them. The whole point of these grammatical reminders is to anticipate the sceptic who would say that sensations are private, that only I can know them in my own case, that others cannot know them with any certainty. Wittgenstein is saying that this sort of claim abuses the grammar of knowledge-claims and that if we are using the term 'to know' as it is normally and rightly used, 'then other people very often know when I am in pain' (§246).

Most of these reminders of the proper grammar of knowledge-claims, and of the logical, grammatical connections between the concepts of knowledge, belief, doubt, and certainty seem correct and no longer controversial. But there is no reason why a Cartesian should not accept the grammar of knowledge-claims suggested by Wittgenstein. The whole point, after all, of Descartes' methodic doubt was to determine how far such doubt could be made to go - or, to put it in terms of knowledge-claims, how much of our common-sense or scientific knowledge is actually demonstrable. What the Cogito reveals is that the existence of the thinking self is beyond doubt - and also, by the same logic, beyond demonstration. The existence of the self becomes clearly and distinctly manifest in the context of the methodic doubt - i.e., it it a logical 'precipitate' of the doubt - but it is not the result of any kind of introspective or otherwise empirical investigation. Certain core facts about the nature of the self are also 'given', in the sense that they are appropriately intuited or apprehended. The intuition or apprehension in question must not be understood in any 'mystical' sense but in a sense appropriate to the sort of status that propositions or judgements have in the early stages of Descartes' intuitionist-deductivist system. It is similar to the kind of intuition one exercises in the course of understanding Euclidean geometry or following a logical argument in which the conclusion is implicit in the premises. It is only in the context of the Cartesian method that, as has already been indicated, we can understand his statement that there is nothing which it is easier for him to know than his own mind. The Cogito and the Sum res cogitans are not empirical facts arrived at by some process of introspective inquiry; rather, they are truths whose self-evidence is intuited in the context of the methodic doubt. It would be a mistake, in other words, to say that these truths are discovered or ascertained, since such terms suggest the end of some inductive process. Descartes has no particular interest in claiming that one can have indubitable knowledge of one's particular mental states. He is interested primarily in the indubitability that a thought systematically acquires in the exceptional context of the methodic doubt. A statement like 'I am in pain' has no particular significance apart from such a context, e.g., if it is offered merely as an item of information. The indubitability of a thought or experience only becomes apparent when it assumes the role of the Cogito after the special process of methodic scepticism has begun.

Since first-person present-tense psychological statements - or avowals - have a significance for the Cartesian only insofar as they can be worked into an axiomatic defence against the methodic doubt, it follows that the apparent peculiarity of such expressions should not worry us unduly, or lead us to imagine that we are turning into 'Cartesian' solipsists. Because philosophers have assumed too readily that there is something terribly Cartesian about avowals, they - including some behaviouristic interpreters of Wittgenstein - have gone to great lengths to analyse them out of existence. Wittgenstein himself seems to argue along behaviouristic lines when he suggests, for example, that words are connected with the natural expressions of sensation and used in their place. When a child hurts himself he cries, whereupon adults teach him exclamations and sentences for the expression of pain: 'They teach the child new pain behaviour' (§244). This expressive or behaviouristic conception of avowals effectively implies that such expressions cannot be bearers of truth-values. Avowals look like assertions but they are not, because their 'assertion' is not based on any kind of observation. They are criterionless and cannot therefore be shown to be true or false. P.M.S. Hacker has launched an effective array of arguments against this 'truth-valueless' thesis (1972, Ch. IX). He argues convincingly that avowals are, in certain contexts, informative and can supply important diagnostic data, even though they are not descriptions of observations, and they may be said to have truth-conditions identical with such third-person assertions as 'He is in pain'. He shows that it is possible to accept that avowals are criterionless, yet informative, without committing oneself to the 'Cartesian' model of introspectionism.

Hacker assumes, however, that there is in fact a Cartesian model of introspectionism which we must be careful to avoid. The purpose of this chapter has been to show that such fear is unwarranted. There is nothing particularly Cartesian or dualistic about avowals or about the idea of self-knowledge. Avowals still retain the peculiarity that they are informative without being based on observation or criteria, but this peculiarity - which will be discussed again in later chapters - is not a pernicious legacy of Cartesian dualism. Avowals, self-knowledge, and inner processes are perfectly defensible by non-Cartesian and post-Cartesian philosophers for the simple reason that these concepts were never particularly Cartesian concepts in the first place. We are perfectly justified in returning to our original hunch that privacy is after all a mark of the mental while at the same time denying that we must be Cartesian dualists. (We may of, course, insist on being Cartesian dualists but the point is that a commitment to privacy does not commit us to such a dualism, nor will it follow from the fact that we are dualists that we are committed to privacy.) Neither do we have to adopt an Inner Eye model of a self-introspective mind in order to maintain a distinction between the private, 'inner' self and the public, 'outer' body. We can appeal to the sort of alternative 'linguistic powers' model suggested by, for example, Richard Rorty (1980). We may accept Rorty's claim that there is no Inner Eye, no Inner Mirror or Glassy Essence - no such process as looking inward at private representations or mental entities which possess ineffable, incommunicable, unsharable phenomenological qualities. We may even give up the notion of privileged access, at least insofar as that notion depends on a picture of access to private entities in a private mental theatre. To give up this Inner Eye model, however, does not mean giving up the concept of privacy. It means only that we should abandon the notion that we possess direct or incorrigible knowledge of something 'by virtue of a special relation to a special kind of object called "mental objects"' (Rorty, 1980, p. 95). Privacy may be considered the mark of the mental in the sense that mental states are those states about which their subjects are normally capable of making incorrigible first-person contemporaneous reports. What makes an internal state mental is not whether it is something that can be experienced in a special way by the person who has it but whether it is something that can be spoken of in a certain way by the one who has it.

To grant that persons have minds is to grant them the power and the right to make incorrigible reports concerning their thoughts, intentions, feelings, and sensations. It is to say that incorrigible knowledge is a matter of linguistic and social practices, in which case we do not need to presuppose that whenever someone makes an incorrigible report she must be experiencing or introspecting some property or 'raw feel' which causes or justifies the report and which only the reporter is then in a position to verify. It is true that only the reporter is in a position to make the incorrigible report, only not because of an ability to introspect an object of some kind, but because of an ability - made possible by language and social practice - to make noninferential reports of a certain kind which are not corrigible by others. This is not to say that first-person reports are incorrigible in some absolute sense. The first-person reporter herself may realize that she has misreported or mischaracterized an internal state, and in that sense first-person reports are effectively corrigible - by the first-person reporter. This, one might say, is a rule of the language-game, and is bound up with the sort of respect that we pay to people who are talking about themselves, about their intentions, dreams, memories, feelings, needs. The point is that to respect

22

another's autonomy is to respect to some significant degree her self-characterizations. This means that self-characterizations are, as a rule, corrigible by the reporter herself, rather than by others, although the comments and behaviour of other people will frequently prompt a change of characterization. The last word remains with the self-describer, however. Other people may try to convince us that we are merely infatuated when we report that we are in love, but they cannot know that they are right unless and until we change our characterization of our feelings. If we continue to believe and to report that we are truly in love, then third parties, insofar as they recognize our autonomy and respect our judgement, will have to take our word for it even while they continue to make knowing prognostications. Such 'knowingness', however, is not the same thing as knowledge.

We may go further than Rorty and insist that if we were to lose this power and this right, or if this power and this right were over-ridden by the use of a technology of cerebroscopes which enabled others to read off all our internal states, we should have to deny that we still possessed minds or inner lives in any familiar or meaningful sense of those terms. Rorty thinks that a culture of totally intrusive surveillance - by cerebroscopes, for example - would not violate us profoundly:

> The secret in the poet's heart remains unknown to the secret police, despite their ability to predict his every thought, utterance, and movement by monitoring the cerebroscope which he must wear day and night. We can know which thoughts pass through a man's mind without understanding them. Our inviolable uniqueness lies in our poetic ability to say unique and obscure things, not in our ability to say obvious things to ourselves alone. (1980, p. 123)

But this is not a consolation to those of us who may not be poets. Ironically, it suggests that in such a high-surveillance culture people could attain privacy only by developing something like a private language, i.e., a language that would be known only to the poet, remaining unintelligible to the secret police (who might in an extreme circumstance constitute the poet's only public). It is against a conception such as this that Wittgenstein's arguments might be profitably directed. If the private language argument is valid, then the escape route proposed by Rorty could not be usefully pursued. The poet can escape the gaze of the secret police only by inventing a language that is wholly obscure or unintelligible to others. The very idea of such a language in such a circumstance is incoherent, if Wittgenstein is right. Moreover, if the poet's internal states and thoughts *are* known to the secret police, then they are known. To suggest that there is further deep-down, hidden, encrypted set of internal meanings which is in some sense inaccessible to the police implies the possibility of a poetic private language. If we are to accept that the private language argument is valid we must reject Rorty's scenario. At the same time we are entitled to argue that privacy (in the special sense of incorrigibility) is indeed the mark of the mental, and that if circumstances were to occur in which the ability to make incorrigible first-person reports was lost or denied - in which others than ourselves became the authorities on our 'innermost' states - then we would no longer know what it meant to say that persons had minds or inner lives, or even what it meant to be a person.

Notes

1. For an account of the private language argument which emphasizes the idea that language cannot be necessarily unteachable, see David Pears (1971, Ch. 8).
2. This synopsis of Kenny's interpretation of Descartes' philosophy of mind is based on his early paper, 'Cartesian Privacy' (1966), and on his more recent work, *The Metaphysics of Mind* (1989).
3. In keeping with current practice, references to Descartes' texts and translations are made by means of the following abbreviations:- AT: Charles Adams & Paul Tannery, eds., (1897-1913); CSM: John Cottingham, Robert Stoothoff & Dugald Murdoch, eds., (1985, 1991).
4. See Bernard Williams (1978, Ch. 8) for a finely detailed analysis of how Descartes perceived pieces of wax and other physical objects. See also John W. Yolton (1984, Ch. 1) on 'perceptual cognition' in Descartes.
5. The claim that mind is better known than the body elicited from Gassendi, in his correspondence with Descartes, the objection that 'your conclusions about the wax merely establish your perception of the existence of your mind and not its nature' (AT VII, 275; CSM II, 191). See Margaret Dauler Wilson (1978, pp. 95-9) for a valuable discussion of Gassendi's objection and Descartes' unconvincing reply.
6. According to Locke, our ideas have two sources, namely external sense and internal sense. In the course of remembering our sensations of external objects we come to notice this internal act of remembering and derive therefrom the idea of memory. Our ideas of perception, thinking, doubting, believing, reasoning, knowing, willing, and other mental processes are formed in the same way, i.e., by the activity of 'internal sense'. See John Locke (1894), Bk. II, Ch. 1, §4.
7. For a comprehensive history and analysis of the concept of introspection see William Lyons (1986). Lyons's account of the development of the concept of introspection deals mainly with the role it has played in empiricist philosophical and psychological theories, from Locke and Hume to William James and Bertrand Russell; and he finds versions of it in the work of contemporary behaviourists, materialists and functionalists,

including B.F. Skinner, D.M. Armstrong, Hilary Putnam and Daniel C. Dennett. Significantly, his discussion of the concept in Descartes is brief and general, and does not undermine the argument developed here.

2 The elimination of the inner process

Although Gilbert Ryle's philosophical behaviourism no longer receives as much attention as it once did, it nevertheless remains one of the most radical attacks on the concept of 'the inner process' that any philosopher has produced. While very few contemporary philosophers would describe themselves as Rylean behaviourists, quite a number would accept that Ryle, for all the shortcomings of his approach, successfully isolated, cordoned off, and exploded the Cartesian Myth. Ryle's contribution to philosophy is of more than just historical importance, however. When Daniel C. Dennett (1991) takes it upon himself to expel the 'central meaner' from the 'Cartesian Theatre' and then sets about replacing the Cartesian Theatre with what he calls a 'Multiple Drafts' model of the consciousness, we are entitled to feel that Ryle's campaign against the Cartesian Myth is still being fought, albeit in appropriately modish terms. Indeed, Dennett rightly places all modern philosophy of mind in a Rylean perspective when he notes that 'ever since Gilbert Ryle's classic attack ... on what he called Descartes' "dogma of the ghost in the machine," dualists have been on the defensive' (1991, p. 33). It is not only dualists, however, who have been put on the defensive. Anyone, including any materialist, who wishes to defend the notion of a self or of an inner mental life must also settle accounts with Ryle.

While there are certain 'family resemblances' between Rylean behaviourism and the Wittgensteinian argument against privacy, Ryle's stance and style are sufficiently distinctive and original to warrant independent analysis. For one thing, his hostility to the putatively Cartesian notion of inner processes is more explicit, unequivocal, and sustained than Wittgenstein's. The challenge, then, is to defend the notion of an inner process against Ryle's cogent philosophical behaviourism - and to do so without being dismissed as a defender of 'the Official Doctrine'. I hope to show that the Cartesian myth is to a large extent a creature of Ryle's particular interpretation of Descartes' philosophy, and that this interpretion has led to the positing of an alternative philosophy of mind which owes its identity - and its inadequacy - to the 'myth of a myth'.

Privileged access: an anti-Cartesian myth

Like some Wittgensteinians, Ryle (1949) assumes that our conceptions of mental privacy, introspection, self-knowledge and inner process are bound to be objectionable because they are essentially dualistic, Cartesian notions. Early in his summary of the Cartesian philosophy of mind, he imputes to it the following claims:

(a) that a person has 'direct knowledge of the best imaginable kind of the workings of his own mind' (p. 13), i.e., his present thinkings, feelings and willings, his perceivings, rememberings and imaginings are all intrinsically 'phosphorescent';

(b) that a person is also able to exercise a special kind of perception - namely inner perception, or introspection - which is immune from illusion, confusion or doubt;

(c) that, on the other hand, no person has direct access to the events of the inner life of another, i.e., he cannot do better than make problematic inferences from the observed behaviour of the other person's body to the states of mind 'which, by analogy from his own conduct he supposes to be signalised by that behaviour' (p. 14).

Imputations (a) and (b), however, are based on the questionable assumption that Cartesianism is predicated on a particular theory of self-reflexive consciousness, in the form of either a self-intimacy or an introspectionist theory of mental states. Ryle's 'infinite regress' argument is directed specifically against such a theory of self-reflexive states. His reasoning is as follows: If the fact that I am conscious of my state of mind is a necessary condition for its being considered a state of consciousness, then each self-reflexive act must itself, in order to qualify as a state of consciousness, be monitored by yet another self-reflexive act. Since this would imply an impossibly infinite regress of self-conscious acts, Ryle argues that there must be some elements of mental processes which are not themselves things we can be conscious of, namely those elements which constitute the supposed outermost states or acts of consciousness. If there is such an outermost sphere of non-self-reflexive states which are still states of consciousness, then self-reflexivity could no longer be retained as part of the definition of the 'mental'. The mind, he concludes, is not characterized by an immediate self-intimating awareness of itself and its states.

But does Descartes need a self-intimacy or 'phosphorescence' thesis along the lines imputed by the Rylean model? Certainly, there are passages in Descartes which invite such a thesis, such as his reply to Arnauld's fourth set of objections, in the course of which he declares:

27

As to the fact that there can be nothing in the mind, is so far as it is a thinking thing, of which it is not aware, this seems to me to be self-evident. For there is nothing that we can understand to be in the mind, regarded in this way, that is not a thought or dependent on a thought. If it were not a thought or dependent on a thought it would not belong to the mind *qua* thinking thing; and we cannot have any thought of which we are not aware at the very moment when it is in us. (AT VII, 246; CSM 171)

We must be careful how we interpret such a passage, however. It can hardly be denied that for Descartes it is a matter of self-evidence that a mind is always conscious of its present contents. But it is worth noting that Descartes does not undertake to say how such content-consciousness is possible. He does not say that it requires an act of introspection, but nor does he explain it in terms of a mechanism of self-intimacy in the Rylean sense. He merely takes it as axiomatic that a thinker, in order to be said to be conscious, or to have a thought, or to be in a particular mental state, must also be said to be conscious of that thought or state. To be conscious of a thought is not necessarily the same thing as being conscious of having a thought - the latter locution may be understood to imply an act of introspective self-awareness while the former need not be so understood. Although Descartes is by no means as clear and distinct here as we might wish him to be, he can be interpreted to mean that 'S is thinking that p' is interchangeable with 'S is aware that p'. The fact that we may still be puzzled by his claim that the mind is always conscious of its contemporaneous mental state(s) does not justify our superimposing on Descartes either a self-intimacy thesis or an introspectionist thesis. We might just as well impose upon him a behaviourist thesis. Indeed, a latter-day Cartesian might seek to clarify his mentor's position by showing that the special relationship between consciousness and mental content (or between thought and thinker) can be established by behaviouristic criteria, such as linguistic criteria. The ability of S to answer questions concerning p could be taken as evidence either that S thinks that p or that S is aware that p. The exercise by S of this ability does not imply the ability of S to introspect in the sense that Ryle attributes to Descartes, nor does it imply some mechanism of self-intimacy or self-luminosity in the sense imputed by Ryle. It implies only that there is a mental state which S has or is aware of. All that Descartes wants to do, arguably, is to establish a conceptual link between conscious states and the state of being conscious. Mental states are modes of consciousness; consciousness consists in current mental states or states of awareness, such that it will be a contradiction to say either 'S thinks that p but is not aware that p', or 'S is aware that p but does not think that p'. This equivalence may not accord with normal usage but in order to make sense of it we do not need to have recourse to a self-intimacy or an introspectionist thesis in the sense that Ryle imputes to Descartes.

The case against (b), the introspectionist imputation, is even stronger than that against the imputed self-intimacy thesis. A claim made in Chapter 1 - that introspection is a concept more appropriate to an empiricist than to a rationalist epistemology - may be iterated here. An empiricist such as Locke (1690; 1959) is perfectly entitled to his inner-sense concept of introspection since it enables him to give a coherently empiricistic account of how people form their ideas of their own mental acts and processes. Inner sense 'introspects' and forms concepts of internal mental states or activities in much the same way as external sense-organs perceive and form concepts of external objects. But it would be inconsistent of a rationalist and an innatist like Descartes to offer a similar account of how our ideas of internal states are formed. Descartes believes that ideas, including the idea of self, are innate, being made present to mind on the occasion of certain experiences - that is, they are not derived or abstracted from experiences. Just as he does not regard perception as a source of ideas about the external world, so he does not regard inner sense as a source of ideas about the mind or self. He does not therefore need the notion of introspection in order to ground his foundational propositions, viz., the Cogito and the Sum res cogitans. Descartes' references to an inner sense must be interpreted in the context of the methodic development of an intuitionist-deductivist epistemology rather than in terms of an empiricistic psychology. To iterate another point made in Chapter 1, Descartes is primarily an epistemologist engaged in the search for foundational truths and certainties, and not at all a latter-day seeker of self-knowledge, or a latter-day phenomenologist or philosopher of psychology seeking an account of the nature of consciousness. He recognizes the existence of inner sense but does not regard it as the source of certain self-knowledge, any more than he regards the external senses as the source of knowledge of the physical world. Once again: the Cartesian self is not the discovery of inner sense; rather, it is the logical posit or 'precipitate' of that exceptional project of pure enquiry, viz., the methodic doubt.

Ryle's third imputation is also based on a questionable reading of Descartes. It assumes that the argument from analogy is the only way in which a Cartesian egoist can justify knowledge of others, and that a Cartesian must assert the absolute certainty of self-knowledge *vis-à-vis* the absolute uncertainty of our knowledge of others. But this is not the case. Descartes is not primarily concerned with either the certainty of self-knowledge or the uncertainty of knowledge of others. I have already argued that the problem of other minds is not a serious problem for Cartesianism; that it has in fact no special significance for Descartes; that the argument from analogy, as a supposed solution to the problem of other minds - 'the making of problematic inferences' - is not contained explicitly or implicitly in Descartes' writings; and that even if that scandalous problem had arisen for Descartes he would have approached it differently, since the argument from analogy, like the problem it was intended ot solve, is more at home in an empiricist than in a rationalist epistemology.

29

The infallible self-knower: another anti-Cartesian myth

Having read Descartes as a self-conscious introspectionist, and having assumed that Descartes' system is based on a theory of self-knowledge, Ryle then proceeds to deny that self-knowledge can be characterized in terms of any kind of privileged access to the 'contents of consciousness', either by means of introspection or some kind of immediate self-awareness. His criticism of the self-intimacy model of consciousness amounts to an attack on the notion of private or privileged access to consciousness. On Ryle's interpretation, the self-luminous model suggests that every conscious individual has immediate acquaintance with, and therefore certain knowledge of, his own mental states or processes. Ryle's objections to this model are very similar to Wittgenstein's and may be summarized as follows: To suppose that my being conscious of my own mental states is identical with knowing them, or that it is the necessary and sufficient ground for my knowing them, is to 'abuse the logic and even the grammar of the verb "to know"' (p. 161). To know, or to be ignorant of, is to know, or not know, that something is the case. One hears a clap of thunder, but one cannot be said to 'know' the clap of thunder; one feels a pain or an emotion, but one does not 'know' one's pain or emotion. It is meaningless, according to Ryle, to speak of knowing in these circumstances. Here Ryle is presenting a variation on Wittgenstein's idea that one cannot properly speak of knowledge at all unless one can also speak of the possibility of doubt or uncertainty. If one claims to know something in a situation where the expression of uncertainty would be meaningless, then one is not making a correct, 'grammatical' use of the verb 'to know'. Statements like 'I know I'm in pain' or 'I know I intend to go home' may have contexts in which they make sense but these would be the exception rather than the rule. In other words, the kind of relation which obtains between oneself and one's conscious states is not a proper cognitive subject-object relation, which means that one cannot sensibly speak of self-knowledge at all insofar as one is talking about the 'contents' of consciousness.

In making these points, however, Ryle is really arguing at cross purposes with Descartes. He is interpreting Descartes in terms of a model which just will not fit down over the Cartesian materials. The subject-object relation as understood and applied by Ryle is essentially an empiricist one and does not reveal a proper appreciation of Descartes' concept of the relation between thought and thinker, between *cogitatio* and *res cogitans*. It is especially wrong to impute to Descartes the claim that conscious states are essentially or necessarily cognitive, as if it were this property which yields the putative certainty of the Cogito. A *cogitatio* is primarily a state of awareness or mental act which may take the form not only of a clear and distinct intuition but also of an obscure and indistinct experience or image. Since some experiences, images, or thoughts can be unclear and indistinct it follows that *cogitationes* are

30

not necessarily or characteristically cognitive. Descartes describes intuition and deduction as the only intellectual activities or procedures by means of which one can attain to knowledge. Intuition is described as being

> not the fluctuating testimony of the senses, nor the misleading judgment that proceeds from the blundering constructions of imagination, but the conception which an unclouded and attentive mind gives us so readily and distinctly that we are wholly freed from doubt about that which we understand. (AT X, 368; CSM I, 14)

This is the case whether the object of understanding is an inner psychological state, a concept or thought, or a material object. Descartes does not say - or need to say - that doubt is impossible in the case of our unsystematic knowledge of our own mental states. Knowledge is what we get when we make a certain kind of effort, primarily when doubt is removed, and then only on condition that the mind is unclouded and attentive. This consideration applies as much to the deliverances of inner sense as it does to the deliverances of external sense. It is not the propositional content of mental states that is relevant, but rather the fact of their existence in the context of the methodic doubt. Someone who is in a mental state - who is 'thinking', in Descartes' broad sense of the term - cannot purport to doubt the fact that he exists and that he thinks. Such thoughts are indubitable, moreover, only in the extraordinary context of the methodic doubt. It is arguable that knowledge and doubt belong to the same language-game for Descartes as much as for Wittgenstein, albeit in different measures. Descartes comes to need the secure foundation of the Cogito only because he has raised the possibility of universal scepticism and has thus let the evil genius out of the bottle. The great doubt of the First Meditation calls forth, elicits, precipitates the great certainty - the Cogito - of the Second Meditation. The source of this great certainty, however, has nothing to do with any infallible deliverances of inner sense, or with the supposedly self-intimating nature of mental states, but with the logical fact that one's thinking implies one's existence in the context of the methodic doubt. What makes this difficult to see is the fact that Descartes is not in any sense an empiricist, either with regard to external sense or internal sense, and his conception of knowledge, including self-knowledge, is very different from that of an empiricist.

Ryle's questionable account of Descartes' concepts of consciousness and self-awareness may owe something to Descartes' claim that any kind of thought or conscious state can take the form of the Cogito. But it does not follow from the fact that 'I think' can be replaced by 'I doubt' or 'I am deceived' or 'I imagine' that every conscious state somehow involves a continual reiteration of the Cogito. In Descartes' philosophy the very fact that one thinks, regardless of what one thinks, will enable one to resist hyperbolic doubts about the fact or basic nature of one's existence, but it does not follow that such resistance is a perpetual state or activity of mind. It does not follow that one is always in a state of hyperbolic self-assurance, a constant mental pinching of oneself. The certainty of one's own existence as a thinking thing is a methodic certainty that makes sense only in the extraordinary context of the methodic doubt; it is not a real, constantly recurring feature of actual psychological states. In reality, therefore, it is perfectly acceptable to Descartes that a person might engage in mental activity without being self-conscious in the sense in which the Cogito posits self-consciousness, i.e., in the sense of a methodically self-positing self-consciousness. Consciousness in the special Cartesian sense implies a capacity to think the Cogito formally in the face of philosophical doubt but does not imply the endless, moment-by-moment iteration of the Cogito. The Cogito itself is not an act of self-consciousness in the conventional sense of that term - it is primarily a methodic intuition, inference or 'performance' situated in the foundational stages of a burgeoning system of certain propositions.[1]

Even if we retain a conventional conception of self-consciousness or self-knowledge, it is still possible, as William Lyons has shown, to argue that Ryle's interpretation of Descartes is mistaken here. Lyons first examines Ryle's assertion that the Cartesian account of self-consciousness amounts to a claim that mental activities give off a 'fluorescence' or 'refulgence' such that the mind cannot help being aware of itself and its contents. There may be doctrinaire Cartesians, according to Lyons, who hold that we are always in fact self-consciously and infallibly aware of our mental activities - and infallibly aware of their true nature - but a Cartesian need not, he believes, hold such immoderate views. A moderate Cartesian could hold that mental events are phosphorescently or fluorescently noticeable in principle, though not necessarily in practice, and yet hold that not only are we not conscious of them some times but that, even when we are, we can be mistaken about them. A Cartesian could quite easily hold, without contradiction, that we can in principle be aware of most mental states, but be mistaken about them from time to time in at least two different ways: 'We can notice them but generate false beliefs about them, and we can notice them and generate true beliefs about them, but make errors when reporting on them' (Lyons, 1980, p. 93). The moderate Cartesian will also be untroubled by Ryle's regress argument whereby it was suggested that if a mental event 'fluoresces' and is automatically noticed then this noticing must itself be a second-order mental event which in turn must automatically ensure that it is noticed, and so on. The moderate Cartesian escapes this criticism by simply denying that mental events are automatically or invariably and infallibly noticed, since Ryle's counter-arguments depend on pointing out the implausibility of 'invariably noticing first-level fluorescing' (p. 94).

Lyons also defends a 'Cartesian' notion of introspection against Ryle, although it is has been argued above that such a notion is not central to Descartes' philosophy and should not therefore be dismissed as Cartesian. Ryle argues that the Cartesian account of introspection must be wrong because,

32

while entailing that every mental event is introspectible, it also entails that a person's mental capacity to introspect is either finite or infinite. But such a conception of the mental capacity to introspect is untenable. If the capacity to introspect is finite, then the Cartesian must admit that beyond the limit of his introspective powers there are non-introspectible mental happenings. If infinite, the Cartesian is forced to admit that humans have at least one infinite capacity. To this argument, in Lyons's view, a Cartesian could reply that his position is not that there are no particular mental events which cannot be introspected but that no type of conscious state as such is immune from introspection. Conscious states are introspectible but not necessarily introspected.

The Cartesian, in sum, need not concede all ground but simply retreat to the position that only some inner states are conscious, that only in certain circumstances are some inner states open to introspection or inwardly-directed attention, and that, even when they are, we can be mistaken about them. While the views of Lyons outlined above are not entirely in accordance with the view of Descartes being developed here they nevertheless show, from another perspective, the extent to which Ryle has based his own concepts of self, interiority and self-knowledge on a tendentious reading of Descartes. It will be argued in the forthcoming sections that the alternative concept of mind proposed by Ryle runs into difficulties which are no less serious than those imputed to Descartes' - difficulties which Ryle brings upon himself because of his construal of the Cartesian concepts of consciousness and 'privileged access'.

The hypothetical other

Ryle's behaviouristic concepts of mind, self and the inner life may be summed up in the following theses:-

(1) The so-called inner life of the self, as defined traditionally in the language of mental predicates, is nothing more or less than a range of behavioural dispositions - that is, the mind or inner life is not the topic of untestable categorical propositions but the topic of testable hypothetical propositions.

(2) Avowals, or first-person, present-tense psychological statements, are not indicative or narrative propositions about the activities or states of a mind or self but rather constitute a kind of expressive verbal behaviour.

(3) There is no essential difference between the ways we acquire knowledge of ourselves and the ways we acquire knowledge of others, except that the method of acquiring self-knowledge may be called retrospection, where this signifies a form of self-observation or reflection on one's own behaviour.

(4) The kind of awareness one has when one is said to 'know what one is doing' may be understood in the short-term dispositional sense of being prepared for the next step in a serial action.

Knowledge of mind, in Ryle's view, means chiefly knowledge of character, personality, and intellect. By these, in turn, he means those sets of dispositions, tendencies, liabilities and potentialities which may be attributed to an individual either by himself or by others on the basis of the observation of overt behaviour. Ryle denies that this process involves the making of inferences from behaviour to some essentially inscrutable self which initiates and controls that behaviour. He argues instead that the assessment of a person's (including one's own) mental capacities and propensities is an inductive process, involving the subsumption of behaviour under law-like propositions, i. e., 'an induction to law-like propositions from observed actions and reactions' (p. 172). In other words, there are no self-intimating conscious states or privately introspectible mental acts to which mental terms refer; there is no inner, substantially spiritual self which they characterize or describe. Those terms which seem to be predicable of an inner self are really dispositional concepts which are used properly to explain and predict overt behaviour, especially to make hypothetical-type statements about it. Terms like believing, attending, expecting, and contemplating do not denote the acts of a mind or self but rather serve to define or isolate dispositions to behave in certain ways. Items of behaviour are not merely signs that individuals are in certain mental states but constitute the putative mental state: 'the styles and procedures of people's activities *are* the ways their minds work' (p. 58). The statement 'A believes in God' looks like a categorical statement about a mental process - i. e., a process taking place in someone's subjective psychological life - but what we really have, if we ignore the misleading surface grammar, is a disguised hypothetical statement which explains the nature and predicts the course of someone's overt behaviour in relation to certain social practices. Thus the mind, self, or person, in the final analysis, 'is not the topic of sets of untestable categorical statements but the topic of sets of testable hypothetical and semi-hypothetical propositions' (p. 46). In appearing to talk about mental processes we are really talking about behavioural dispositions; in appearing to make categorical judgements about minds we are really making hypothetical statements about behaviour. To ascribe a disposition or power is to say no more than that it is possible or probable, on the basis of observation, that an individual will perform a determinable range of actions if certain conditions are satisfied. The disposition is reduced in some sense to the conditional, hypothetical responses of an agent. Ryle says, for example that

> To possess a dispositional property is not to be in a particular state, or to undergo a particular change; it is to be bound or liable to be in a particular state, or to undergo a particular change, when a particular condition is realised. (p. 43)

It seems to be Ryle's view that dispositional terms do not refer to physical states as such. His objective, after all, is to show that mental terms do not refer to mental acts, events, or states, or *other* inner causes. He would hardly have achieved this objective if he translated mental terms into dispositional terms and then allowed the latter to refer to any sort of actual internal states. We may take it that categorical statements containing dispositional terms are wholly reducible to hypothetical propositions about actual behaviour, i.e., propositions to the effect that an individual will, on the basis of observation of his past or present behaviour, behave in a certain way if certain conditions obtain. If this is so, however, then it is arguable that Ryle has created for himself a problem about our knowledge of other minds or other persons. It is arguable, indeed, that his non-realist, reductionist, 'operationalist' account of dispositions leads to the same kind of scepticism about other persons as did the traditional 'argument from analogy' which he is so anxious to avoid.

The classical objection to the so-called argument from analogy is that it puts our knowledge of others on a purely inferential basis. According to the argument, we cannot have direct or certain knowledge of other minds but must make do with analogical inferences. That is, I observe certain connections in my own case between my inner states and my public behaviour, and, assuming that others have minds and bodies like myself - and this can only be an assumption - I can infer mental states similar to my own from behaviour similar to my own. But since there is, at least from the putatively Cartesian point of view, only a contingent relation between bodily behaviour and mind, we can never be certain that our inferences are right. It is therefore logically possible to doubt that we ever really know other people's minds, or even be sure that they have minds. This is the 'scandalous' consequence of accepting the argument from analogy as an account of how we acquire knowledge of other minds.

Ryle's view, however, has similar consequences because he translates mental concepts into dispositional terms which are in turn analysed into open hypothetical statements about behaviour. His thesis, we must remember, is that both self-knowledge and our knowledge of others consist in inductions to law-like or hypothetical propositions. Arguably, Ryle's inductions are no less problematic than the 'problematic inferences' of the mythical Cartesian or solipsist. Inductive generalisations or hypotheses will not enable us to account for the sorts of conclusive judgements we make about others or, for that matter, oneself. Ryle, like the mythical Cartesian, fails to account for what Wittgenstein calls 'the certainty [that] resides in the nature of the language-game' (1969, §454). The mythical Cartesian puts our knowledge of others on a problematic inferential basis, much to Ryle's disapproval. But Ryle himself puts the whole of personal knowledge on an equally problematic hypothetical basis. According to neither the 'Cartesian' nor the Rylean view are we entitled to make certain categorical statements about others. Both views run counter to our everyday usage of mental terms and fail to account for the nature of interpersonal

35

knowledge. In the course of human interaction we make a range of judgements about personality, rationality, intelligence, and character which are categorical rather than hypothetical. This does not mean that we cannot be wrong, since there is nothing essentially untestable about categorical judgements. What it does mean is that, when we are wrong, it is not because a hypothetical proposition has been falsified, but rather that we have been deceived, or deceived ourselves, or made a rash judgement, and now a new judgement forces itself upon us. The most revealing situation is one in which we are obliged to make a new judgement without having to acknowledge that our earlier judgement was false. An individual of whom it was last year true to say 'He believes in God' may undergo a change of mind to the extent that it is now true to say 'He does not believe in God'. The original judgement does not go the way of a falsified hypothesis - its truth (for the past) remains intact. Hypotheses are not suitable in circumstances in which unforeseen changes in behaviour and attitude do not signify inadequate prediction on the part of the observer but rather signify changes of mind on the part of the observed.[2]

A case can be made for saying that in the interactive process of 'getting to know' ourselves and others we are concerned more with ascriptive or descriptive uses of concepts than with induction to law-like hypothetical propositions. Our concepts of persons are developed, not in ways analogous to abstraction from inductive observations, but more in ways analogous to the gradual stroke-by-stroke completion of portraits (of friends), sketches (of acquaintances), and caricatures (of enemies), where rightness and wrongness may have connotations of justice and injustice as well as truth and falsity. Persons are rendered intelligible through the characterizations, descriptions, classifications and judgements of others. This will include reference to abilities, propensities and dispositions but these terms are normally understood in a 'personal' rather that in a behavioural sense, i.e., as features of persons rather than of their behaviour.

Lyons has suggested that Ryle's account of dispositions is in any case ambiguous as to what sort of account it is. He argues that if Ryle's account is understood as a semantic one, then it is acceptable. It is a reasonable account of 'X has a disposition Y' to say that this means 'whenever circumstances C occur, X will do Y or a variety of things M, N, O and P which could be said to be of type Y'. But if Ryle's account is also meant to be a 'genetic' account of dispositions - that is, an explanation of what they are ontologically - then, in Lyons's view, it is inadequate. A semantic account of dispositions neglects the causal processes in which dispositions are, as it were, grounded. A proper account of what dispositions are and how they work should alert us to the fact that there must be some categorical factor at work:

> The true genetic account of dispositions makes it clear that dispositions are not just potentialities. They are potentialities based on the existence of real

factors. Thus, [the] causal factor, which lies dormant or is presumed to be lying dormant in the person or thing to which a disposition has been attributed, is often called the structural or categorical basis of the disposition, because it will often turn out to be a structural property of the thing to which the disposition is attributed, and because to refer to an actual property is to refer categorically rather than hypothetically. (1980, p. 51)

Lyons effectively places Ryle in a dilemma. If Ryle opts for a semantic account only, then all his explanations will be pseudo-explanations, since they involve no reference to causes. Dispositions will be attributed only to behaviour and not to persons, as if there were no causal connections between the person to whom the disposition is attributed and the behaviour which exhibits it. This is in keeping with Ryle's determination to avoid reference to 'any hidden internal causes', for a disposition is 'neither a witnessable nor an unwitnessable act' (p. 33) - it is not an act at all. A disposition, in Ryle's account, 'is a factor of the wrong logical type to be seen or unseen, recorded or unrecorded' (p. 33). The price of this ontological purity is, as we have seen, an explanatory poverty. On the other hand, if Ryle were to opt for a more complex account in which there *is* reference to a structural basis, then he would be obliged to concede the existence of 'something inner'. Lyons concludes that Ryle's account will not do in any case as a genetic account 'and so will not do the Occamist dirty work he asks of it' (1980, p. 50).

Language, self-testimony, and the problem of autonomy

In his conception of language, and despite his credentials as a logical or philosophical behaviourist, Ryle finds himself behind the banner of those scientific behaviourists who thrive on making extrapolations from animal to human behaviour. In order for these behaviourists to make their extrapolations pertinent to the scientific study of human behaviour, it has been necessary for them to minimize the specific difference of human language. Due to the fact that vocal sounds play a rather small part in the behavioural responses of animals, behaviourists cannot afford to consider language an absolutely distinct or autonomous source of information. If discoveries based on the study of animals are to have any explanatory value in human psychology it is necessary to 'demystify' the phenomenon of human speech. This demystification has been carried out by regarding speech not as an irreducible alternative to behaviour, but as a subtle form of behaviour consisting in the arrangement of sounds rather than of bodily parts. Speech remains a major source of information only because it happens to present a greater concentration of significant variables than the grosser movements of the body. Thus language becomes, in Ryle's own words, 'one tract of human behaviour on which we pre-eminently rely for our knowledge of ourselves and others' (p. 181). This does not mean that people volunteer privileged information about themselves, but that they inadvertently reveal, disclose, or 'betray' things about themselves in their unstudied talk. Though people may be wary of doing this in certain circumstances, nevertheless, according to Ryle, the natural and normal thing to do is to speak one's mind, while the abnormal and sophisticated thing is to refrain from doing so: 'We have to take special pains to keep things back, because letting them out is our normal response' (p. 181).[3] Normal unstudied utterances, therefore, constitute 'our primary evidence for making self-comments' (p. 183) or for making comments about others. These utterances themselves do not *per se* contain information, nor do they constitute information - they may simply be construed as evidence for the presence of a certain disposition or set of dispositions. Phrases such as 'I want' or 'I hope' or 'I wonder' serve to introduce avowals or expressions of feelings or inclination, but they do not report or describe any inner happenings or processes.

Ryle does not offer a clear line of demarcation between behaviourally expressive utterances on the one hand and narrative, reportive, or descriptive utterances on the other. It is not even clear whether all utterances, not just avowals, are in some sense forms of vocal or verbal behaviour. Even mathematical formulae may be spoken in such tones of voice as might be evidence of anything from boredom to rage. If an avowal is no more intrinsically informative than a spoken formula, then there is no clear basis for the distinction which Ryle presumes to exist between expressive and narrative statements. In fact, the distinction may even be an untenable one. A statement with an informative content may be spoken very expressively - for example, through clenched teeth - to an inattentive student. Conversely, a statement in the form of an avowal may be spoken inexpressively - for example, by someone learning a language. The statement 'I feel very angry', if spoken out of context and dispassionately, would be less expressive than the formula $e=mc^2$ spoken in anger. The expressiveness resides in the mode and context of utterance rather than in the syntax or semantics of the uttered sentence. There are, it would seem, no strictly linguistic criteria which would serve to demarcate a clear-cut essential difference between subjective avowals and other more 'objectively' informative utterances. The scientist reporting a reading and an agent declaring her intention are alike in using vocal sounds which are either syntactically and semantically correct or incorrect, and which, if they constitute certain kinds of sentences, are either true or false. If a sentence is one which can be shown to be true or false, regardless of its mode of utterance, then it can be taken to be more than mere expressive vocal behaviour. As linguistic utterances, avowals have more in common with other sentences or other linguistic acts than they have with expressive vocal behaviour such as cries and shouts.

One way of bringing out this contrast between meaningful speech-acts and expressive vocal behaviour is by noting the difference between sign-language and expressive behaviour. Sign-language has meaning in virtue of its status as a language and not in virtue of its being behaviourally expressive. The user of sign-language who painfully moves his hands to say 'My arms are aching' is doing more than behaviourally expressing his pain - he is also *stating the fact* that his arms are aching. When he drops his arms to massage one with the other he is no longer moving them symbolically, or according to rules, or to state anything. Likewise, the person who uses his vocal chords to say that he has a pain is doing more than groaning elaborately - he is stating or articulating a fact about himself.

Of course, expressive behaviour often depends for its expressiveness on the utterances which accompany it, while utterances often depend for their complete meaning and veracity on the behaviour which accompanies them. There is a sense, however, in which any utterance, *qua* utterance, is essentially distinguishable from any form of behaviour, *qua* behaviour. It can hardly be denied that avowals belong to language. As speech-acts they are not correctly described as behaviour.[4] Neither can it be denied that, as Hampshire puts it, 'an avowal may be false and may be discovered to be a lie or a misdescription by a careful collection of evidence' (1972, p. 105). A piece of behaviour may also, of course, be misleading or deceitful, but only in the sense that any apparent piece of evidence may be said to lead one to make a wrong judgement. There are no good grounds for depriving avowals of the status of indicative, informative statements, although they may also play the kind of 'performative' roles identified by Austin.[5]

Ryle himself, in his essay 'Phenomenology vs. *The Concept of Mind*', published thirteen years after the book, admits that his 'assimilation of avowals to ejaculations or complaints will not do' (1971, pp. 195-6). While he still maintains that 'in avowing my depression I speak not as an angelically well-situated reporter on my depression but simply as a depressed person' (p. 195) he nonetheless acknowledges:

> An avowal may be a reply to a question; it may even be meant to provide a doctor or an oculist with information that he requires for his diagnosis. If I say 'I have a shooting pain in my eyes,' while I may be complaining, I am also reporting. Avowals seem then to be like reports, and yet not to be reports of anything discovered or established; to merit being received as incontestable, and yet not to issue from any kind of certitude on the part of the authors. (p. 196)

This admission, however, presents Ryle with the difficulty of how to account for avowals in his scheme of things. If they are genuine reports, it must be possible for them to be true or false. If so, it should be possible to verify them, in which case it should make sense to consider each subjective 'reporter' the best and sometimes the only authority in his or her own case. This line of argument is precisely what Ryle wants to avoid, since it suggests (to him) that people have privileged access to their own subjective states. While he proceeds to acknowledge that his concession on avowals obliges him to re-consider his position on privacy and consciousness, he is still insistent that self-knowledge is a matter of induction to open hypothetical propositions, and that subjective experiences are not things that one can know. Others may 'believe or know that I am in pain but I just have the pain - and the words for it' (p. 195).

This is right, of course. If knowledge is a matter of reasons and evidence, and I do not, strictly speaking, have reasons or evidence for saying that I am in pain, then an avowal of pain is not a datum of self-knowledge. Even if I could be said to know that I have a pain, an avowal to that effect would hardly constitute an increment in self-knowledge. Neither would declarations of intention or expressions of hope constitute increments in self-knowledge. Such an increment would only occur, for example, if I was told, or realized it myself, that I have a disposition to complain too much or tend to declare intentions which I seldom carry out. Such facts, however, are as much the concern of others as myself, both in the sense that it is other people who are the objects of my plaintiveness or absent-mindedness, and also other people who are in a position to judge my behaviour, to determine its significance for *them*. Insofar as I am the 'author' of my behaviour I am no more in a position to judge its significance for others than an author presenting his work to the public. Insofar as I am the source or author of my behaviour I cannot be outside it, judging it. This is even more so in the case of feelings or emotions.[6] The significance of my having certain feelings or emotions may elude me if I fail to communicate them to others, since even emotion-concepts, as Errol Bedford has suggested, are not purely psychological: 'they presuppose concepts of social relationships and institutions, and concepts belonging to systems of judgement, moral, aesthetic, and legal' (1964, p. 98).

Nevertheless, one's reports of one's subjective life are not to be construed as merely circumstantial evidence for the hypothetical propositions of others, as if one were nothing more than a problematic object for others. If we are to account for a being's status as a subject and a person we must credit her or him with what Malcolm (1964) calls 'an autonomous status', i.e., we must maintain a distinction between the first-person and third-person perspectives, between self-testimony and behavioural observation, even to the point of saying that self-testimony is one of the most essentially human uses of language. That is, we must grant that some non-trivial truths about a person cannot be inferred from the third-person scrutiny of her behaviour (no matter how thorough) but must be volunteered by her in first-personal terms. That we can do this, without at the same time holding that self-testimony is based on introspective observation, will be argued later. In the meantime, it is enough to have argued that, under

40

normal conditions at least, a person has a fundamental *say* in the story of her own psychological life. She does not have the only say, as the solipsist or mythical Cartesian might argue, but neither do others have the only say in the determination of her subjectivity or the contents of her mind.

Self-acquaintance and self-observation

Given Ryle's view that mind is not something autonomous that we can refer to but simply a collective term for a plethora of behavioural dispositions, it follows for him that all questions about the relationship between a person's behaviour and his mind are meaningless. A person's mind is not part of her, much less identical with her. The problem of self-knowledge is therefore not reducible to such questions as 'What knowledge can a person get of the workings of her own mind?' or 'How does she acquire this knowledge?' These are impossible questions which suggest that an individual somehow looks into 'a windowless chamber' to which only she has privileged access. Equally absurd, then, is the question of how I can get to know the workings of another mind. Ryle, of course, acknowledges that the problems of self-knowledge and knowledge of others are genuine problems but maintains that they are reducible to 'the methodological question of how we establish and how we apply certain sorts of law-like propositions about the overt and silent behaviour of persons' (1949, p. 169). He will not accept any significant difference between one's own situation and that of others. The problem is not, on his analysis, a two-fold one concerning self-knowledge and knowledge of others but rather a single problem concerning knowledge of persons. In one of the most remarkable but exemplary applications of his theory in this context he writes:

> I learn that a pupil of mine is lazy, ambitious, and witty by following his work, noticing his excuses, listening to his conversations and comparing his performances with those of others. Nor does it make any important difference if I myself happen to be that pupil. I can indeed listen to more of his conversations, as I am the addressee of his unspoken soliloquies; I notice more of his excuses as I am never absent when they are made. On the other hand, my comparison of his performances with those of others is more difficult, since the examiner is himself taking the examination, which makes neutrality hard to preserve and precludes the demeanour of the candidate from being in good view. (p. 169)

We are not faced any longer, it seems, with the traditionally abstract, general question of how I come to know my own mind and the minds of others, but with a range of specific questions such as: 'How do I discover that I am more unselfish than you?' or 'How do I decide that I am more easily irritated than

41

most people but less subject to panic?' 'How do I find out that your action took more courage than mine?' Ryle insists that questions of this sort are no mysteries, that we have no doubt about what kinds of information would satisfy our requirements - though we may not be always in a position to carry out the necessary tests. His main argument is that the same kinds of tests apply in one's own case as in someone else's. At one point he puts forward what looks like a verificationist theory of the meaning of statements which ascribe mental predicates: 'It is part of the *meaning* of "you understand it" that you could have done so-and-so, and would have done it if such-and-such; and the *test* of whether you understand it is a range of performances satisfying the apodoses of these general hypothetical statements' (1949, p. 170). The important point is that these tests apply not only to others but to oneself also. For example, in order to ascertain whether or not I am creative in some area of activity it is not enough for me to look into my own soul, as it were - I have to subject myself to certain public tests of a formal or informal sort. Of course, there are numerous qualities of intellect, personality, and character which cannot be explicitly tested for. Nevertheless, I discover my own or another's qualities in much the same way, through the observation of conduct in public or (in one's own case) in private. In one's own case this will mean judging one's own conduct in retrospection or catching oneself doing something which one suddenly realizes to be, say, vain, envious, or shameful. In short, the ascertainment of a person's (including one's own) mental capacities and propensities is an inductive process, 'an induction to law-like propositions from observed actions and reactions' (1949, p. 172). This inductive process, however, operates outwardly and not inwardly. It is not carried out through introspection, which would imply that one had some sort of privileged access to one's own consciousness.

Ryle's alternative to introspection is what he calls retrospection, which he regards as 'a genuine process and one which is exempt from the troubles ensuing from the assumption of multiply divided attention' (1949, p. 166).[7] Moreover, there is nothing intrinsically 'mental' about the objects of retrospection. In the same way that I can catch myself engaged in a piece of 'silent soliloquy', I can also catch myself saying something aloud. The objects of retrospection are necessarily elements of my autobiography, but they will equally be overt actions as well as sensations and emotions, or calculations done on paper as well as calculations done in the head. Most significant of all for Ryle is the fact that a retrospective theory of self-knowledge precludes us from holding that we have infallible sources of knowledge about our own minds, because 'even prompt recollection is subject both to evaporation and to dilutions', and no matter how vividly I recollect an action or feeling I may fail to identify its nature: 'Chronicles are not explanatory of what they record' (1949, p. 167).

Ryle does not elaborate on how the concept of retrospection relates to the concept of self-observation. Since he argues in favour of the idea that we can and do observe our own behaviour, he cannot be interpreted as simply eliminating the concept of self-observation and replacing it with that of retrospection. He appears to be faced with two possible conceptions of the relationship between self-observation and retrospection. He may hold (a) that retrospection is a form of self-observation; or (b) that it is a privileged form of recollection which does not require prior self-observation and is a kind of substitute for it. Alternative (b) would be clearly unacceptable to Ryle, since this would give a unique character to self-knowledge by implying that it is non-observational. We should remember that his objective is to make self-knowledge as much a matter of observation as knowledge of others. This leaves us with the thesis that retrospection is a form of self-observation. But just how useful is this conception of retrospection to Ryle? Does it not perhaps attract some of the same difficulties that attend the much-maligned notion of introspection? Is the claim that retrospection is a form of self-observation even very plausible?

It is true in a general sort of way that the significance of certain actions and experiences is sometimes realized only 'on retrospection'. Psychoanalytic theory could be said to be based on the premise that our understanding of the past (and subsequently of the present) can be altered through controlled recollection and reflection. Similarly, reflection on historical events often enables us to make new observations about the nature of certain institutions and practices. But this type of retrospective analysis is not to be understood as a primary mode of observation or as some kind of substitute for observation. If we have anything more than a metaphoric use of the term 'observation' it is, at most, in the sense of a secondary or a derivative mode of observation. Retrospection, like memory or reflection, has to be a function of foregoing observations or experiences which are subsequently remembered and reflected on. We cannot recollect, reflect on, or otherwise 'retrospect' what we were not previously conscious of or acquainted with in some way. Retrospection is, we may say, a secondary or higher-order activity, and cannot carry the same semantic or conceptual load which was traditionally borne by the concept of introspection. Retrospection presupposes prior self-observation, and is not itself either a form of direct observation nor a substitute for it. Rather than constituting a mode of self-observation it effectively presupposes it; and while retrospection can be included among the sources of self-knowledge it cannot be offered as a primary account of the self-observation which leads to self-knowledge.

There are even more fundamental difficulties with Ryle's account of self-awareness or self-consciousness, i.e., the kind of awareness a person has when she may be said to know what she is doing at any particular moment. Ryle's account is that doing something consciously or knowingly means being prepared to take the next step, or meet the next eventuality, in a serial action. While engaged in any given step, a person is prepared for what should or may follow, and when it does follow, she is not surprised. In other cases, as when someone suddenly makes an unpremeditated witticism, he is surprised to find what he has done 'and would not describe himself as having known what he was doing, while he did it ....' (1949, p. 177). The same thing is true of other sudden acts performed on the spur of the moment. The action may be the right one to perform, but the agent does not know how he came to perform it, as he was unprepared for it. Only in the conduct of serial operations can we talk of the agent being conscious of what he is doing in the sense of being prepared for the next step in the series.

This account is inadequate for a number of reasons. The converse of a serial action is not, as Ryle seems to think, an impromptu or spur-of-the-moment movement but a 'simple' action, i.e., an action consisting in only one movement. Raising one's arm in a gesture is not normally a serial action, yet it is surely one that I may perform consciously and knowingly. Seriality has to do with the numerical stages in an action, not with the suddenness of its execution. It is, of course, less likely that I will be asked what I am doing while performing a simple or non-serial action, since I will normally have completed the action before the question can arise. But if I am asked what I was doing, I will be able to answer without having to reflect on the fact and also without having been disposed to carry out another stage in a multi-stage process. Ryle is unable to explain how I knew what I was doing though I did not go through before-and-after stages in my performance. He cannot make being able to answer the question 'What are you doing now?' a criterion for acting consciously since there are non-sudden, non-serial actions that are performed knowingly and which do not allow for such a question. The fact that there is not time to allow the question to be asked does not mean that the action is sudden or impromptu - it may be done after lengthy deliberation and after much practice. Ryle might argue that every action is, in principle, divisible or interruptible, including quick, single-movement actions, and that any action which is not interruptible is too sudden to have been consciously performed. But even if we should allow that all actions are divisible and interruptible, this still leaves Ryle unable to explain how the first stage, prior to interruption, is consciously performed. It would be absurd to enter into an infinite regress of 'serializations' of the first stage. This would in any case leave the basic problem unresolved. Ryle may argue that an agent is *au fait* not only with what remains to be done but also with what he has done, i.e., he attends retrospectively to what he has done while he is preparing himself for the next stage. But, as already indicated, a coherent theory of retrospective attention presupposes states of awareness which are not retrospective. There seems no obvious way in which an account in terms of behavioural dispositions and retrospective

44

attention can adequately explain the relationship between agency and primary states of awareness.

Ryle fails equally, though for different reasons, to explain the nature of the attention which we pay to other people's behaviour. He claims that 'in almost the same way as a person may be ... alive to what he is doing, he may also be alive to what someone else is doing' (1949, p. 179). Here Ryle has in mind the 'serial operations' of listening and looking. He maintains that the difference between the attentiveness of a listener and that of a speaker is a difference of degree, not of kind. But this is at least wrong in implying that there is no essential difference between the awareness I have in performing my own actions and the awareness I have of someone else's. For one thing, the former is non-observational, the latter observational; for another, the state of my mind in performing an action bears intrinsically on the nature of that action, while the state of my mind need have no bearing at all on the action of someone else. If it does have a bearing, it will necessarily be an extrinsic one.

A final point that should be made in this context is that Ryle is mistaken in identifying 'acting consciously' with 'acting knowingly'. To act consciously means to be prepared for the next appropriate step in a serial action. It is obvious, however, that I need not always take the appropriate steps, or succeed in meeting eventualities, in order to be said to have acted attentively or consciously. A child at play is behaving consciously and even intently but there may be no criteria for deciding whether or not all or many of his moves are appropriate, or even whether he meets eventualities. Innovative, imaginative, and creative work in general does not require that one be prepared for appropriate steps - the point may be to take new steps, to surprise even oneself in the course of doing so. In a sense, the experimenter or artist does not know what she is going to do next but this is not to say that she is somehow unconscious or inattentive. Acting consciously does not necessarily mean knowing what one does. We might say that 'they know not what they do' does not mean 'they are acting unconsciously'. On Ryle's premises, a person who played a game badly would simply be less conscious or attentive than someone who played well. But clearly an inability or unpreparedness to take appropriate steps here could be due to a number of reasons; lack of consciousness or awareness would not necessarily be among them.

In conclusion, then, let us say that the relation of an agent to her own actions and conscious states is significantly different from the relations perceived between other people and their actions and conscious states. In fact, in one's own case one should not speak of a relation at all, if this implies a relation between an observer and a kind of object. There is no room for the relation of observer-and-object to arise with respect to one's own psychological life. We *are* our conscious states, intentions, emotions, memories. We may agree with Ryle - as, indeed, even a Cartesian might - that we do not have privileged access to our own minds or selves, but only because there is no question of access, privileged or otherwise, to what is part and parcel of ourselves. Accessibility implies a contingent relation, albeit an intimate one, between one thing and another, but such a relation cannot be said to exist in one's own case. Only others could be said to have (privileged) access to our minds because the conditions of our privacy are contingent on how much we are observed and acted upon by those others. To iterate a point made earlier about self-knowledge and interpersonal knowledge, our friends (and enemies) may know more about us, in the sense of having more information about us, than we do ourselves. It is they who will have worked out our characters, personalities and 'mentalities' in a more or less coherent fashion. The fact that we are 'occult' to most people for most intents and purposes is not simply due to the impossibility of their 'seeing into our minds' but to the impracticability of their coming into such intimate and extensive relations with us as would make us wholly intelligible to them. The fact that some aspects of our psychological lives are unknown to others is not necessarily because they are unknowable but because it has not been practically, or even morally, possible for them to sustain relationships of privileged access with us. This apparent concession to behaviourism should not lead us to compromise our view that we have a power and a right to make first-person statements which are incorrigible by others. But defending the claim that we have this right and this power does not depend on a mythically Cartesian theory of privileged access or introspection

Behaviourism and the disappearance of introspection

Throughout this chapter I have made frequent reference to a concept which has become centrally problematic in contemporary philosophy of mind, especially in the critique of Cartesianism, viz., the concept of introspection. William Lyons (1986) traces the origins of this concept to Augustine's *De Trinitate*, but soon suggests that the beginning of 'the golden age of introspection' was the seventeenth century, and that this age lasted until the first decade of the twentieth century. As one might expect, the *locus classicus* for the concept is held to be Descartes' *Discourse on Method*, but Lyons acknowledges that empiricists, beginning with Hobbes and including Locke and Hume, also contributed substantially to its development. Indeed, it is significant that Lyons's account of the subsequent development of the concept in both psychology and philosophy deals mainly with its treatment by philosophers who were influenced by, or were practitioners of, empiricist epistemologies, viz., Franz Brentano, Wilhelm Wundt, William James, John Stuart Mill, and Bertrand Russell. That introspection was seen as a possible method in psychology is evident from James's claim that :

46

Introspective Observation is what we have to rely on first and foremost and always. The word introspection need hardly be defined - it means, of course, the looking into our own minds and reporting what we there discover. Every one agrees that we there discover states of consciousness. (James, 1950, p. 185)

Lyons shows that the rejection of introspectionism got under way in 1913 when J.B. Watson declared that psychology was a purely experimental branch of natural science. The goal of the new science was the prediction and control of behaviour. Introspection, Watson argued, forms no part of psychology's methods, 'nor is the scientific value of its data dependent upon the readiness with which they lend themselves to interpretation in terms of consciousness' (Lyons, 1986, p. 23). By 1922 E.C. Tolman was attempting to replace private mental 'feels' with internal 'behaviour-acts' and 'potentialities for behaviour', although these terms, in Lyons's view, raised more difficulties than those of a Cartesian sort.

B.F. Skinner, the leading theorist of the next generation of behaviourists, was less dismissive of introspection than his predecessors, though he tried to incorporate it into his functional analysis of consciousness. He pointed out that because some behaviour is inner it should not on that account be thought of as possessing any special structure or nature. Being inner implies nothing more than limited accessibility. Skinner acknowledges the possibility of introspection - or what he calls 'introspective behaviour' - when he says that 'a behavioural theory of knowledge suggests that it is the private world which, if not entirely unknowable, is at least not likely to be known well' (1964, p. 84). He also acknowledges that 'the fact of privacy' cannot be questioned and believes that privacy actually causes problems at the level of interpersonal knowledge. Such privacy may even cause the individual to suffer because 'a person cannot describe or otherwise know events occurring within his skin as subtly and as precisely as he knows events in the world at large' (p. 82).

Lyons identifies three sorts of explanation of inner events in Skinner, which we might label (i) the 'inference from variables' explanation, (ii) the 'covert behaviour' explanation, and (iii) the 'discriminative check' explanation. The first sort of explanation suggests that such apparently inner events as 'intending' or 'deciding' are not what they appear to be. In declaring that 'I am on the point of going', one is simply making a prediction on the basis of one's own knowledge of one's environment and past behaviour. A declaration of intention is an inference from a 'history of variables which would enable an independent observer to describe the behaviour in the same way if a knowledge of the variables were available to him' (Skinner, 1965, p. 258). The inference which Skinner introduces here is arguably less plausible than the notion of introspection which it is supposed to replace. Instead of the problem of other minds we are now faced with the problem of non-other minds, i.e., the problem of accounting for the difference between the observational basis on which we normally ascribe mental states to others and the non-observational basis on which we ascribe them to ourselves.[8] Skinner's explanation 'alienates' us from our own behaviour much more thoroughly than Cartesian dualism, since he places our knowledge of our own behaviour on a par with our knowledge of another person's. He brings about this alienation by using words like 'intention' in a peculiar way, by suggesting that intention is a species of prediction. In normal usage of the term, intention connotes an intimacy of control over our own behaviour which we do not have in the case of other people's behaviour. Moreover, as Lyons suggests, 'we do seem to have a privileged knowledge of the existence of that control' (p.38). It is a fact of experience, or at least of language-use, that decisions are *made* and intentions are *formed* - they are not inferred or discovered. It is also a fact of grammar, in a Wittgensteinian sense, that the language of decisions and intentions is significantly different from the language of inference or observation. Others can be said to infer my intentions from my behaviour but I cannot be said to do so. Language-use could, of course, change to such an extent that we would cease to talk in terms of decisions or intentions but this is not the kind of 'eliminative' case that is being made by Skinner.

In rejecting the theory of the introspective origin of mental concepts, behaviourists seem forced towards the conclusion that the meaning of mental terms is entirely exhausted by their reference to observable behaviour. They make, as Malcolm puts it, 'the natural assumption that ascription of mental predicates to oneself and to other persons would be symmetrical in respect of verification' (1972). But this assumption is, in Malcolm's view, mistaken:

> People do not base their announcements of their intentions on their awareness of events in their bodies .... If I intend to go home I should be able to announce this straight off, without recourse to observation of my behaviour. Indeed, if my remark were truly based on such observation of myself, it would not be an expression of intention. (1972, p. 84-5)

Skinner's conjecture is, as Malcolm adds, 'wildly remote from the facts', and is generated by the false assumption that a speaker's true statements about what he intends, thinks, or wants 'must be based on the speaker's observation of something' (1972, p. 85). The fact is, however, that no such observation is carried out. No one knows what the internal physical variables would be which are supposed characteristically to precede or accompany my going home or any other action which I may announce myself as about to do. Malcolm observes that it is a basic feature of many mental concepts that

> there is a radical asymmetry between their application by oneself to oneself, and their application by oneself to other persons .... Mental

48

concepts are applied by us to other persons on the basis of behavioural criteria, that is, on the basis of some change of countenance, or utterance, or physical action. But we do not apply them to ourselves on this basis. Thus logical behaviourism gives an incorrect account of one part of their use. (1972, p. 86)

The second type of explanation of mental, 'inner life' concepts suggested by Skinner is that they refer to 'covert behaviour'. The private event is nothing more or less than 'incipient or inchoate behaviour', which can be further explained in terms of the internal movements which usually precede overt behaviour. These inchoate, truncated, internal movements are accompanied by 'proprioceptive stimulations' i.e., the sorts of feelings that accompany the fully overt movement. Introspection, then, is merely the reportings of these internal, unexpressed movements and their accompanying proprioceptive feelings. The difficulty with these re-descriptions, however, is that they do not undermine the mythical Cartesian whose concept of privacy is under attack! The re-descriptions do not eliminate Cartesian privacy (so-called) or even the notion of privileged access. As Lyons points out, the proprioceptive 'feels' of which Skinner speaks 'look very like raw Cartesian awareness' (1986, p. 40). The re-description changes the vocabulary but the concept of the 'inner process' remains curiously intact.

The third type of explanation - the 'discriminative checks' explanation - is related to the Wittgensteinian notion of criteria and to the Rylean account of perception and understanding as 'achievement' words. We accept (according to Skinner) that someone has heard or seen something only if they can perform pertinent discriminative tasks, and we grant ourselves the same claim to perception on the same grounds. There is, in other words, no act, mental or otherwise, to which a perceptual term refers - there is only the declaration of an ability to make a certain identification of an object or event. Saying 'I heard the oboe just there' is not a report of an inner experience but a challenge to oneself or others to pass a test in identifying a particular sound. The test might include humming or otherwise producing the notes contributed by the oboe player in an orchestra. By so arguing, Skinner proposes to empty such statements of their inner, introspective connotations - to turn them 'inside out', as it were. But again this account is at odds with the facts of experience and, more significantly, with the grammar of self-ascriptions. While sometimes one may be asked to 'prove' that one has heard the oboe, or had some other particular experience, this is not always or typically the case. People may talk about seeing and hearing things without having any notion of checking on it by noting their own discriminative behaviour. They would only do so if they had some doubt about the accuracy of their perception. The discriminative checks themselves are an additional procedure and are not part of the meaning of what it is to announce a perception of something. Indeed, the discriminative procedure is itself a perceptual process. Must *it* be analysed further in terms of further second-order discriminative procedures? An opening is effectively created here for a 'Cartesian' intervention. Even if I announced a perception and attempted a discriminative task which failed, it would not follow that I did not have a perceptual experience. If I failed to hum the oboe player's notes, or if it transpired that the oboe was silent at the time I announced my perception, I could still claim, significantly and truthfully, that I *thought* I heard the oboe, i.e., that I 'heard' notes which seemed to me to issue from the oboe. The gap in the behaviourist re-description is filled by a Cartesian *cogitatio*.

Despite the broad similarities between the views of the behaviouristic psychologists and the philosophies of Ryle and Wittgenstein, there are important differences. These differences are often expressed as the difference between methodological and logical behaviourism. Ryle may be distinguished from a methodological behaviourist for the reason that his position is more conceptually 'eliminative' than theirs. The psychologists from Watson to Skinner have attempted to demonstrate experimentally and theoretically that the empirical observation of overt behaviour is superior to introspection as a method of acquiring reliable, comprehensive knowledge of human nature. Ryle, on the other hand, regards introspection not merely as an unscientific procedure but as an impossible concept in itself. Skinner, as we have seen, acknowledges the possibility of 'introspective behaviour' and allows for the existence of an inner world which is not entirely knowable. Ryle, by contrast, makes no such concession and does not offer a behaviouristic re-description of introspection or privacy.

It is in the area of avowals that Ryle differs most obviously from the Wittgensteinians. While Malcolm, for example, would agree with Ryle that first-person utterances are not made on the basis of introspection, he refuses at the same time to reduce them to merely expressive or behavioural phenomena. As we saw above, he regards self-testimony as an autonomous and important source of information about persons, and denies 'even a theoretical possibility that this self-testimony could be supplanted by inferences from external or internal physical variables' (1964, p. 153). Indeed, the category of first-person, present-tense, psychological utterances constitutes one of the most uniquely human uses of language, giving rise to a human being's status as 'a subject and person' (1964, p. 154). As a Wittgensteinian, he argues for a conceptual tie between the language of psychological phenomena and outward circumstances and behaviour, but this is in order to account for how psychological concepts are learnt, not for how they are normally used. This particular view of Malcolm's seems entirely correct. While he shares with the psychological and philosophical behaviourists a refusal to draw clear boundaries between the public and the private, between the mental and the behavioural, between self and the society of others, between thinker and doer, he does not insist on abolishing 'the inner life' in the name of abolishing

Cartesian scepticism, Cartesian egoism, or the Cartesian ontology. Such a view is strengthened if we further insist that the concepts of privacy and interiority have been mistakenly 'Cartesianized' in any case, leading us to shy away from developing a proper philosophy of subjectivity for fear of re-instating the ghost in the machine.

Notes

1. For the argument that the Cogito should be understood as 'performance' rather than inference, see Jaakko Hintikka (1967) who also argues that it is very misleading to appeal to introspection in explaining the meaning of the Cogito: 'The reason why Descartes could not doubt his own existence is in principle exactly the same as the reason why he could not hope to mislead anybody by saying "I don't exist." The one does not presuppose introspection any more than the other. What the philosophers who have spoken of introspection here are likely to have had in mind is often performatoriness rather than introspectiveness,' (p.125).
2. Cf. Stuart Hampshire (1972, p. 36): 'To attribute a disposition to someone is never to preclude that he may on some occasion act, or have acted, in some way contrary to his general tendency or disposition.... It is typical of human character (as we actually conceive and describe it) that it allows of lapses, and that people sometimes behave in a way which is not in accordance with their character.'
3. A similar position is taken by Hampshire (1959, p. 164) who argues that the inner life is the 'obverse of social restraint and convention'.
4. Cf. J.L. Austin (1962). Although Austin does not demarcate explicitly between speech acts and behaviour, it is clear enough that the sorts of 'dimensions' he attributes to all speech acts, including stating and describing, are not appropriately attributable to non-linguistic behaviour, e. g., 'illocutionary force,' a 'truth/falsehood dimension,' and 'a locutionary meaning (sense and reference)' (p. 145).
5. Avowals would be most likely to serve as perlocutionary acts, i.e., 'what we bring about or achieve by saying something, such as convincing, persuading, deterring, and even surprising or misleading' (Austin, 1962, p. 109).
6. Dispositions, as Hampshire has pointed out, are not necessarily behavioural: 'one can have a disposition to think in a certain manner and also to react emotionally in a certain manner' (1972, pp. 35-36).
7. One of Ryle's objections to the theory of introspection is that it must hold that, in an act of inner perception, the observer 'could attend to two things at the same time' (1949, p. 164). That is, the mental process under observation would have to be complete and not modified by the equally

complete and concomitant act of introspection. According to Ryle, this is either impossible or else 'there must be some mental processes which are unintrospectible, namely those introspections which incorporate the maximum number of synchronous acts of attention' (p. 165) which would mean that a person's knowledge of his own mind could not always be based on introspection.

8. Cf. R.C. Buck (1986, p. 43) on the problem of 'non-other minds': 'The argument from analogy proposes a route of shaky inference to probable knowledge about the minds of others. Gradually, however, it is realized that this argument is a red herring, that the behaviour ... of others provides the only possible criteria for what one means when he ascribes mental predicates to them. With this realization the argument from analogy collapses, and the problem of other minds dissolves. But a discomfort remains. If mental predicates have their criteria in behaviour, what of self-ascriptions of such predicates. Does one observe his own behaviour, listen to his own utterances, in order to find out that he is angry, has a toothache, etc.? Clearly not! Yet if the words he uses are not significant of behaviour, what are they significant of? How can you contradict my claim that I have a headache, unless you and I are talking about "the same thing"? The dissolution of the "other minds" problem generated a problem about "non-other minds"'.

3 The materialization of mind

Our everyday language is full of mentalistic or psychological terms which feature prominently in the sorts of accounts we give of ourselves and others. Until recently, materialists were happy to acknowledge and accept a linguistic dualism, i.e., a distinction between mind-talk and body-talk - between, on one side, talk about one's memories, dreams, and feelings and, on the other, talk about one's weight or height or colouring. Indeed, it is, as we shall soon see, one of the intriguing ironies of contemporary philosophy of mind that one branch of modern physicalism, the mind-brain identity theory, cannot get started unless it accepts, at a linguistic or conceptual level, the mental/physical distinction. What are the implications of accepting and maintaining this conceptual distinction; and what would be the implications of trying to eliminate it? Will those who insist on maintaining the distinction find that their physicalism is rendered problematic; and will those who seek to eliminate it find that there are features of reality whereof they can no longer speak? A close look at the course of modern physicalism - the history of the 'materialization' of mind - will yield the observation that only a subtle and resourceful version of physicalism is going to be capable of giving an adequate account of what it means to have a mind and be a self.

In one of the canonical texts of modern physicalism, U.T. Place (1962) defends an early version of the mind-brain identity theory. Place, who sees himself as complementing behaviourism rather than providing a complete alternative to it, accepts that the analysis of core cognitive concepts (such as 'knowing', 'believing', 'understanding', 'remembering') and of core volitional concepts (such as 'wanting', 'intending') in terms of dispositions to behave is 'fundamentally sound'. On the other hand, he argues that there is 'an intractable residue of concepts clustering around the notions of consciousness, experience, sensation, and mental imagery, where some sort of inner process story is unavoidable' (p. 101). That is, statements about pains, about how things look, sound and feel, about things dreamed of or about pictures in the mind's eye, are statements referring to events and processes 'which are in some sense private or internal to the individual of whom they are predicated' (p. 102). Place then proceeds to argue that an acceptance of inner processes does not entail dualism (as the behaviourists assume), and that his own thesis that consciousness is a process in the brain cannot be dismissed on logical grounds. He stresses from the outset that in defending the thesis that consciousness is a brain-process he is not arguing that when we describe our dreams, fantasies, and sensations we are talking about processes in our brains. He is not claiming that statements about sensations and mental images are simply reducible to, or analysable into, statements about brain-processes *qua* brain-processes:

> To say that statements about consciousness are statements about brain-processes is manifestly false. This is shown (a) by the fact that you can describe your sensations and mental imagery without knowing anything about your brain-processes or even that such things exist, (b) by the fact that statements about one's consciousness and statements about one's brain-processes are verified in entirely different ways, and (c) by the fact that there is nothing self-contradictory about the statement 'X has a pain but there is nothing going on in his brain.' What I do want to assert, however, is that the statement 'Consciousness is a process in the brain,' although not necessarily true, is not necessarily false. 'Consciousness is a process in the brain,' is neither self-contradictory nor self-evident; it is a reasonable scientific hypothesis, in the way that the statement 'Lightning is a motion of electric charges' is a reasonable scientific hypothesis. (p. 102)

In his search for a suitable analogy in the physical world for the mind-brain identity relation, Place rejects the identity between 'cloud' and 'mass of water particles' in favour of the identity between 'lightning' and 'motion of electric charges.' In the former case, the fact that something is a cloud and the fact that something is a mass of suspended particles are both verified by the same normal process of visual observation or inspection. Given that statements about brain-processes and about mental states are verified in two different ways, a more suitable analogy resides in the identity between lightning and a motion of electric charges. However closely we scrutinize an instance of lightning we shall never be able to observe the electric charges, since their occurrences can be established only by special scientific procedures. Analogously, no matter how closely we scrutinize our states of consciousness we shall not be able to perceive brain-processes, since their nature too can only be observed by special procedures. Yet this anomaly in procedures of verification does not prevent us declaring an identity of reference. Just as we may say that flashes of lightning are *in fact* motions of electrical discharges in the atmosphere, so we may say that mental states are *in fact* brain-processes.

A similar conclusion is reached by another classical identity theorist, J.J.C. Smart (1970), who sees himself, indeed, as taking his departure from Place's article. For Smart (who focuses mainly on sensations) the identity thesis does not claim that sensation-statements can be translated into statements about brain-processes. Nor does it claim that the logic of a sensation statement is the same as that of a brain-process statement: 'All it claims is that insofar as a sensation statement is a report of something, that something is in fact a brain-process. Sensations are nothing over and above brain-processes' (p. 56). A similar position is summed up with similar brevity by Herbert Feigl: 'We may say that neurophysiological terms and the corresponding phenomenal terms, though widely differing in sense, and hence in the modes of confirmation of statements containing them, do have identical referents' (1969, p. 38).

The significance of the identity thesis as stated by Place, Smart and Feigl is that inner processes, experienced subjectively as mental states, are strictly identifiable with brain-processes in the sense that there is no need to postulate the existence of entities other than physical events in giving an exhaustive account of such processes. Does this mean that the interiority which we experience as a feature of our psychological processes is really just a physical innerness? The identity theorists claim that there is no need to deny either the occurrent, episodic nature of such processes - or their private, subjective, phenomenal qualities. Yet it is precisely these latter qualities which create most difficulties for the traditional identity thesis. Kai Nielsen (1971), for example, though committed to a materialist ontology, endorses a classical objection to the identity thesis when he accepts that it runs adrift on Leibniz's Principle of the Indiscernibility of Identicals, i.e., the principle that two objects are numerically identical just in case all properties possessed by one are also possessed by the other. In claiming that mental state x is identical with brain-state y, reductive materialists must be claiming that anything which is a property of x is also a property of y. Just as the properties of the Morning Star are identical with the properties of the Evening Star; and just as the properties of flashes of lightning are identical with motions of electrical discharges in the atmosphere, so the properties of mental states are identical with those of brain-states. But Nielsen thinks that this analogy does not hold. Certain characteristic properties of mental events are not characteristic properties of brain-states. Sensations, feelings, and images have an inherently private, phenomenological quality and are unobservable by others, while brain-processes are public in principle and hence observable by others. Reports of inner processes are incorrigible by others than myself, while accounts of brain-processes are as corrigible as other statements about the world. Moreover, brain-processes may be described in unequivocally objective terms - in terms of electrical activity, EEG graphs, blood-flow, and chemical or hormonal levels - whereas mental states cannot be so described.

There seems to be a radical discontinuity, in other words, between the two modes of characterization, which is not the case with the difference between the mode of characterization of lightning and the mode of characterization of electrical discharges. There is no reason, for example, why a person should make any significant distinction at all between lightning and electrical discharges, if she has a knowledge of physics and meteorology. It is indeed an implication of Leibniz's Law that once we know that there is numerical identity where we once thought there was difference, then one mode of characterization is sufficient. When we say that the terms 'the Morning Star' and 'the Evening Star' have different senses but the same reference, we are really saying that we can talk about the Morning Star and the Evening Star in the same descriptive terms - e.g., in terms of gravity, luminosity, distance from Earth, etc. There is, in fact, only one star which is observable (for astronomically complex reasons) in different positions relative to an Earth-bound observer. The terms 'Morning Star' and 'Evening Star' are not themselves predicates but context-dependent names. Similarly, in the case of lightning *vis-à-vis* motions of electrical discharges, the phenomenon picked out by both nominal phrases is describable by one set of predicates, although not all predicates may be known to every conceivable observer. Regardless of which nominal phrase we are using and regardless of the context in which it is appropriately used, we can go on to describe the referent in terms drawn from just one class of predicates.

This does not seem to be the case with the semantic disparity between mental-state and brain-state predicates. The disparity or discontinuity between the senses of the nominal or identifying terms carries over into the process of predication and characterization. While we can talk about both the Morning Star and the Evening Star in terms of luminosity, mass, and gravitational pull we cannot talk about both mental state x and brain-process y in terms of one type of predicate. That is, if we attempt to describe a thought or sensation in terms of electrical activity and physiological characteristics only, then it seems that certain features of the mental state *qua* mental state will be left out. If a neuroscientist is probing the brain of someone who is dreaming, he may be able to give a lot of information about the state of the dreamer's brain but this physiological account of the dreamer's brain-processes will not be an account of the dreamer's *dream*. To get that account it will be necessary to wake the dreamer and ask her. The dreamer's account will not be in physiological terms, even if she is herself a neuroscientist, but will be in terms appropriate to the narration of dreams. The dream-telling neuroscientist may, of course, make references to brain-processes in the course of her narration, but there is a significant difference between her references to her dream and her references to the brain-processes which occurred at the same time. The difference consists in the fact that the dreamer's account of her dream as experienced and remembered by her is incorrigible by others, while her references to brain-processes *are* corrigible by (other) neuroscientists. This incorrigibility - or what Kurt Baier (1970) calls this 'epistemological authority' - suggests that there is a degree and a quality of subjectivity or privacy which is predicable of dreams considered as

56

mental states but which is not predicable of dreams considered as brain-processes. The subjective process of dreaming seems to be more private and 'inner' than the identity thesis wants to admit. It is mentally and subjectively inner, and not merely deep in the brain or 'difficult to get at' in the sense of requiring special instruments. We are close to saying that the dream of the neuroscientist is a *cogitatio* in Descartes' sense, although the feature of incorrigibility as such does not commit us to dualism. It commits us only to the view that the identity thesis has failed to recognize the qualitative difference between a physically inner process and a mentally or subjectively inner process.

A recent defence of the identity thesis against this type of argument has been made by Paul Churchland (1984) who, though not an identity theorist himself, maintains that the argument from private properites fails to undermine the identity thesis because it commits an intensional fallacy. He formulates the argument as follows, with a view to exposing its invalidity:

1. My mental states are introspectively known by me as states of my conscious self.
2. My brain-states are *not* introspectively known by me as states of my conscious self.
Therefore, by Leibniz's Law (that numerically identical things must have exactly the same properties),
3. My mental states are not identical with my brain-states. (p. 32)

To emphasize the fallacious nature of this form of argument, Churchland asks us to consider the following logically parallel arguments:

1. Muhammed Ali is widely known as a heavyweight champion.
2. Cassius Clay is *not* widely known as a heavyweight champion.
Therefore, by Leibniz's Law,
3. Muhammed Ali is not identical with Cassius Clay.
   or,
1. Aspirin is recognized by John to be a pain reliever.
2. Acetylsalicylic acid is *not* recognized by John to be a pain reliever.
Therefore, by Leibniz's Law,
3. Aspirin is not identical with acetylsalicylic acid. (p. 32)

Despite the truth of the premises of these arguments, the conclusions in each case are clearly false, and the identities in question are in fact genuine. The problem, according to Churchland, is that the putative 'property' ascribed in premise (1) and denied in premise (2) in each example, consists only in the subject item's being *recognized, perceived,* or *known* as a something-or-other. But such recognition is not a genuine property of the item itself, fit for divining identities, 'since one and the same subject may be successfully recognized

57

under one description, and yet fail to be recognized under another (accurate, coreferential) description. Bluntly, Leibniz's Law is not valid for these bogus "properties'" (p. 32). The attempt to present these bogus properties as genuine comprises the intensional fallacy. The premises reflect, not the failure of certain objective identities, but only our subjective failure to appreciate them.

Churchland's critique of the argument from private properties is not as strong as it looks. In the first place, the private properties argument does not require its proponents to hold that the properties of mental states are necessarily knowable by introspection, as if introspection involved a special inner faculty on a par with the perception of external objects. There is no such faculty because, as Searle rightly says, the model of 'specting intro' requires a distinction between the object spected and the specting of it, 'and we cannot make the distinction for conscious states' (1992, p. 144). The fact that we experience some of our internal states in ways which are qualitively private to each one of us - private in the sense that they are not accessible to others - does not imply that there is any sort of perceptual relationship between subjects and their conscious states or experiences. All that the critic of identity needs to do is to claim (as Malcolm does) that there is a radical asymmetry between the ways in which we ascribe mental concepts to others and the ways we ascribe them to ourselves, such that the sort of identity desired by the identity theorist cannot be established. This asymmetry consists in the fact that self-testimony is not based on inferences from external or internal physical variables, either behavioural or cerebral, whereas ascriptions of mental states to others is based on such inferences. The observer of brain-processes, even if he is a neuroscientist observing his own brain, has a capacity for self-testimony which is not based on his observation of these processes - or on any kind of introspective observation of his mental processes. Self-testimony is a feature of the first-person usage of mental terms, and introspectionism is just one theory, favoured by some empiricists, about how this self-testimony is possible.

A cogent alternative to the introspectionist account of self-testimony is suggested by Searle. What is special about first-person reports may be best understood in terms of the time-honoured appearance-reality model. This model applies to our perceptual relationships with the world at large but not to our 'relationship' with our own internal states. In our reports of the world at large, there is a distinction between how things seem to us and how they really are:

> It can seem to me that there is a man hiding in the bushes outside my window, when in fact the appearance was caused by the peculiar pattern of light and shadow on the shrubbery. But for how things seem to me, there is no reality/appearance distinction to be made. It really does seem to me there is a man hiding in the bushes. Where intentional mental states are concerned, the states themselves are constitutive of the seeming. The origin, in short, of our conviction of a special first-person authority lies

simply in the fact that we cannot make the conventional reality/appearance distinction for appearances themselves. (1992, p. 146)

This is a better account of the special status of first-person statements and the private or subjective ontology which they report. It weakens the force of Churchland's intensional fallacy argument in so far as it shows that the privacy or inaccessibility argument against the identity thesis need not be couched in terms of a 'bogus' relational property like knowability or introspectibility.

Qualia: a matter of life and death?

A recent criticism of classical identity theory which remains within the terms of reference of Leibniz's Law without seeming to appeal to the 'bogus' property of introspectibility is Frank Jackson's 'argument from Knowledge' (1990, pp. 469-477). Jackson's criticism of the mind-brain identity theory and of physicalism generally does not depend on a theory of introspectibility, but on the putative reality of the felt, phenomenal properties or 'qualia' of mental states themselves.[1] This looks like a version of Nielsen's inaccessibility argument but Jackson's position can be stated independently of a theory of access. What matters is not whether (or how) qualia are introspected or accessed but the fact that experiences exhibit phenomenal properties. His main point is that no amount of physical information can reveal the qualitative character of a person's experiences. This is illustrated by the story of Mary who has lived from birth in a black-and-white environment. As a scientist she is confined to a black-and-white laboratory and obliged to view the world through a black-and-white monitor. As a specialist in the neurophysiology of vision, Mary possesses all the physical information there is to know about what goes on when people have visual experiences. She discovers, for example, just which combination of wavelengths from the sky stimulates the retina, and exactly how this produces, via the central nervous system, the sorts of processes which result in the uttering of the sentence 'The sky is blue'. Despite all her physical information, Mary, on leaving her laboratory and walking into a coloured world, begins to have experiences which she did not previously know about and which she did not infer from her information. Since she acquires new experiential knowledge of the world, it is inescapable that her previous knowledge was incomplete, not because she lacked physical, objective information but because there were certain experiences she did not have. Ergo, Jackson concludes, there is more to be had than physical information, and physicalism must be incomplete or even false (1990, p. 471).

It does not seem necessary to claim here that this experiential knowledge or knowledge of phenomenal properties must be inaccessible to others. It may be true that knowledge of qualia is, as a matter of fact, obtained from the inside but it is not this fact which gives experiences their phenomenal properties (See Macdonald, 1989, pp. 20-7). It is conceivable that while some people have the ability to introspect their experiences, there could be others who do not have this ability but who could still be said to have experiences, phenomenal properties and all. In order for the story about Mary to make sense it is not necessary that she have the ability to introspect. It is not even necessary that there be such a thing as introspection or even privileged access. It is important to emphasize this point if Jackson is to be defended against the kind of criticism made by Dennett (1990). According to Dennett, qualia are supposed to be ineffable, intrinsic, private and directly or immediately present to consciousness. But Jackson need not accept any of these characterizations of qualia since they are all part of the attempt to impose a perceptual or access model on the relationship between qualia and subjects. It might seem that Jackson must at least accept that qualia are intrinsic or private but this is not so. At least, he need not accept these terms in the sense in which Dennett understands them. For example, 'intrinsic' for Dennett means 'unanalyzable' or 'simple' but that is not the only sense in which the term can be understood. In fact, when Dennett says that qualia do not exist (in the sense in which he has characterized them), it is open to Jackson to agree.

The strength of Jackson's view of qualia is that it does not depend on notions of inner sense or a theory of access, but simply on a distinction between the experiential (or mental) and the physical, a distinction regarded as conceptually fundamental by philosophers as different as Jaegwon Kim (1972) and Donald Davidson (1980). Kim, for example, acknowledges that any version of the identity theory that tries to avoid the objection from phenomenal properties by denying the existence of mental phenomena will only do so at the cost of denying the fundamental tenet of the identity theory, i.e., that mental phenomena are in some sense real, or real enough to be perceived as identical with physical states:

> As I see it, the fundamental tenet of the [identity] theory is that it is *a physicalist monism that retains mental events as legitimate entities in the world.* That is both its central attraction and the source of its gravest difficulties. And it may prove to be the cause of its downfall. But if you take it away, you take away the identity theory. (p. 180)

Davidson's name is associated with a version of physicalist monism which defends a 'token-token' conception of the identity relation, to distinguish it from the 'type-type' conception of classical identity theory. Instead of making the strong claim that there is an identity of types of mental events with types of brain events, token-token identity theory asserts only the existence of particular identities between individual tokens or instances of mental and physical states. Davidson's 'anomalous monism' is intended to emphasize the fact that while each token mental event is a physical event, mental types or properties are at the same time not reducible, in any deterministic, law-like or nomological fashion, to physical ones. If it is a feature of physical reality that physical change can be explained by laws that connect it with other physical changes and conditions, it is a feature of the mental that the attribution of mental phenomena must be responsible to the 'intentional background' - reasons, beliefs, and intentions - of the individual: 'There cannot be tight connections between the realms if each is to retain allegiance to its proper source of evidence' (1980, p. 222). He insists that there is a 'nomological slack' between the mental and the physical and that this is essential 'as long as we conceive of man as a rational animal' (p. 223). His position is, in a sense, an ethical rather than a metaphysical one. As long as we have a certain conception of ourselves we must acknowledge the categorial difference between the mental and the physical, and acknowledge by implication that there are no strict laws on the basis of which we can predict and explain mental phenomena. We could, as it were, give up such a stance and adopt an altogether different one, but it would have to be a stance in which the constitutive ideal of rationality was abandoned and in which the distinction between the mental and the physical was not made. Davidson's view is not in any sense anti-scientific. Mental events as a class cannot be explained in strictly causal, nomological terms by physical science, but particular events can when the identities are known. The dependence or supervenience of the mental on the physical does not entail reducibility through law or definition; but this irreducibility does not entail some kind of dualism either. The anomalousness of the mental is not maintained against science but simply as a necessary, Kantian-style condition for conceiving human agency as autonomous. Though intended as a contribution to the theory of action, Davidson's paper is an important milestone on the path towards a philosophy of mind in which the acknowledgement of the mental/physical distinction is not assumed to involve a commitment to a problematic dualism.

But how are we to understand the mental/physical distinction in a way which does not involve either a problematic substance dualism or a dualism of properties? If we want to maintain a distinction between the 'inner' and the 'outer', between the subjective and the objective, between the 'spiritual' and the 'material', can we do so without recourse to some form of Cartesian dualism? Can we be some sort of materialists and yet retain a coherent conception of the self, of a subjective interiority which is more than just a physical innerness? A case can surely be made for an affirmative answer to the last question. It seems obvious that we have inner lives or 'interiorities' in a sense in which inanimate objects do not. The fear of death may be understood not just as the fear of losing consciousness but more poignantly as the fear of losing one's inner life. Death may be understood not as the end of bodily life (since the body of a dead person continues to exist, even to 'live', organically) but as the end of a very particular inner life - the 'going out' of an interiority, of the light of a uniquely individual consciousness. We know that part of the answer to the childish question, 'Where does the light go when it goes out?' is to say that light is not a something which goes anywhere. A materialist will want to say the same about consciousness - that consciousness doesn't *go* anywhere when someone dies (e.g., in the form of a dear, departing soul). But we want to say, paraphrasing Wittgenstein, that while consciousness or interiority is not a something, it is not a nothing either. If self, mind, consciousness, and the inner life were nothing to begin with, then death would not be a reality. But death *is* a reality, therefore that which comes to an end at death is in some sense a reality - a reality, moreover, which is other than the reality of the body.

It is the fact of mortality which is to be wondered at here. The fact that persons rather than bodies go out of existence points to the reality of the inner, subjective life. The death of persons seems to fly in the face of physics itself in the measure that something quite real (a self, a consciousness, a subjectivity) goes out of existence, while the matter of the body continues to obey the law of conservation of energy. Clearly, the grieving materialist cannot conceive of death as the literal separation or departure of soul from body. But neither ought she to say that there is no difference, except a physically functional one, between the interior of a body (or brain) and the interior of a person. At a particular level of physical description, the interior of the body remains materially the same after death as before, while the interiority of the person-as-subject is no longer a fact in the world. The materialist who does not accept the notion of an afterlife or the notion of an immaterial soul can only do full justice to the reality of individual subjectivities, and to the reality of personal life and death, by accepting the idea of an interiority which is neither the interiority of a body nor the interiority of a soul, but which is rather the interiority of a uniquely individual mortal self. In order to appreciate the concept of interiority in this context it seems that we must go as far as we can with the dualist who believes in the soul's survival of death - and then stop short of accepting the dualist's ontology, his literal picture of souls existing in a remote and attenuated duplicate of earth. In thus acknowledging the spirit but not the letter of dualism we begin to have the sense of a self which is more than a body but less than a Cartesian soul, i.e., the sense of a self that is as mortal as it is real.

To say that the self is mortal is to say that its existence depends on the proper functioning of the body, and that when the body ceases to function in a person-sustaining, self-sustaining, mind-sustaining way, then person, self and mind cease to exist. Contrary to what Platonists and Cartesians have claimed, minds and selves are not essentially immortal but are, rather, essentially mortal. They are the kinds of things that emerge out of the living masses of cells, tissues, chemicals and hormones which constitute a living, properly functioning body, which continue to exist in and through that body until it begins to malfunction, and then one day that body is no longer able to sustain a consciousness and a self - and the result is mortality. The result is also grief and a sense of loss for all those, dualists and materialists alike, who find only a lifeless body where they used to find the vital body of a loved one. Only those who are committed to a certain kind of religious world-picture can enjoy the very real and enviable consolation of thinking that an omnipotent deity will some day, somehow, restore the absent loved one to a new state of being.

Emergentism: the case for a first-person ontology

This way of thinking about 'inner life' consciousness or subjectivity could be described as a form of emergentism, namely, the belief that the mind is a higher-level emergent property of the brain. According to John Searle (1984; 1992), consciousness is a higher-level or emergent property of the brain in the sense of 'higher-level' or 'emergent' in which solidity is a higher-level emergent property of H_2O molecules when they are in a lattice structure (ice), or in the sense in which liquidity is a higher-level emergent property of H_2O molecules 'when they are, roughly speaking, rolling around on each other (water)' (p. 14). Consciousness is a mental property, but also, at the same time, a physical property of the brain in the sense in which liquidity is a property of systems of H_2O molecules. When Searle goes on to characterize consciousness in some more detail, we find him speaking in terms of 'an ontology of the mental'(1992, p. 95), namely, an ontology of subjective states, an irreducibly first-person ontology. Subjectivity, as the term is used by Searle, refers not to an epistemic mode but to an ontological category. The ontologically subjective is not to be understood therefore in terms of the contrast that we often make between subjective and objective judgements. It is not a matter of someone's opinion that I have a pain, but a matter of fact. When I say that I have a pain in my lower back, that statement is completely objective in the sense that it is 'made true' by the existence of an actual fact and is not dependent on any stance, attitudes, or opinions of observers. It is just that the phenomenon itself about which the true statement is made, the actual pain, has a subjective mode of existence. Pains and other mental states are real but they are subjectively real. They have a first-person existence; and this is a mode of existence we should learn to live with instead of denying it as the behaviourists did, or reducing it or eliminating it as some materialists have done. As far as Searle is concerned, this first-person mode of existence of mental states is nothing to be ashamed of, and if we are ashamed of it it is because we are at heart conceptual dualists.

Searle, in arguing for a version of emergent naturalism - for an irreducibly subjective first-person ontology - is presenting a picture with which the grieving materialist can live. By accepting something like the notion of a first-person ontology, we have a sense of what it means to be a mortal self, what it means to talk about an inner life or a 'subjectivity'. To acknowledge that we are mortal selves is to acknowledge that we come into existence as a result of having a certain kind of body - and go out of existence in due course for precisely the same reason, i.e., as a result of having the kind of body which ceases one day to go on delivering the goods that constitute an inner life consciousness. If we cannot help ourselves doing philosophy, if we cannot help pushing against the limits of language in a Wittgensteinian sense, then we can picture the self as an emergent property, or a set of emergent properties, the existence of which depends directly, systematically and causally on a certain degree of interaction and integration among appropriate lower-level physical components. What the grieving materialist has in common with the grieving dualist is the sense of the body as the remains of someone, of a person who has gone out of the world. The difference, of course, is that the materialist, when wearing her philosopher's hat, understands that the person does not literally depart to some ethereal space but has gone out of existence utterly.

This sort of emergentism has been criticized from a Wittgensteinian perspective by Norman Malcolm (1986). The basis of Malcolm's critique is Wittgenstein's well-known observation that 'only of a living human being and what resembles ... a living human being, can one say: it has sensations; it sees, is blind; hears, is deaf; is conscious or unconscious' (1963, §281). All such psychological, mentalistic ascriptions are part of a package, part of a complex network of language-uses that has the human body and its behaviour at its centre. Take away the living human being, take away human behaviour and human speech and the forms of life in which human beings speak to and act upon each other, and our mentalistic language loses its purchase, loses its grip, loses its point. In some contexts, this Wittgensteinian point provides the basis of an attack on dualism, but in other contexts it provides the basis of an attack on certain versions of anti-dualism, including Searle's emergent naturalism. For Searle, consciousness, subjectivity, and intentionality are just emergent properties of the brain. For Wittgensteinians such as Malcolm, however, these terms can only be usefully ascribed to human beings acting and speaking and thinking in particular contexts. Such terms cannot be ascribed to brains or nervous systems, anymore than to pure spirits. A brain, considered in isolation from the situated body, does not resemble a human being; it does not have an expressive face in which we might detect anger or suspicion or understanding; it does not act on or in the world; does not speak or make gestures or sigh or groan or laugh or otherwise generate the sorts of criteria which enable psychological language to be learnt and used. 'It makes as little sense to ascribe experiences, wishes, thoughts, beliefs, to a brain as to a mushroom' (p. 186). In other words, brains do not experience, wish, think, or believe - rather, human beings do.

These Wittgensteinian considerations must give us pause. A clue to an alternative position may be available in Malcolm's own Wittgensteinian notion of innerness. Malcolm accepts that underneath all the confusion in

64

contemporary philosophy about inner states there lies a striking truth about our psychological concepts, namely, that each of us stands in a different relation to his own thinking and feeling than does anyone else. Every philosopher must, he says, have a dim awareness of this truth, since it is embedded in the grammar of the psychological language that we use every day. The fundamental difference is that *you* can have evidence for what *I* think and feel, whereas I cannot be said to have such evidence. You may have evidence for the fact that I intend to go to the cinema this evening, but I just intend to go to the cinema this evening. I can't be said to have evidence for my own intention. The same first-person logic applies to other attributions of mental acts and states, which leads Malcolm to conclude that the metaphorical use of the word 'inner' indicates that 'you and I stand on a different logical level in regard to what I think and feel' (p. 187). This conceptual difference would be abolished if we accepted that mental states are brain-states, because then you and I could in theory stand on the same level in regard to what I think and feel. In order to ascertain my thoughts and feelings you and I could come to rely equally on some advanced brain-reading technology - on a technology of cerebroscopes, for example, as envisaged by Rorty. But such a technology is considered unthinkable for Malcolm since (a) it ignores the logical difference between the non-criterial nature of first-person ascriptions and the criterial nature of third-person ascriptions, and (b) it assumes that mental processes are inscribed in the brain in such a way that they could in principle be read off by a brain-reading technology. For Malcolm, however, the sorts of states that are ascribed to persons on a criterial basis, and self-ascribed non-criterially, are not the sorts of states that can be read off a brain. The idea that you could read a mental state off a brain- state is analogous to the idea that you could understand something about emotions by understanding the anatomy of the heart.

There seems to be something right about Malcolm's rejection of a brain-reading technology, but we can disagree with his assumption that the use of the word 'inner' is or must be metaphorical here. There is no reason why we cannot say that persons have a literally inner life because they, as language-users, have the right and the power to make first-person psychological statements, to ascribe non-criterially to themselves an array of psychological terms. We do not have to account for this fact in dualistic terms, nor in terms of some theory of introspection or privileged access. The innerness of the self-reporting, first-person language-user is an innerness made possible by language and those forms of life in which avowals - i.e., first-person contemporaneous statements - are valued and regarded as informative.

The grammar of psychological language does not of itself convey all that is meant by the term 'inner' in this context. We have to look at the fuller picture, at the values, belief-systems, practices, customs, and institutions in which this language of innerness is itself embedded. The notion of a self with an inner life cannot be understood in isolation from the network of recognitions and non-recognitions that constitute a culture or a community. The self is a not a physical given, nor is it simply a physically emergent property of the brain. It is also, in some measure, a social or cultural construct. Although certain physical conditions must obtain in order for a self to be brought into being, it may be said that whether or not a self is elicited or formed, or what sort of self is elicited or formed, will depend on what sort of social and cultural factors are brought to bear on the individuals in a community. The self does not spring into being, fully formed at the moment of birth - or at any other moment, for that matter. Persons and selves develop in and through the language and practices of the communities into which they are born. To talk about the self here should cause us no more embarrassment than talk about community, or talk about rights, values, social practices, and forms of cultural life. To talk about the self and its privacy or innerness is to talk about the degree to which people's expressions of their thoughts and feelings are respected, or accepted as sincere and true, as informative, as expressions of a subjective life.

To treat people as public bodies only, as public objects only - to treat them wholly from a third-person perspective - is to treat them as devoid of an inner life, which is to treat them with profound disrespect. Something *is* hidden, except not just as a matter of nature but as a matter of right, of nurture and culture. What is hidden is what we recognize as hidden, what cannot be got at, as a rule, except through the first-person statements and self-expressive behaviour of the person before us. The 'cannot' here is a moral, even a historical cannot, and not a physical or a metaphysical cannot. To form a relationship with someone is to recognize that there is no end to their hiddenness, to their innerness, to the things which they may express or conceal, including certain opinions which they may have about ourselves. The idea of a relationship with someone who is equally transparent to everyone should not interest us. Our relationships, when they are at their most respectful, are not with public or transparent bodies but with those persons who use the resources of language and gesture to reveal and conceal, express and suppress, tell lies and tell the truth; with persons who exercise the right and the power to create an inner life, a self, which is never wholly available or accessible to us. That is all that a self is, that aspect of a person which is hidden from us, which we are not sure of, which we forbid ourselves to force into the open. It is the very thing which animates and sustains relationships; it is in some significant measure the creature of relationships, the creature of both nature and nurture, a something never quite fully grasped in life, which goes wholly out of reach at the moment of death.

Over against Searle's cerebral emergentism we can pose a kind of cultural emergentism. But in order to do this convincingly there is one other move which needs to be made. One of the problems with Searle's account of a first-person ontology is that it seems to be based on questionable epistemological assumptions. Searle seems to assume that there is, as Hilary Putnam (1981) would say, a single system which contains all the objects that anyone could refer to - 'all the objects there are' - including, one may presume, the inner objects of a Searlean first-person ontology of the mental. I want to argue with Putnam, against Searle, that there is no such totality of 'all the objects there are', and no description of such a totality (See Putnam, 1981, Ch. 3). There is no absolutely external or God's-eye point of view from which such a totality could be objectively surveyed and exhaustively described. In place of the such an external realist perspective, Putnam proposes an internal realist picture, according to which objects cannot be said to exist independently of conceptual schemes. We cut up the world into objects of different kinds when we introduce one or other scheme of description. Objects and their 'corresponding' signs, signs and their 'corresponding' objects, are alike internal to the scheme of description. What Putnam says of objects, I want to say of psychological subjects. Just as there are no 'pure' objects which exist independently of conceptual schemes or interest-laden descriptions, so there are no 'pure' subjects, no pure Cartesian egos, which exist independently of the conceptual schemes, the social practices and institutions within which references to persons, selves, souls and inner lives have a place. The materialist who wishes to avoid an eliminativist posture - who wishes to participate, for example, in the recognized cultural rituals of grieving - can do so on the basis of a conceptual scheme or description which recognizes the internal reality of a mortal self. For both the grieving dualist and the grieving materialist there is a sense in which a body really is the 'remains' of a person; a sense in which a unique subjectivity - the spirit of a person - goes out of, departs the world.

Mind as inner cause

One materialist philosopher who appears to pay due attention to the 'innerness' of our psychological states is David Armstrong (1968; 1970). Some of Armstrong's views align him with the identity theorists. He is as impressed as they are by what the physical sciences have to say about the nature of mind, and he sympathizes with the view that these sciences can give a complete account of mind in purely physico-chemical terms. While accepting that in the future new evidence may come to light which will force science to reconsider the physico-chemical view, nevertheless 'the drift of scientific thought is clearly set towards the physico-chemical hypothesis' (1970. p. 67). He sets himself the task of working out an account of the nature of mind which is compatible with the view that human beings are nothing but physico-chemical mechanisms.

Armstrong also resembles the identity theorists in sympathising with behaviourism. He sees behaviourism as fitting in with a physicalist, scientific view of human nature. If there is no need to draw a distinction between mental processes and their 'expression' in physical behaviour, if mental processes are

67

indeed identified with their behavioural expression, then the concept of mind is suitably de-mystified and no longer conflicts with the scientific view. But the behaviourists, according to Armstrong, have never fully answered the objection that when my thoughts do not issue in behaviour 'there is still something actually going on in me which constitutes my thought' (p. 72) and this is not reducible to a mere disposition to behave. It is not simply that I would speak or act if some conditions that are unfulfilled were to be fulfilled. Something is currently going on 'in the strongest and most literal sense of "going on", and this something is my thought' (p. 72). Because Rylean behaviourism in particular denies the occurrent, episodic nature of the inner process, it is unsatisfactory as a theory of mind. In more general terms, behaviourism is also a 'profoundly unnatural' account of mind, in Armstrong's view. It is natural to refer to somebody's speech and action as expressions of his thought, but unnatural to think of his speech and action as identical with his thought. The thought is something quite distinct from the speech or action and in some sense lies *behind* behaviour: 'A man's behaviour constitutes the *reason* we have for attributing certain mental processes to him, but the behaviour cannot be identified with the mental processes' (p. 72).

What Armstrong takes from behaviourism is the notion that the concept of mind is logically tied to behaviour, not in the sense that categorical statements ascribing mental predicates are translatable into hypothetical statements about behaviour, but in the sense that mind can be defined as the 'inner cause' of certain behaviour. By re-defining mental states as inner causes of behaviour, Armstrong is keeping faith with behaviourism while at the same time keeping faith with the inner process. He further emphasizes his dual commitment by deciding to treat dispositions as actual states of things. That is, he offers a realist account of dispositions rather than the kind of operationalist account offered by Ryle. Though Armstrong's own distinction between a realist and an operationalist concept of dispositions has been criticized by Lyons (1980), we may nevertheless describe Armstrong's conception as realist insofar as he defines a disposition as residing in the structure of an object and as the topic of categorical rather than hypothetical judgements.

Armstrong encapsulates his position in neatly dialectical terms. The 'thesis' of classical philosophy is that the mind may be thought of as an inner arena of some kind. The 'antithesis' offered by behaviourism is that the mind may be thought of as behavioural dispositions. His own proposed 'synthesis' is that the mind may be properly conceived as an inner principle, but a principle that is identified and characterized in terms of the outward behaviour which it brings about. Significantly, Armstrong concedes that this way of looking at the mind 'does not itself entail a Materialist or Physicalist view of man, for nothing is said about the intrinsic nature of these mental states' (1968, p. 349). But given the general success of the scientific, materialistic theory of the nature of things, including human beings, it is reasonable to assume that mental states are in fact 'nothing but physical states of the central nervous system' (p. 349).

Thus far Armstrong's position has been stated in only general, schematic terms. Nothing very specific has been said about the nature of inner processes. He himself recognizes that his position may share a weakness with behaviourism, viz., that, like behaviourism, it may be a satisfactory account of the mind from a third-person point of view but is not very promising as a first-person account. In other people's case it is appropriate to explain their actions and speech in terms of inner causes or principles, but in our own case we seem to be aware of so much more than mere behaviour. It will not do to say that being conscious is having things going on within us which are apt for causing certain sorts of behaviour. His proposal is that consciousness 'is nothing but perception or awareness of the state of our own mind' (1968, p. 350). Conscious states are states of attention 'directed towards inner states and not to the environment, which enables us ... to behave in a selective way towards our own states of mind' (p. 350). In more physicalist terms, consciousness of our own mental states becomes simply 'the scanning of one part of our central nervous system by another. Consciousness is a self-scanning mechanism in the central nervous system' (p. 351).

This is not just an implicitly introspectionist theory of consciousness. Armstrong expressly conceives of consciousness in the way that Locke and Kant conceived it, as a form of introspective perception. Having referred favourably to Kant's concept of 'inner sense', he goes on to say that we cannot directly observe the minds of others, but each of us 'has the power to observe directly our own minds, and perceive what is going on there' (p. 350). What is significant about this argument is that it finds Armstrong committing the modern philosophical sin of introspectionism, that sin attributed so often to Descartes and punished so often by Ryle and the Wittgensteinians. It also shows him raising the question of other minds and subsequently walking into the briar patch of difficulties usually associated with the mythical Cartesians. That profound privacy which Anthony Kenny was at pains to attribute to Descartes' mentalism is no less attributable to Armstrong's materialism. Kenny and others have tended to assume or argue that the distinction between 'inner' and 'outer' entails a Cartesian dualism of mind and body. The significance of Armstrong's theory, however, is that it shows that a concept of the mind as private and self-introspective is not necessarily inconsistent with materialism, which suggests in turn that critics of Cartesianism cannot assume that in attacking privacy or introspectionism they are attacking the essence of Cartesianism.

One significant difference between Armstrong's and Descartes' conceptions of self-knowledge should be their different approaches to the question of the incorrigibility of statements about one's own current mental states. Armstrong attributes to Cartesians the belief that we cannot be mistaken about our own current mental states, and maintains that if the doctrine of incorrigibility or indubitability were true it would refute his type of central-state materialism. His reasoning here is that if the concept of a mental state is the concept of a state of the person apt for the production of behaviour, then we cannot hold simultaneously that introspection is incorrigible, for the knowledge of causes cannot be incorrigible:

> Surely any statement that one thing is a cause, or potential cause, of another thing, however arrived at, is subject to the tests of future observation and experiment? And if it is so subject, how can it be incorrigible? (1968, p. 103)

Armstrong concludes that the defender of a causal, central-state materialism must show that 'there can be no logically indubitable knowledge of, or logically privileged access to, or self-intimation by, our current mental states' (p. 103).[2] His first argument against indubitable introspective knowledge is that a mental state and one's knowledge of it are temporally distinct existences, so that it is always logically possible that one event, 'pain', might occur but the other - the thought, 'I am in pain' - might not occur, and vice versa. His second argument is that it is (empirically) impossible that our ordinary reports of our current mental states should be indubitable. My 'indubitable' knowledge that I am in pain can surely embrace only the current instant: 'it cannot be logically indubitable that I will be in pain by the time the sentence ['I am in pain now'] is finished' (p. 105).

Armstrong's arguments are perhaps valid against a strong or 'logical' version of the incorrigibility thesis, but it is unlikely that anyone has ever held such positions. It is not claimed by anyone, not even by Cartesians, that people have logically indubitable knowledge of, or logically privileged access to, their current mental states. It is not even clear what this might mean. Armstrong is yet another philosopher who imagines that Descartes' Cogito has to do with indubitable knowledge of a mental state, as if Descartes were engaged in a kind of do-it-yourself, introspective, self-analytical psychology. The Cogito, however, is not an item of psychological, empirical self-knowledge at all, i.e., it is not the outcome of a close encounter with one's self. Notions of 'acquaintance' with objects of knowledge are empiricist notions, not properly rationalist or Cartesian ones. The Cogito, as I have repeatedly argued, is best understood as the end-state of a process of sceptical reasoning, rather than as the record of an act of introspection. The indubitability of the Cogito makes sense only in the context of a methodic doubt about the possibility of cognitive certitude. What matters to Descartes is the unique logical implication of the relation between the existence of a *cogitatio* and the existence of a methodically doubting *res cogitans*. Such statements as 'I am in pain' or 'I am thinking of x' have no particular significance for a Cartesian if they are offered merely as incidental items of psychological information. Their 'indubitability' does not become an issue until the questions of existential certainty are raised in an appropriately systematic and philosophical way.

Privacy, mentality, and incorrigibility

Richard Rorty argues that if Armstrong were right in saying that the concept of a mental state is essentially the concept of an inner cause apt for producing certain behaviour, than we would never be able to make sense of the common contrasts between (a) dualism and materialism, or (b) between the mental and the physical, or (c) between materialism and behaviourism. Rorty's difficulty is with the sort of topic-neutral version of scientific materialism put forward by Armstrong. The topic-neutral materalist seems to think we are being fair to Descartes 'as long as we give an analysis of the mental that leaves it open that mental events are taking place in an immaterial stuff' (Rorty, 1970, p. 402). But this neglects the point that 'immaterial' gets its sense from its connection with 'mental'. If the mental is merely the unknown cause of certain behaviour, 'then no sense is given to "immaterial" because no example of the "nonextended" is available to us' (p. 402). We cannot, in Rorty's opinion, define 'mental' as something that might turn out to be either mental or physical, because we cannot define any term as something that might turn out to refer to what is denoted by a contrary term: 'It is part of the sense of "mental" that being mental is incompatible with being physical, and no explication of this sense which denies this incompatibility can be satisfactory' (p. 402).

While Rorty does not, of course, wish to maintain that mind is an immaterial substance, he does claim that the materialist who wants to maintain that it is an empirical question whether or not the realm of the mental is self-sustaining must insist on preserving mental entities that have characteristics incompatible with being physical. After deciding to regard sensation and thoughts, but not beliefs, moods, or other dispositional states as stereotypical mental particulars, he argues that the feature which sensations and thoughts have in common with each other and not with anything physical is incorrigibility. He rules out intentionality as a distinguishing feature of the mental because 'to have a sensation, unlike having a thought, is not to be in a state which has "aboutness" or which can somehow refer to the inexistent' (p. 409). He also rules out non-spatiality on the grounds that it makes 'excellent sense' to give sensations and thoughts a location, though a vague one, and that this 'vague spatiality' applies equally to one's weight, build and health. Nor can we argue that the mental is unextended and the physical extended 'by claiming that the shape or size of thoughts and sensations is a contentless notion, whereas all physical things have shape or size' (p. 410). No *state* of an object, as distinct from the object itself, has shape or size. To insist that mental events are shapeless and sizeless 'is merely to remind us that they are states of persons' (p. 410). Also rejected

71

is Armstrong's notion that 'innerness' alone is the mark of the mental, since this only comes to mean 'beneath the skin,' i.,e., something 'on all fours' with internal secretions or muscle movements. That is to say, physical 'innerness' does not provide a means for distinguishing the mental from the physical. We cannot, according to Rorty, make Armstrongian 'states apt ...' into *mental* states just by adding an assortment of intrinsic features to them 'unless there is among those features one which separates off all such states from other states we know of, and, thereby, establishes a new category of existence' (p. 413). The only feature which can do this, in Rorty's view, is privacy. By privacy he does not mean incommunicability, or special access, or unsharability. He means privacy in the sense of incorrigibility, which in turn means that mental events are unlike any other events in that certain knowledge about them cannot be overridden: 'We have no criteria for setting aside as mistaken first-person contemporaneous reports of thought and sensations, whereas we do have criteria for setting aside all reports about everything else' (p. 413).

What makes an entity mental is not whether it is something that explains behaviour but whether certain reports of its existence have the special status of incorrigibility in the sense stated above. Incorrigibility is not defined in terms of logical indubitability but in terms 'of the procedures for resolving doubts accepted at a given era' (p. 417). Thus he submits:

S believes incorrigibly that p at t if and only if
(i) S believes that p at t
(ii) There are no accepted procedures by applying which it is rational to come to believe that not-p, given S's belief that p at t. (p. 417)

This definition is immune from the criticism of logical indubitability made by Armstrong and others. It is not being claimed that Armstrong's self-scanning processes cannot possibly be wrong but that there is no assured way of correcting them if they should be wrong. Viewing the matter in this way reduces incorrigibility to what Armstrong calls 'empirically privileged', thus giving incorrigibility 'an epistemological status relative to the state of empirical enquiry, and one capable of being lost if, for example, cerebroscopes should come to over-rule first-person reports' (Rorty, 1970, p. 417).

Rorty's critique of Armstrong is important for (a) its emphasis on the extent to which the mental/physical distinction is embedded in our language, (b) its rejection of a non-mentalistic sense of innerness, and (c) its re-definition of privacy or incorrigibility in terms of procedures and 'corrigibility conditions'. Rorty has shown that in order to define the mental in terms of the power and the right to make first-person contemporaneous reports, it is not necessary to defend any sort of problematic, mythically Cartesian notion of introspection or privileged access. It is also important that in granting incorrigibility an epistemological status in relation to the state of empirical inquiry, Rorty draws attention to the fact that this status could be lost if new brain-scanning technologies were to be developed. In other words, the invention of cerebroscopes could cause first-person reports to be over-ridden and thus alter our conception of the mental. Such a development would raise an ethical question about the right to an inner life, to a 'mind' of one's own, to a fundamental level of privacy, viz. privacy of thought, intention and decision.

What Rorty does not acknowledge, however, is the fact that this ethical question is not something which arises only in the event of a futuristic brain-scanning technology. It is always possible to bring about situations in which first-person reports are ignored or devalued, in which the right to an inner life or even an inner self is denied or systematically frustrated. Sandra E. Marshall has argued that those who wish to exercise control over others, to use them as public objects subject only to their will, have always known that the way to achieve this is to bring about in individuals a loss of the sense of self, to get them to see themselves as public objects: 'One way of doing this is to subject them to a regime in which all privacy is lost' (Marshall, 1991, p. 266). Though she finds it impossible to imagine a community in which everyone knew everyone else's thoughts, she makes it clear that there are logical or conceptual links between self, community and privacy, including, we would argue, that fundamental degree of privacy that is guaranteed in the right to make incorrigible first-person reports on one's own mental states. The right to privacy, according to Marshall, is important to our status as persons or selves, in that if we are to have some sense of our selves 'there must be some things which are recognized as ours, in the sense that these will form the content of the idea of self' (p. 268). The 'some things' of which she writes are facts about ourselves in the sense of the sorts of facts that a doctor or psychiatrist may know about us in normal circumstances. The same moral reasoning which applies to confidential information possessed by another person may also apply to the even more 'intimate' sort of information which is contained in first-person reports. We can readily agree with Marshall when she concludes: 'If we are to have control over our selves, to be autonomous, then these are the things over which we must have control; and these may include facts about us. To respect privacy will be one of the ways in which we show respect for one another as persons' (pp. 268-9).

But how well-founded is this talk of privacy, first-person reports, autonomy? Despite all that has been said hitherto, could it be that this sort of idiom is seriously 'theory-laden'? Could it be that it belongs to a conceptual framework which is pre-scientific or unscientific - a framework which is open to revision, even elimination? Such doubts as these have been triggered by one of the most controversial developments in recent philosophy of mind, namely, eliminative materialism, which looks forward to the decline of mentalistic terminology and the 'folk' psychology in which it is embedded. This will be the topic of the next chapter.

Notes

1. One of the clearest accounts of the nature of qualia is given by Gerald Edelman (1992, p. 114): 'Qualia constitute the collection of personal or subjective experiences, feelings, and sensations that accompany awareness. They are phenomenal states - 'how things seem to us' as human beings. For example, the 'redness' of a red object is a quale. Qualia are discriminable parts of a mental scene that nonetheless has an overall unity. They may range in intensity and clarity from 'raw feels' to highly refined discriminanda.... In general, in the normal waking state, qualia are accompanied by a sense of spatiotemporal continuity. Often, the phenomenal scene is accompanied by feelings or emotions, however faint. Yet the actual *sequence* of qualia is highly individual, resting on a series of occasions in one's own personal history or immediate experience.'

2. Armstrong (1968, p. 103) distinguishes between the notion of indubitability and self-intimation in the following way. The proposition p is logically indubitable for A if, and only if:

    (i) A believes p,

    (ii) (A's belief that p) logically implies (p).

    We can say that p is self-intimating for A if, and only if:

    (i) p,

    (ii) (p) logically implies (A believes p).

    According to Armstrong, in saying that introspective awareness is incorrigible we are simply saying that any belief we have about our own current mental state is inevitably true. Error is thus ruled out but not ignorance. In saying, however, that our current mental states are self-intimating we rule out this possibility of ignorance. Taken together, the notions of incorrigibility and self-intimacy give us the doctrine of the perfectly transparent mind. Armstrong notes that while this doctrine is associated with Descartes, 'it stands in no necessary relation to Cartesian Dualism' (p. 102).

4 The case against folk psychology

The eliminative materialist does not look forward, as a mind-brain identity theorist might, to a tit-for-tat substitution of brain-process terms for mental terms. According to Paul Churchland, such a substitution would presuppose that mental concepts are already doing a good job of identifying certain phenomena, that a nice match-up could in principle take place 'between the concepts of folk psychology and the concepts of theoretical neuroscience' (1984, p. 43), and that a better job could be done, conceivably, by brain-process language alone. Churchland's own eliminativist hypothesis is that our common-sense, mentalistic, psychological framework will not undergo a reduction to a more scientific one 'because our common-sense psychological framework is a false and radically misleading conception of the causes of human behaviour and the nature of cognitive activity' (p. 43). Consequently, we must accept that the older framework will simply be eliminated, rather than 'reduced', by neuroscientific theory. The ontology of an older theory concerned with mental entities will give way to the ontology of a new and superior theory concerned with cerebral and neurological entities. This shift in conceptual frameworks will resemble the shift in our recent conceptual history from caloric-fluid theory to kinetic energy theory as an account of heat; or the shift from phlogiston theory to oxygen theory as an account of combustion; or the shift from witch theory to psychosis theory as an account of mental disturbance. The concepts of folk psychology - 'belief', 'desire', 'pain' - await a similar fate, in Churchland's view. With the development of the neurosciences we shall be able to set about reconceiving our internal states and activities within a more adequate framework. Our explanations of one another's behaviour will appeal to such things as our neuropharmacological states. Our own private introspection will also be enhanced and transformed, 'just as the astronomer's perception of the night sky is much enhanced by the detailed knowledge of modern astronomical theory ... ' (p. 45).

75

Churchland offers three reasons for claiming that an eliminative materialism is preferable to a reductive materialism. There are, first, the widespread 'explanatory, predictive, and manipulative failures of folk psychology' (p. 45). We do not know, in folk-psychological terms, what sleep is, or how learning is possible, or how differences in intelligence are grounded, or how memory works, or what mental illness is. In other words, the most central things about us remain mysterious from within folk psychology. Second, there is an 'inductive lesson' to be learnt from our conceptual history. Our folk theories about other, simpler aspects of the world have proved false, so we should expect that folk theories about something as complex as conscious intelligence will also prove wrong. Third, the *a priori* probability of eliminative materialism being true is higher than that of either the identity theory or functionalism because eliminative materialism does not depend on the demanding requirements of finding 'match-ups' between folk psychology and a matured neuroscience.

Churchland's most radical claim is that our common-sense terms for mental states are in fact theoretical terms embedded in a theoretical framework, and that the meanings of these terms are fixed in the same way as are the meanings of theoretical terms in general. Like any theory which consists of laws and operates according to a deductive-nomological model of explanation, folk psychology serves an explanatory-predictive function and postulates the existence of laws of nature and of theoretical entities. Folk psychology consists of hundreds of 'rough-and-ready general statements or laws' (p.59) which amount to explanations of human behaviour. Collectively, these constitute a rough-and-ready theory which postulates 'a range of internal states whose causal relations are described by the theory's laws,' (p. 59) and it is this framework of accumulated wisdom which Churchland labels 'folk psychology'. If our common-sense folk psychology is a theory, then the question of the relation of mental states to brain states becomes a question of how an old theory (folk psychology) relates to a new theory (matured neuroscience). The four major positions on the mind-body issue emerge as four different 'anticipations' of how the problem is to be resolved. The identity theorist expects that the old theory will be 'smoothly reduced' by a matured neuroscience. The dualist maintains that the old theory will not be reduced by a matured neuroscience, on the grounds that human behaviour has non-physical sources. The functionalist also expects that the old theory will not be reduced 'because too many different kinds of physical systems can produce the exact causal organisation specified by the old theory' (p. 61). The eliminative materialist also rules out reduction but on the grounds that the old theory is too mistaken to begin with.

Could the eliminativist be right, conceivably? Could it be the case, conceivably, that our familiar, time-honoured ways of talking about our psychological lives are as mistaken as the alchemist's way of talking about matter, or the witch-doctor's way of curing sickness, or the flat-earther's way of envisaging the world? Could it be the case that our concepts of mind, self, and 'the inner life' belong in the same category as the gods of the classical pagan theologies or the demons and spirits of tribal animism? Is the concept of mind or self as much a folk-theoretical concept as that of demon or tree-spirit?

Science, folk theory, and theoretical folk

Churchland's eliminative materialism depends largely on his two-edged claim (a) that the mentalistic terms of ordinary language constitute a *folk* theory, and (b) that the mentalistic terms of ordinary language constitute a folk *theory*. Let us look first at claim (a). It is not at all clear what a folk theory is, or what the relationship is between folk theories and scientific theories. Are we to assume that folk theories are essentially vulgar pre-scientific or unscientific theories? Are we to take it that alchemy, for example, was a kind of primitively vulgar precursor of chemistry - a kind of folk chemistry - or simply an utterly pre-scientific theory which has now been effectively replaced by the science of chemistry? Just what is it that makes alchemy (but not chemistry) so folksy?

Whether we describe alchemy as a vulgar precursor of chemistry or as a kind of folk chemistry, it does not seem right to refer to it as a folk theory. It may be true that it was a kind of pre-scientific theory rather than a primitive science but it is not correct to call it a *folk* theory since it was not popularly or commonly practised and was in fact surrounded by a good deal of hermetical secrecy. The concepts and practices of alchemy were no more widely understood in the pre-scientific era than those of modern chemistry are widely understood in our time. Hermeticism has been a distinctive feature of most pre-scientific theories, i.e., theories pre-dating the emergence of the modern sciences. It is inferable from the historical work of Thorndike (1967), Rossi (1968), and Webster (1980) that practices such as astrology, necromancy, demonology, and natural magic were not popular in the sense of being commonly practised but were in fact esoteric, hermetic, occult practices.[1] While such practices were, of course, 'believed in' by the wider community - and their practitioners regularly consulted as therapists, forecasters, or oracles - the esoteric 'knowledge' itself was not more widely understood than the 'knowledge' possessed by a modern scientist. The relationship between the public and practitioners of alchemy in late medieval and Renaissance society would not have been more intimate than that between the public and, say, chemists in our own era. Indeed, because of the absence of a system of public education, the pre-scientific specialist was perhaps even more remote from his general public - illiterate ordinary folk - than is the modern scientific specialist. Any theory can become a folk theory if there is a lay public which has limited access to the work of a society's theorizing specialists. 'Folk' is not the antithesis of 'scientific'; it comes close to meaning 'vulgar' or

77

'popular', in the sense in which people in our own era could be said to have a 'popular' understanding of modern physics ('the Big Bang', 'black holes', 'quarks'). The modern sciences can give rise to vulgar, popular, or 'folk' versions of themselves. Indeed, we can say that this is just how we demarcate and identify folk theories and beliefs - namely, in relation to the specialist or scientific practices which generate them. Folk theories do not necessarily or typically pre-date scientific theories. In the pre-scientific era, folk theories were posited or generated by pre-scientific theories and practices such as natural magic, alchemy, and astrology. The common-sense wisdom or lore of the time would have included unquestioning acceptance of some of the vocabulary and conceptual frameworks of these occult practices. The common-sense laity would have had no good reason to disbelieve the claims of alchemists, natural magicians, and the rest. It would have believed in the reality of demons and astral influences and in the seriousness of the alchemist's project. Most people would have entered into a pragmatic, common-sense liaison with these occult specialists who might, after all, have the sort of power that could be used against you if you rejected them out of hand. What we now call superstition was, in the pre-scientific era, a form of common-sense discretion or wisdom, i.e., a form of that 'acknowledgement without knowledge' which informs the minds of all those who are not themselves experts or specialists but who have to stay on the right side of the experts and specialists. The folk theorist in the pre-scientific era is not the alchemist or magician. Rather, the folk theorist is the non-specialist who has only a common-sense or 'vulgar' understanding of the arcane specialism of the alchemist and magician. Folk means non-expert, non-specialist, non-arcane; folk theory means the vulgar understanding that the non-expert has of the concepts, techniques, and practices of all the specialists who claim to be able to cure him, to predict his future, to save his soul, to protect him from demons or diseases, to make his land fertile, to make himself fertile.

Folk belief, then, whether pre-scientific or scientific, consists of terms and concepts which have percolated down unreliably into common usage; it is often a mixture of the old and the new, of hand-me-down superstition and popularized versions of current state-of-the-art theorizing. The distance between the common-sense folk theorist and the specialist has not narrowed in the scientific era. Those of us who would have been non-experts in alchemy are now non-experts in chemistry; those of us who would have been non-experts in natural magic are now non-experts in medicine; those of us who would have been non-experts in astrology are now non-experts in astronomy; those of us who would have been non-experts in divination and prophecy are now non-experts in economics and meteorology; those of us who would have been non-experts in demonology or exorcism are now non-experts in psychoanalysis or clinical psychology. The content of common sense may have changed as the content of the various specializations has changed, but the nature of the relationship between the common-sense laity and the specialist has not substantially changed, and will not substantially change. The modern folk theorist is still gathering crumbs from the tables of the specialists; in the future there will be more - and harder - crumbs from more tables. The specialists themselves are still doing the same sort of thing they always did, only more successfully than their pre-scientific predecessors. They are still in the business of selling cures and remedies, of saving our souls, of prediction and control, of converting base metals into gold.

There is no doubt, then, that common sense contains theoretical concepts, but at least some of those concepts are present in common sense because they have percolated down from the theories and practices of the specialists. Many, if not all, of the modern sciences generate folk versions of themselves, just as earlier, pre-scientific theories generated folk versions of themselves. In the scientific era, folk versions of magical or pre-scientific theories have been largely replaced by folk versions of scientific theories. When we talk about folk physics or folk chemistry we are not necessarily talking about something which is antithetical to modern physics but about something which owes its existence to modern physics, and which is facilitated by popular science magazines and TV series. The same fate could befall a matured neuroscience, i.e., it could become a folk neuroscience. The elimination of folk psychology in that event would not mean the complete and successful elimination of popular ignorance about the determinants of human behaviour - it would mean, rather, the replacement, or partial replacement, of one folk theory (folk psychology), by another (e.g., folk neuropharmacology). If some unscientific theory like witch-theory or demon-theory has already been replaced at a popular level it is not by a well-distributed, well-understood scientific theory but by an unevenly distributed constellation of scientific-sounding notions about brainwaves, electrical stimulation, mind-expanding drugs, shock treatment, Pavlov's dogs, etc. This is also what folk psychology is like in the modern era - it comprises bits of Freudianism, Jungianism and behaviourism, just as in earlier times it comprised bits of demonology and astrology. Folk psychology in this sense is not something which antedates and is completely replaced by scientific theory but something which comes after scientific theory, that 'falls out' from it. In other words, at the level of common sense, a folk science will have taken the place of witch theory, or astral influence theory, or the theory of humours. This is the most that eliminativism can look forward to. It can only look forward to the elimination of unscientific folk theories, not to the elimination of folk theories as such. As long as there exists a general public - a common sense laity of non-experts - then it is very likely there will exist folk theory. The most that the eliminativists will get is folk versions of various scientific theories, including the neurosciences.

The reason that folk theorizing cannot be eliminated has to do with both the nature of specialization and the nature of common sense. The modern sciences by their nature involve not only specialist vocabularies and conceptual frameworks but also specialist methodologies and technologies. Eliminativists often talk as if the only difference between scientific theories and common sense theories lay in a difference of conceptual frameworks or ontologies. They fail to adequately acknowledge the fact that any science is also a highly technical practice, i.e., a practice involving the mastery of instruments and methodologies, often applicable only within severely controlled environments, such as laboratories. The problem for the eliminativists is that whereas concepts and frameworks can be popularized to some degree, techniques, technologies, and methodologies cannot. Even the popularizability of concepts is limited for the reason that most technical vocabularies and frameworks depend for their proper and accurate use on techniques which are in turn dependent on the application of instruments and technologies. Scientists themselves, once they leave their laboratories or controlled environments, are not going to be able to accurately apply technical or theoretical concepts unless they have access to special instruments. The astronomer without her telescope and charts is, in many cases, not much better off than the layperson when looking at the stars through her unaided eye; the microbiologist without his microscope may not be much better at spotting and identifying bacteria than anyone else; the engineer without her theodolite may not greatly excel the layperson when it comes to measuring angles with the naked eye.

Such considerations render particularly questionable some of Churchland's illustrations of what elimination might involve. These are simple examples of what it would mean to use scientific concepts in place of folk-psychological ones, especially in the context of introspective consciousness. He suggests that internal states now introspectible under descriptions provided by folk psychology could be better discriminated under descriptions provided by the neurosciences. All those internal states currently lumped together under the concept of 'pain' can be more finely discriminated as sundry modes of stimulation in our A-delta fibres and/or C-fibres, or in our thalamus and/or reticular formations. What are commonly referred to as 'after images' can be more penetratingly analyzed as 'differentially fatigued areas in the retina's photochemical grid' (1979, p. 119). Sensations of acceleration and falling are better grasped as deformations and relaxations of one's vestibular system. Rotational dizziness is more effectively introspected as 'a residual circulation of the inertial fluid in the semi-circular canals of the inner ear' (p. 119). The familiar sensation of 'pins and needles' is more usefully apprehended as oxygen deprivation of the nerve endings.

The main problem with these examples of possible elimination is the assumption that all there is to the practice of the neurosciences is a conceptual framework, as if one may simply learn off a certain technical vocabulary and then go around applying it as one sees fit. But the conceptual framework of the neuroscientist depends for its proper application on techniques and instruments that are not available to the person in the street. They are not even available to the specialist once she leaves her laboratory and joins the rest of us in the street. The language of A-delta fibres, reticular formations, and vestibular systems can only be used effectively and accurately if it is used in conjunction with the investigative technology of the neuroscientist, the application of which may sometimes involve surgical procedures, and sometimes include the use of X-ray and brain-scanning technology. The more that a scientific idiom is separated from this sort of investigative observational technology, the more likely it is to become a kind of folk idiom itself - that is, a kind of folk science. The terms used, if they are used independently of the appropriate technology, may come to be used even more accurately than less scientific common-sense terms. All we are likely to get is a kind of hit-and-miss folk usage which will only be an irritant to the fully-equipped specialist whose job it is to apply the appropriate technology according to the appropriate manual.

The dependence of conceptual frameworks on technical methodologies and instrumentation provides us with an important clue to the nature of folk theory. What makes folk theory folksy is not the fact that is unscientific but the fact that the person in the street is always travelling light - that is, she is not packing the battery of investigative or observational technologies that have been generated by modern scientific practice. There is therefore a serious practical limit to the extent to which folk theorizing can be eliminated. Folk theorizing is always theorizing at a remove from the technical hardware that is central to scientific theorizing. It is theorizing without benefit of specialist knowledge and specialist methodologies; it is the theorizing of the layperson who may have a little knowledge of a range of scientific vocabularies but little or no access to the techniques, instruments, and technologies that would enable him or her to use this knowledge accurately and effectively. Indeed, it is quite possible that such a little knowledge, like a little learning, could be a dangerous thing, especially if it led to people diagnosing and subsequently attempting to treat their own medical conditions. As a rule, people should perhaps be advised to make do with older, cruder, less precise frameworks which do not require highly specialized, deeply theory-laden methodologies and technologies.

One of the significant differences, then, between common sense and scientific practice is that common sense is non-technical, non-methodic and non-specialist, and involves unaided observation. Most of the observations that most of us make outside the specialist environments of the laboratory or research institute are going to be unaided, for the very simple reason that we cannot carry any or all of the technologies around with us; and also for the reason that most of us are not capable of being specialists in all the areas of specialization that now exist. Recognition of this fact is part of what we might mean by practical wisdom in the modern era. Practical wisdom in the pre-scientific era consisted in not dabbling in magic yourself, in knowing when to take your problem to the local magician who knew precisely how to call spirits from the vasty deep or wherever; practical wisdom in the scientific era, on the other hand, consists in knowing when to consult the doctor or engineer, or some other specialist, instead of dabbling in these things yourself. Common sense in our era defers to the specialist and regards the specialist as a consultant, just as common sense in more magical times deferred to, and consulted, the practitioner of some specialized hermetical practice. This suggests that the best way to envisage or model the relationship between common sense and the specializations is in terms of a consultancy model, a model which would place the sciences, including the neurosciences, on the same footing as, say, medicine or civil engineering. No one seriously argues that the layperson should diagnose and treat all her own medical conditions; no one recommends that people become amateur engineers and go around building their own bridges. Likewise, given that neuroscience is just one specialization among an increasing plethora of specializations, it is unwise to suggest that people should set about mastering and applying the neuroscientific framework by themselves, to themselves. The role of the neuroscientist is that of consultant, not that of a proselytiser whose mission is to rid the world of folk theories. If we were to re-model the relationship between the specializations and common sense in the form of a consultancy model we could eliminate the sort of proselytizing model on which eliminativism is predicated.

We should introduce a qualification into the distinction between the specialist and the layperson. It is misleading to talk as if there were two kinds of people, namely, 'specialists' who are good at scientific theorizing and 'lay people' who are capable only of more lowly forms of 'folk' theorizing. Since no one can be a specialist in everything, it follows that all specialists are also, for many practical intents and purposes, members of the common-sense laity. All specialists are folk theorists in all those areas in which they are not specialists. The neuroscientist, for example, is likely to be a folk theorist as far as nuclear physics, botany, or astronomy is concerned. This gives us another clue to the nature of common sense. Common sense is where we all go when we come out of our specialist shells, when we leave the laboratory, the ivory tower, the library, or the research institute. Common sense is the great leveller in the measure that it constitutes the common ground on which people are reduced to sharing the judgments of their unaided senses. A good example of this is in the matter of everyday perceptual judgements, such as the judgements we make about the world around us - judgements in terms of horizons, the sky, the sun, the moon, the stars, the seasons, the weather. As far as the everyday phenomenal world is concerned, we are all still practicing geocentrists, even flat-earthers. We know theoretically that the earth is round, that the earth is not stationary, that it is the sun which is stationary relative to the earth, and that we are the ones who are in motion around this local star. But still we see the sun rise in the east, move slowly across the sky, set in the west. Conversely, we fail to experience the movement of the earth, either its orbital or its rotational motion. Our perceptual faculties seem to be, as Fodor puts it, 'cognitively

82

impenetrable', i.e., to be impervious to theory and information (1984, pp. 23-43). And it is because this is the case that, despite what the astronomers tell us, we continue to talk about sunrise and sunset. For most practical intents and purposes we get away with it, just as our ancestors did. Our common-sense perceptual faculties are much the same as those of our ancestors, and that is why our common-sense language about the common-sense world remains - and will remain - much the same, despite advances in observational technologies and in cosmos theory.

The eliminativist will not accept this sort of approach, of course. Churchland insists that if our perceptual judgements must be laden with theory in any case, 'then why not have them be laden with the best theory available? Why not exchange the Neolithic legacy now in use for the conception of reality embodied in modern-era science?' (1979, p. 35). He even devises a sort of mental and physical exercise for putting Copernican theory into observational practice. This exercise - which may be carried out 'some suitably planeted twilight' - involves identifying the solar planets by sight, determining the plane of the elliptic in which these planets revolve, then tilting one's head to one side so that the elliptic becomes a horizontal in one's visual field. If you get this right, you will begin to form a sense of the Copernican cosmos - you will come to see that the Earth's axis of rotation is to your right, roughly parallel to the axis of your tilted head. By keeping the stars as your fixed frame of reference, you can 'observe' the rotation of the earth as it carries you away from the planetary formation in question, and in 24 hours you will be able to see that the position of the Earth has translated to the right a visible degree. In other words, the shifting configurations of the solar family will become apparent to you, 'a vertiginous feeling will signal success' (p. 34), and you will be at home in the solar system for the first time.

What is so questionable about this way of supposedly experiencing the Copernican cosmos is that it is really rather folksy. It doesn't involve any of the methodologies or observational technologies that are normally used by scientists to confirm and demonstrate the Copernican theory. It relies, moreover, on something as folk-psychological as a 'vertiginous feeling' to signal the success of the exercise. This sort of feeling is very surely not what scientists would use as the criterion of the successful outcome of an experiment of this nature. In any case, this exercise in revisionary perception doesn't really produce the sort of experience that would corroborate, at a perceptual level, the Copernican theory. Nothing that an unaided earth-bound observer can do can cause him to experience the orbital and rotational motion of the earth. At best, these motions can only be inferred. Over against Churchland it is arguable that most people, for most of the time, are not in a position to accurately apply the heliocentric or Copernican framework, or to perceive the cosmos as it is modelled within that framework. Most people, most of the time, do not have a complete grasp of the theory, and - more importantly - do not have access to the technology, including the vast communications technology, that would enable them to apply it adequately. Given the very limited availability of that technology, it is wiser to stay with the vocabulary that best accords with the deliverances of the unaided eye (which happens to be a geocentric vocabulary) than to adopt some kind of folk heliocentrism. The practical wisdom of modern common sense consists in not using the deliverances of unaided common-sense perception to challenge, or try to disprove, the claims of the experts, in this case the claims of the Copernicans; and that wisdom is all that should be expected of folk-astronomers, which is what most of us are, most of the time. To put this in terms suggested by Wilfrid Sellars (1963), we are better advised to stick with the language of the manifest image which we have mastered, than to go over to the language of the scientific image which we have not mastered, and which most of us are unlikely to master, given the nature of modern scientific specialization.

But to say things like this is still to put the case too defensively. It is arguable not only that elimination is not a practical possibility but also that it would be undesirable in some cases. It is arguable, in other words, that common sense should sometimes set limits to the progress of the sciences, especially the human or 'mind' sciences. As a variation on Feyerabend's plea for the separation of science and the state (1975, Ch. 18), we might argue that common sense is central to the process of science-state separation and to what we might wish to call theory-pluralism. Common sense may be regarded as the public cultural space - the 'res publica' - in which people may be maximally noncommittal, in which they are free to accept or reject a particular account of the world, whether it be a particular religious account or a particular scientific account. A common-sense discourse which was largely composed of the terms of reference of one science would be as undesirable as one which was dominated by the terms of reference of one religion; freedom of conscience (which may be taken to include freedom of 'theoretical' conscience) would be curtailed, even eliminated. Eliminativism doesn't just have implications for the content of thought. It also has implications for freedom of thought - in this case, freedom of theoretical thought. Of course, the eliminativist may not see that there is any kind of real choice between a common-sense framework and a scientific one. The choice between folk theory and scientific theory looks like a choice between ignorance and knowledge. But to present the choice in such stark terms is to beg the question and to make precisely the sorts of assumptions that people ought to be free to question. These assumptions are unlikely to be questioned within the specialisms themselves, so it is important that there should remain a region in which they may be questioned - and this region we may call common sense. It is the space in which individuals become mature citizens, in Feyerabend's sense. A mature citizen, Feyerabend suggests, is not one who has been trained or instructed in a special methodology or ideology but one who has learned to make up his or her mind 'and who has then *decided* in favour of what he thinks suits him best' (1975, p. 308).

There is a feature of folk psychology in particular which suggests that scientific frameworks and practices might be a potential threat to a certain kind of privacy and a certain, very fundamental kind of freedom of expression. This threat is hinted at but not taken up by Richard Rorty (1970) in an article in which the eliminativist idea made one of its earliest appearances:

> [T]o say that it might turn out that there are not mental entities is to say something not merely about the relative explanatory powers of psychological and physiological accounts of behaviour, but about possible changes in people's ways of speaking. For as long as people continue to report, incorrigibly, on such things as thoughts and sensations, it will seem silly to say that mental entities do not exist - no matter what science may do. The eliminative materialist cannot rest his case solely on the practice of scientists, but must say something about the ontology of the man in the street. (1970, pp. 422-3)

The pertinent sentence here is the penultimate one: 'For as long as people continue to report, incorrigibly, on such things as thoughts and sensations, it will seem silly to say that mental entities do not exist - no matter what science may do.' As we saw in Chapter 3, Rorty maintains that privacy is the mark of the mental; and by privacy he means incorrigibility in the sense that we have no criteria for setting aside as mistaken first-person contemporaneous reports of thoughts and sensations. This incorrigibility is not absolute but is relative to 'the procedures for resolving doubts at a given era' (p. 417). It is not being claimed that a subject's self-scanning processes cannot be mistaken but that there is no assured way to set about correcting them if they should be mistaken. So far, so good. In the previous chapter, we saw Rorty making important points about the relationship between mentality, incorrigibility, and privacy. But Rorty subsequently goes on to allow for a possibility that is quite alarming. In the course of clarifying what he means by incorrigibility, he emphasizes that it has 'an epistemological status relative to the state of empirical inquiry, and one capable of being lost if, for example, cerebroscopes should come to overrule first-person reports' (p. 417). Cerebroscopes are brain-scanning, brain-reading machines which would enable neuroscientists to determine what exactly was going on inside one's brain, making possible an account of a person's internal psychological states which could be superior to one's own account in traditionally first-person mentalistic terms. Even one's claim that one had a pain, or one's report of a dream, could be overridden by the neuroscientist equipped with a cerebroscope.

The possibility of cerebroscopes overruling first-person accounts is, as we have already seen, a possibility which has questionable ethical and political implications. What looks like the replacement of one set of theoretical terms by another, or the replacement of one mode of verification by another, is also the suppression of a whole mode of expression and even of a form of life, i.e., that form of life in which first-person reports of internal states are acknowledged and valued. What has to be defended here is a freedom of speech at a very fundamental level, i.e., the level of first-person present-tense accounts of current mental states! It is the possession of the language of these mental states - a 'folk-psychological' language - which makes the first-person account possible. If that language and ontology were eliminated, then the wherewithal of the first-person account would be eliminated also and a new moral and political era as well as a new scientific era would be entered.

This may sound like an alarmist exaggeration but it can be defended on the basis of the Wittgensteinian observation - reiterated most recently by Norman Malcolm (1989) - that each of us stands in a different relation to his own mental or psychological states than does anyone else. The difference between first-person ascriptions and third-person ascriptions is that the latter are criterial (based on evidence, usually behavioural) while the former are non-criterial (not based on evidence at all). This logical difference between self-ascriptions and other-ascriptions would be abolished if we accepted that some new technology could put first-person ascriptions on the same criterial footing as third-person ascriptions. A new framework and technology of self-observation would put third parties on the same footing as oneself with regard to what one feels or thinks. In order to ascertain my thoughts and feelings both myself and some third party could come to rely equally on some advanced brain-reading technology. Such a technology would override the conceptual difference between the non-criterial nature of self-ascriptions and the criterial nature of third-person ascriptions.

But it would do a great deal more than that. It would blur the ethical and political differences between a society which accepts and values incorrigible first-person talk and one which does not. It is possible to imagine a society in which such first-person reports or avowals are not valued in any case, in which avowals are over-ridden not by a brain-reading technology but by a cultural or political regime which systematically denies the right to certain forms of avowal or self-expression. It is conceivable that there would be no significant difference between a society which made systematic use of cerebroscopes and a society which systematically ignored first-person expressions or self-ascriptions. In both sorts of society people are regarded only from a third-person perspective, from the perspective of the cerebroscope, the expert, and technocrat. By making first-person psychological reports corrigible in this way, our traditional notions of self, self-knowledge, and self-expression would be radically undermined. The private, subjective ontology of the person in the street would be replaced by the public, objective, 'technical' ontology of the expert with a cerebroscope - the expert who can know more about the exact nature of your inner life than you can, and who can 'correct' or simply ignore any statement you care to make about your internal states.

In a culture of cerebroscopes, a very fundamental freedom of expression would be lost or compromised, namely, the freedom to express or not to express one's own private or internal states. As things stand, thought and feeling are private, not as a matter of nature or necessity, as the mythical Cartesians might want to say, but as a matter of right. What is private is what is recognized as private, and includes those psychological states which can only be 'accessed' through the first-person statements and self-expressive behaviour of the person before us. Our relationships, when they are at their most civilized and respectful, are not with public or transparent bodies but with private citizens, i.e., with relatively opaque persons who use the resources of language and gesture to express or suppress the truth about themselves, and who are thus enabled to cultivate and protect an inner life - a self - which is never wholly available or accessible to us. By contrast, a world in which the first-person account of internal states could be overridden by the accounts of experts using cerebroscopes would be a kind of technocracy, a world in which the technical devices of prediction and control could be taken right into the very interiority of the individual.

Demons, mental states, and other theoretical entities

So much for the eliminativist's concept of *folk* theory. We need now to examine the claim that the mentalistic terms of ordinary language constitute a folk *theory*. Churchland, as an advocate of the theory-ladenness thesis, rejects the idea that there is 'a theory-neutral or intensional-dependent relation that connects words to unique natural sections of the world' (1989, p. 281), and argues that most of the kinds we regard as natural kinds are not natural kinds at all but merely 'practical' kinds. This is a somewhat modified version of a bolder claim made in *Matter and Consciousness*:

1. Any perceptual judgement involves the application of concepts (for example, *a* is F).
2. Any concept is a node in a *network* of contrasting concepts, and its meaning is fixed by its peculiar place within that network.
3. Any network of concepts is a speculative assumption or *theory*; minimally as to the classes into which nature divides herself, and the major relations that hold between them.

Therefore,

4. Any perceptual judgement presupposes a theory. (1984, p. 80)

87

This argument turns on a questionable assumption made in the course of formulating the third premise, i.e., that any network of concepts is 'a speculative assumption or theory.' Without knowing precisely what a 'meaning network' is, or how many concepts it takes to make up a network, we cannot know how best to evaluate the claim made here. Certainly, it is not obviously true that the concepts deployed in observation-statements are theoretical, unless it is obvious that the observations occur within a theoretical framework to begin with. Thus the observation-statements made by a physicist in her laboratory may contain references to such theoretical entities as electrons and neutrinos but the physicist's observation-statement that the grass in her lawn is long and needs mowing does not deploy theoretical concepts in anything like the same sense, if at all. The mere addition of related common-or-garden concepts such as 'flower', 'water', 'rain' does not establish a network that magically transmutes all the concepts into theoretical ones. Such concepts can, of course, be put to a theoretical use, and can be introduced into theoretical discourse but they are not theoretical in virtue of being concepts. We could argue, following van Fraassen (1980), that theoretical discourse arises out of attempts to answer why-questions, i.e., attempts to provide explanations. We could also argue, following Wittgenstein, that the meaning of theoretical terms is their *use* in a particular kind of discourse, i.e., in the language-game of 'forming and testing a hypothesis', as distinct, say, from the language-game of 'describing the appearance of an object' (1963, §23). There is, in other words, no theoretical 'essence' which terms have in virtue of designating concepts or in virtue of belonging to a network of concepts. Even conventionally theoretical terms like 'electron' or 'atom' might lose their theoretical status if they began to occur in other kinds of discourse. If there were creatures who could detect electrons with their electron-detecting antennae, then the term 'electron' might be normally deployed in observation-statements! It is wiser to argue, though, that the objects to which 'untheoretical' terms refer are 'untheoretical' entities, not simply because they are observable, but because there are no major why-questions to which their existence provides an explanation. In the human world and in our era, theoretical entities like electrons are explanatory objects as a rule, while such observable things as lawns, trees and stones are not - as a rule. 'Theoretical' in this sense means 'explanatory' rather than just 'unobservable' or 'conceptual'.

Peter Alexander's neglected distinction between descriptive and theory-laden statements is particularly useful in this context. In reply to N.R. Hanson's claim (1958) that seeing is a theory-laden activity, Alexander argues that some descriptions are not theory-laden and may even be regarded as 'pure' descriptions in the sense that they are not interpretative or explanatory (1963, pp. 79-98). We could not, in Alexander's view, even perceive that one theory differed from another (for better or worse) unless we could perceive that both were rival interpretations of the same situation. There must be some agreement therefore on what 'the same situation' actually is, and such agreement is possible only if interpretation-free descriptions are possible. The theoretical or interpretative statement, 'John is possessed of a devil', is (in)commensurable with a rival statement, 'John is having an epileptic seizure,' only if it is agreed by both parties that such statements as 'John is writhing on the floor with clenched teeth and making strange noises' are accepted as true or descriptively apt. The rival theorists can accept this description in a way that they cannot accept each other's theories. Indeed, their disagreement at the level of theory presupposes agreement at the level of description. The why-question to which they offer different answers may be stated in purely descriptive terms, e.g., 'Why is John writhing on the floor, etc?'

If there is disagreement between our two theorists over the details of the description or over the terms of the question, it will be a disagreement about the aptness of language-use. It is possible to wonder, for example, whether John is writhing or squirming - accuracy here might affect accuracy of diagnosis - but insofar as there is a conceptual issue here it can be resolved within the conventions of language-use. Descriptions may be said to be convention-laden rather than theory-laden, i.e., their acceptability to all parties depends on the appreciation and 'grasp' of linguistic conventions. Although Alexander ignores the 'creative' or otherwise non-conventional uses to which language can be put, he does seem justified in distinguishing between convention-ladenness and theory-ladenness. The concepts deployed to describe or report John's behaviour are not theoretical, while the concepts used to answer the question 'Why is John writhing on the floor?' posit the existence of theoretical entities or processes (demons, epilepsy) and are therefore theoretical.

Alexander raises another important issue which should prompt us to question Churchland's claim that perceptual judgements are theory-laden or presuppose a theory. To what extent, for example, is the judgement 'The sun is on the horizon' theory-laden, as it stands? If one spectator perceives a neighbourly star, another a god, and yet another a shining flat disc, can all three be said to see the same sun? Alexander thinks that all three *do* see the same sun in some sense of the term, 'the same sun'. One's belief or knowledge does not alter the signification of the term 'sun' as used in the description of the sun's perceived position. All three may agree that the sun is on the horizon, that this is the best way to report or describe the situation in view. The fact that each has a different *theory* of the nature of the sun and the cosmos does not alter the fact that the sun is perceived to be on the horizon. The signification of a term does not change just because our account of the situation to which it refers changes. Indeed, in order for there to be 'an account of the situation', there must be some agreement on what that situation is, hence agreement on such perceptual judgements as 'the sun is on the horizon'. The fact that someone has constructed a theory to answer certain questions that have arisen about the sun does not mean that the term 'sun' must be dissolved into the terms of the subsequent theory, or that the term loses its descriptive function.[2] This is the reason that modern heliocentrists can still permit themselves to speak of the sun rising and setting. Such phrases are not unscientific or pre-scientifically theoretical but are quite appropriate in situations which do not call for anything more than a 'pure' description or a perceptual judgement. The need for a theoretical account only arises if someone wants to know what prevents the sun from falling out of the sky. The reply of the heliocentrist will then, of course, be different from that of the sun-worshipper or the Ptolemaic astronomer.

Given that we are not compelled by either logical, linguistic or empirical considerations to accept that all perceptual judgements involve theoretical concepts, neither are we compelled to accept that mental concepts are essentially theoretical. A compelling case has not been made for accepting that mental states are theoretical entities in the sense that electrons or quarks are theoretical entities. But if mental states are not theoretical entities it is not because we are somehow 'directly acquainted' with them. Rather, it is because there are no theoretical why-questions to which their existence is pertinent, as a rule. To simply insist that they *are* theoretical entities, while at the same time insisting that they do not do the job of theorizing very well, is an exercise in ground-shifting. It is like claiming that our concepts of such things as tree, lawn, stone, cloud, and rain are folk-theoretical concepts which are just not much use when it comes to theorizing about the origins of the solar system, as if they must therefore be replaced by more explanatory sorts of concepts.

Eliminativists talk as if mental concepts were used mainly to explain human behaviour but this seriously misrepresents their usage. Human behaviour, understood as the behaviour of individuals in normal circumstances, is not theoretically problematic. Bearing in mind Wittgenstein's observation 'My attitude towards [a friend] is an attitude towards a soul. I am not of the opinion that he has a soul' (1963, p. 178), we may take it that 'opinion' here could be replaced by something like 'theoretical belief'. The point is that we do not in normal circumstances opine or speculate or hypothesize that someone is conscious or rational or depressed or elated or in pain. Our perceptual judgements about other people's mental states or 'souls' are more like observations than forms of hypothesizing or theorizing. But even to call our judgements perceptual or observational is not quite right. Our judgements are recognitions or confirmations of the forms of life in which we are situated, and within which our ascriptions of mental states acquired their meaning in the first place.

This, of course, is not to deny that some human behaviour triggers off why-questions. The kind of human behaviour, however, which invites theoretical explanation is abnormal behaviour. Abnormal behaviour is clearly problematic; and it is abnormal and problematic precisely to the extent that normal mental concepts do not apply to it and do not even adequately describe it. This does not indicate the theoretical poverty of normal mental concepts but highlights their convention-laden or 'practical' character. One of the features that neuropharmacology shares with a pre-scientific ancestor such as demonology is the fact that both go outside the class of normal mental concepts for their explanations of (abnormal) behaviour. The terms of reference of demonology do not belong to the class of mental concepts any more than do the terms of reference of neuropharmacology. It is also significant that both demonology and neuropharmacology are, in their different ways, third-person accounts of behaviour. They are accounts which are typically offered in the absence of a first-person account. The person whose behaviour is a problem has lost, inter alia, the power to give an intelligible account of her own behaviour. The demonologist implicitly recognizes this by introducing a third party - the demon - into the causal account. The neuropharmacologist also recognizes a loss of mind or self by looking for causes which indicate a lapse of voluntary control or 'overdetermination' by involuntary neuropharmacological processes. To suggest that all behaviour in all circumstances needs be explained in wholly neuropharmacological terms is to suggest (a) that all behaviour is theoretically problematic, i.e., the topic of why-questions, and (b) that the first-person account is systematically negligible. Suggestion (a) is objectionable on the grounds that it ignores the difference between normal and abnormal behaviour; suggestion (b) is objectionable on ethical, even political, grounds. A universally neuropharmacological account of all behaviour, even if it were possible, should be no more desirable than a universally demonological account. In both approaches the self which would volunteer a first-person account in mental terms is marginalized, even suppressed or eliminated. The fact that we might learn to speak in neuropharmacological terms about our own mental states, (with the aid, perhaps, of Rorty's cerebroscope), would have about the same significance as our giving up the right to a first-person account and learning instead to speak in the tongues of Beelzebub.

The ineliminability of the subjective view

So far we have concentrated on finding fault with the eliminativist's conception of folk theory. Now we need to present a more positive and substantive case for a non-eliminativist philosophy of mind and subjectivity. Fortunately, we do not have to start from scratch. In the work of a small number of philosophers, most notably Thomas Nagel (1970; 1979; 1989) and Colin McGinn (1983; 1991), we have conceptions of subjectivity which are post-Cartesian without being dismissive of privacy or interiority. Nagel cogently argues that the subjective character of conscious experience cannot be captured by any of the recently devised reductive analyses of the mental, 'for all of these are compatible with its absence' (1979, p. 166). The subjective character of experience is not analysable, for example, in functional terms, no matter how explanatory such an account might be, 'since these could be ascribed to robots or automata that behaved like people though they experienced nothing' (p. 167). If physicalism is to succeed it must be able to give, in Nagel's view, a physical account of the phenomenological features of experience. But when we examine the subjective character of these very features such an account seems impossible. The reason is that every subjective phenomenon is essentially connected with a single point of view, 'and it seems inevitable that an objective, physical theory will abandon that point of view' (p. 167). By their very nature, physicalist accounts are objective and therefore must exclude the subjective. Persons, unlike physical things, possess the sorts of subjective features which do not lend themselves to the physical account - that is, they have the type of 'internality' or interiority which physical things lack. This has to do with the 'mineness' of one's mental or subjective states. In addition to the connection which all mental states have with my body there is the fact that they are also mine - 'that is, they have a particular self as subject, rather than merely being attributes of an object.' (1970, p. 226). Since all mental states must have a self as subject, they cannot be identical with mere attributes of some object like a body, 'and the self, which is its subject cannot therefore be a body' (p. 226). The belief that physicalism leaves out of account the essential subjectivity of psychological states is the feeling that 'nowhere in the description of the state of a human body could there be room for a physical equivalent of the fact that I (or any self), and not just that body, am the subject of those states' (p. 227).

Nagel tries to convince us of the irreducible, ineliminable reality of subjectivity by inviting us to consider the differences between our (human) experience and the experience of bats. We generally assume that bats *have* experiences; we have no difficulty in believing that 'there is something that it is like to be a bat' (1979, p. 168). Bats perceive the world primarily by sonar or echolocation - by sending out high-frequency sounds and attending to the subsequent echoes as these sounds are deflected off objects within a certain range. Their brains are designed to correlate the outgoing impulses with the subsequent echoes, and this information enables them to estimate distance, size, shape and movement. Their discriminations are comparable to those we make by vision or by a combination of the senses. But bat sonar, as far as we can tell, is not similar in its operation to any sense that we possess, 'and there is no reason to suppose that it is subjectively like anything we can experience or imagine' (p. 168). This creates difficulties for any attempt to extrapolate from our experience to the inner life of the bat. It is impossible for us to know what it is like for a bat to be a bat. We can imagine ourselves hanging upsidedown, catching insects in our mouths, and using our ears rather than our eyes, but this only tells me what it would be like for *me* to *behave* as a bat does. If extrapolation from our own case is involved in the idea of what it is like subjectively to be a bat, then the extrapolation must be incomplete. The specific subjective character of this 'alien' form of life is beyond our ability to conceive.

From the impossibility of such extrapolation, Nagel concludes that a realism about the subjective domain in all its forms 'implies a belief in the existence of facts beyond the reach of human concepts' (p. 171). We are compelled to recognize the existence of 'alien' subjectivities without being able to wholly comprehend them. The relevance of this point to the mind-body problem is that the facts of experience - facts about what it is like for the experiencing organism - are accessible only from one point of view, and it becomes a mystery 'how the true character of experiences could be revealed in the physical operation of that organism' (p. 171). The latter belongs to the domain of objective facts - the kind that can be observed and understood from many points of view and even by individuals with different perceptual systems. The subjective character of experience, by contrast, is fully comprehensible only from one point of view, and any shift to greater objectivity does not take us nearer its real nature but rather takes us farther away from it.

Nagel's insistence on the 'mystery' of subjectivity does not lead him to embrace dualism. He merely says that physicalism is 'a position we cannot understand because we do not at present have any conception of how it might be true' (1979, p. 176). Ascribing mental properties to an immaterial thing is no solution because there is just as much difficulty in understanding how *it* could have a point of view as there is in understanding how a material thing could have a point of view. A non-corporeal substance seems safe only because, in retreating from the physical substance as a candidate for the self, we are so much occupied with finding a subject whose states are originally mine that we simply postulate such a subject 'without asking ourselves whether the same objections will not apply to it as well: whether indeed any substance can possibly meet the requirements that its states be *underivatively* mine' (1970, p. 227).

The position taken by Colin McGinn (1983) does not quite coincide with Nagel's. While Nagel seriously wonders whether subjective properties can be accommodated within an objective conception of the world, McGinn is more concerned to ask whether we can 'make sense of a representing mind which does not ascribe subjectively constituted features to the (external) world' (p. 74). McGinn contrasts two types of 'subjective representation' with more objective ways in which the world is represented. The two types of subjective representation in question are what he calls 'indexical thought' and the experience of secondary qualities. McGinn's primary concern is not with the semantics of indexical expressions but with indexical thoughts - or, rather, with 'the indexical modes of presentation which enter thoughts' (p. 17). That is, he is concerned with what it is to think of things as *I, here, now*, etc. His reason for making this distinction between indexical expressions and indexical thoughts is that if we concentrate on the former we will be apt chiefly to notice that they are *occasional*, in the sense that their reference varies from occasion to occasion; but when we turn to indexical thoughts it is their *perspectival* character which stands out - that is, the way in which they incorporate and reflect a 'point of view' on the world. This perspective is something possessed by a psychological subject 'and it is the subjectivity of the subject that makes it proper to regard the indexical modes of presentation constitutive of a perspective as themselves subjective' (p. 17). To think of something indexically is to think of it in relation to oneself: 'all modes of presentation go back to, and are anchored in, conscious presentation of the subject of the indexical thought in question' (p. 17). Indexicals are subjective in basically the same way that secondary qualities are. Given the Lockean conception of secondary qualities as those qualities 'whose instantiation in an object consists in a power or disposition of the object to produce sensory experiences in perceivers of a certain phenomenological character' (p. 5), and given also that the experiential facts are *constitutive* of the presence of the quality in question, then the analogy between indexicals and secondary qualities may be put as follows: 'to grasp what it is for an object to have a secondary quality or an indexical property one needs to appreciate what it is like to perceive secondary qualities or entertain egocentric modes of presentation - that is, appreciate this "from the inside"' (p. 20). In both cases the world is represented as having attributes or perspectives the very existence and identity of which have their source in subjective aspects or capacities of the 'representer'. Without subjective representers there are no secondary qualities nor indexical, first-person thoughts.

The similarity between indexicals and secondary qualities is reinforced by three further parallels. First, the relativity of both has the consequence that a difference of representation does not imply a genuine disagreement. The fact that a Martian calls green what we call red does not imply error on either part. It implies only different instantiations of the powers of objects to produce certain sensory experiences. More obviously, two people do not disagree if one calls 'here' what the other calls 'there'; there would be disagreement only if both referred to the same place as 'here'. Second - and most significantly in the context of a critique of the eliminativist thesis - indexicals are like secondary qualities in not figuring in causal explanations of the interactions of physical objects. Physics omits them not just because they are egocentric and relative but because they do not constitute the sorts of explanatory predicates that we would expect to find in a theory of the causal workings of nature. This 'explanatory idleness' stems from the very self-referring, subjective character of indexicals. Indexical and secondary-quality predicates do not attribute intrinsic physical properties to things - and do not therefore contribute to an account of the causal powers of things. And, third, neither indexicals nor secondary qualities purport to denote real essences or natural kinds. Indexical and secondary-quality words do not function in this way but serve rather to express a subject-involving, experience-involving perspective on the world.

When an aspect of our means of representing the world has been shown to have a subjective nature, it is natural, according to McGinn, to ask whether that

94

aspect is eliminable from any true account of the nature of things. The motive for such elimination would be to represent things as they are in themselves, not as they strike a mind which receives, interprets, and perhaps distorts them. Is it possible, however, to form a conception of a type of mind whose representations are free of secondary-quality perceptions and indexical modes of presentation? Perceptual experience which represented the world only in terms of primary qualities would have an entirely objective content. The world would not be perceived to have qualities which depend upon the perceiver's sensory make-up. The condition of possessing an 'observer-independent conception' of the world will be that you can employ primary-quality concepts in judgements other than those made in direct response to experience. We only begin to think of the world objectively when we employ primary-quality concepts in judgements which are *not* made in response to sensory experience. In other words, primary-quality concepts are non-sensory in origin and in usage, and the whole 'absolute conception' of which they are a part cannot be given a sensory interpretation at all. On the other side, secondary-quality classifications do not purport to fit what is objectively present in the world independently of experience, 'and so cannot be criticized for failing to conform to classifications arrived at on objective grounds - their role is rather to classify objects by way of their sensory appearance' (p. 72). In general, if a kind of representation has a subjective source, then it is not required that it fit what is objectively the case in the world.

McGinn's claim, then, is that secondary-quality concepts only are derived from experience of secondary qualities, and can be derived only from such experiences, whereas primary-quality concepts can be possessed in logical independence of specific sensory experiences. Martians with different senses from ours, or no senses at all, could (conceivably) understand our scientific theories, but they could not grasp our concepts of secondary qualities. Insofar as a being possesses secondary-quality concepts it necessarily has a subjective perspective on the world, and insofar as it has a subjective point of view it necessarily possesses, or has the capacity to possess, secondary-quality concepts. The claim that a certain type of property is inherently subjective naturally raises the question of whether it is possible to misidentify the indexical properties and the secondary qualities, and McGinn argues that the ascription of both is incorrigible. In the case of secondary qualities, the ascription of 'experientially constituted' qualities does not require us to look beyond what is given 'from the inside'. If we have the experience of red and the word for it, 'red', then we cannot be mistaken in ascribing the secondary quality, redness, although we might have to be more careful than McGinn realizes in how we make our ascription. We may take it, however, that certain careful ascriptions of secondary qualities are incorrigible. In the case of indexicals, the matter, as McGinn admits, is not without complexity, but he soon makes the strong claim that (a) we could not think or speak indexically unless there were incorrigible uses, and that (b) the corrigible uses are dependent upon the incorrigible uses. He accepts Wittgenstein's distinction between the two sorts of use to which 'I' can be put. That is, 'I' can be used 'as subject' or 'as object' (1972, pp. 66-7). 'I' is used as subject in 'I am in pain', 'I am trying to raise my arm,' and other self-ascriptions of psychological states. 'I' is used 'as object' in 'I am bleeding', 'I have grown six inches', and other self-ascriptions of bodily states. The as-subject uses do not allow for the possibility of misidentification, whereas the as-object uses do. You can know of someone that he is bleeding and wrongly think that someone to be yourself; but you cannot know of someone that he is in pain and wrongly take that someone to be yourself:

> In general, there are two possible sources of error in any subject-predicate judgement, corresponding to the predication component of the judgement and the identification component. In the case of 'I am bleeding' the mistake can lie in the identification component, as well as in the predication component; in 'I am in pain' it can lie in neither. (1983, p. 48)

McGinn concludes that the egocentric character of indexical thought makes it 'peculiarly subjective', in much the same way in which the experiential associations of thoughts about secondary qualities confer subjectivity upon them. Both features of subjectivity create a problem for physicalism. The existence of first-person, incorrigible perspectives on the world is difficult to accommodate within an objective physicalist account of reality. All that physicalism can do is suppress or marginalize the subjective account but it cannot reduce or eliminate it. Nagel, as McGinn notes, tries to express this 'uncapturability' thesis by claiming that no amount of information expressed non-indexically could ever entail 'I am X', where X is the name of the speaker. There is the same irreducibility about secondary qualities - the subjective experiential content of redness cannot be transferred onto the world of physically comprehensible objects. We may say, therefore, that being red is not an objective physical property. One can only eliminate such qualities by denying the reality or usefulness of the experiences which contain them, but there is no question of getting primary qualities, natural kinds, or theoretical entities to replace subjective, secondary-quality concepts as such. There is no question of the subjective and the objective view being commensurable with regard to verisimilitude:

> The objective view does not have the relativity of the subjective view, but it purchases this absoluteness at the cost of removing itself from the perceptual standpoint. There can be no question of selecting one kind of view and abandoning the other: to abandon the subjective view is to abandon the possibility of experience of the world; to abandon the objective view is to abandon the idea of an observer-independent unitary

96

reality. Neither view can serve the purposes of the other, and neither can be construed as setting a standard which the other can be criticised for failing to meet. (1983, p. 127)

Subjectivity as a property of brains

It is instructive to compare the views of Nagel and McGinn with a somewhat different defence of the notion of subjectivity put forward by Searle (1984). Searle's first thesis towards providing a non-dualist, yet non-reductionist, answer to the mind-body problem is that 'all mental phenomena, whether conscious or unconscious ... are caused by processes going on in the brain' (1984, p. 18). All the evidence of neurology and related sciences indicates that mental states do not occur independently of brain processes. There is, however, no question of saying that mental events, so conceived, are conceptually eliminable. To avoid any such misunderstanding, Searle adds a second thesis: 'Pains and other mental phenomena just are features of the brain (and perhaps of the rest of the central nervous system)' (p. 19).

At first sight this seems inconsistent with his first thesis. The first thesis claims that mental events are caused by brain processes, which suggests that mental events are distinct from these processes. But now we have Searle denying such a distinction by insisting that mental phenomena are features of the brain. At the basis of our puzzlement here, according to Searle, is a misunderstanding about the nature of causation. It is tempting to think that whenever A causes B that there must be two separate things involved, as in the classical example of one billiard ball striking another. This, however, is only one of the ways in which things are causally related. There are other sorts of causal relationship in nature, such as the relationship between the microscopic properties and the macroscopic properties of a system. Searle accepts the physicist's theory that all objects are composed of microscopic particles, namely, molecules, atoms and sub-atomic particles. These micro-particles have features appropriate to their scale - features that can only be detected by sophisticated technical instruments. But physical systems also have features in their large-scale dimensions, such as the solidity of the table, the liquidity of water, the transparency of glass. Every physical system, therefore, can be said to have two sets of properties, micro-properties and macro-properties. The language that is appropriate to talking about the one is not necessarily appropriate to talking about the other, and yet the two sets of properties belong to the same system *and* are also causally related. The macro-properties are causally explained by the behaviour of the elements at the micro level, e.g., the liquidity of water at normal temperatures is caused by the lattice structure of molecules of H_2O. But not only are the macro-features causally explained by the behaviour of particles at the micro level, these macro-features belong to the very same system as the micro-elements which cause them. The largescale, global, surface macro-features are both caused by the behaviour of micro-elements and are at the same time realized in the system that is composed of these elements.

What we have here, according to Searle, is a useful model for determining the relationship between mind and brain, viz., the micro-macro model. If we regard mental phenomena as akin to largescale or macroscopic features, then we can say that mental phenomena are caused by processes going on in the brain at the microscopic, neuronal level, and are at the same time realized or 'expressed' in the system that is constituted by neuronal processes, i.e., the brain. Consciousness, then, is caused by the neuronal activity of the brain, and is also a feature of the brain. Consciousness is to neuronal activity what liquidity is to the molecular activity of H_2O, or what crystaline graininess is to the activity of molecules of NaCl.

What Searle has to say about subjectivity as a feature of the brain is of particular interest in this context. It is, for Searle, a mistake to have ever supposed that a definition of reality should or could exclude subjectivity: 'If "science" is the name of the collection of objective and systematic truths we can state about the world, then the existence of subjectivity is an objective scientific fact like any other' (p. 25). If a scientific account of the world attempts to describe how things are, then one of the features of that account should be the subjectivity of mental states. It is an objective fact about biological evolution that it has produced brains which exhibit subjective features. Thus the existence of subjectivity is an objective fact of biology, and if this fact runs counter to a certain definition of science, then it is the definition and not the fact which we will have to abandon. Instead of reducing or diminishing our concept of mind, as some materialists have done, Searle suggests that we should expand or extend our concept of the brain to include the phenomena of subjectivity, consciousness, intentionality, and mental causation.

One of the things which Searle takes for granted is that mental phenomena are in fact related to neuronal brain processes *in the same way* that the macro-properties of objects are related to the micro-properties of those same objects. This is a questionable assumption. Strictly speaking, the largescale or global properties of brains considered as physical systems or objects, are not mental phenomena but rather the observable surface properties of the 'grey matter' which the neurosurgeon sees when he probes a person's brain. The peculiarity of *mental* phenomena is that they are not observable as properties by the neurosurgeon or anyone other than the subject who has them. The relationship between mental states and neuronal processes is not logically equivalent to the relationship between the macro- and micro-properties of physical systems. In any physical system other than the brain the two levels of properties are equally physical, equally objective, equally accessible to inspection by third parties.

This is true of the brain in the case of its global 'grey matter' properties *vis-à-vis* its neuronal properties, but it is not so obviously true of the brain in the case of its mental properties. If mental properties are among the global properties of the brain, they do not sit well among its other global properties, viz. its grey matter properties. It looks, in fact, as if we have a third set of properties for which there is no equivalent in the normal micro-macro model of a normal physical system. These properties seem to be the properties of a 'subject' rather than of an object called the brain. If subjectivity itself is a property of the brain it is not like any of the other properties of the brain - it is not a public, inspectible, objective one but one which can only be experienced uniquely 'from within'. As John Wisdom says, 'The peculiarity of the soul is not that it is visible to none but that it is visible only to one' (1962, p. 53). The same sort of point is made by McGinn when he writes:

[T]he property of consciousness itself (or specific conscious states) is not an observable or perceptible property of the brain. You can stare into a living conscious brain, your own or someone else's, and see there a wide variety of instantiated properties - its shape, colour,, texture, etc. - but you will not thereby *see* what the subject is experiencing, the conscious state itself. Conscious states are simply not, qua conscious states, potential objects of perception: they depend upon the brain but they cannot be observed by directing the senses onto the brain.... In other words, consciousness is noumenal with respect to perception of the brain. (1991, pp. 10-11)

It is too easy to assert, as Searle does, that subjectivity 'just is' a feature of the brain. This is not to deny that there is a causal relationship between neuronal and mental events but rather to suggest that the micro-macro model of this relationship is not as insightful as it looks. We are still left with the kind of intuitions articulated by both Nagel and McGinn - that the true character of subjective experience is not revealed in the physical operation of the experiencing organism; that no amount of information about neuronal processes, expressed in non-indexical terms, could ever entail 'I am X', where X is the name of the speaker; that the existence of first-person, incorrigible perspectives cannot be accommodated within a corrigible, scientific, physicalist account, no matter how broad or 'deep' that account may be.

Notes

1. Thorndike suggests that magic was originally popular in the sense that everyone was a magician but argues that its practice became increasingly specialized as societies evolved. By the early Renaissance period, and

under the influence of Neoplatonism, it had become profoundly esoteric and hermetic, the monopoly of a priesthood (1967, pp. 29-32).

2.　Cf. Hilary Putnam (1975, p. 381), where he argues that accepting a theoretical identification - e.g., 'Pain is stimulation of C-fibres' - does not commit one to interchanging the terms 'pain' and 'stimulation of C-fibres' in idiomatic talk.　The identification of 'water' with 'H_2O' is by now a well-known one but no-one says 'Bring me a glass of H_2O', except as a joke.

5 The mechanization of the inner life

Long before the era of Artificial Intelligence Descartes was arguing for the conceivability of machines which could impressively imitate the behaviour of animals and human beings. He maintained that in the case of animal-seeming automata we would not in fact have any means of ascertaining that they were not of the same nature as the animals which they simulated (See AT VI, 56-9; CSM I, 139-41). On the other hand, automata that were designed to imitate human behaviour could be distinguished from actual persons by applying two tests. The first test - the linguistic or 'semantics' test - should show 'that they could never use words, or put together signs, as we do, in order to declare our thoughts to others' (AT VI, 56; CSM I, 140). The reason is that while we may easily conceive a machine that is designed to emit speech-sounds, we cannot conceive that it should be so made as to arrange words variously in response to the meaning of what is said in its presence, 'as the dullest man can do' (AT VI, 57; CSM I, 140). The second test - the 'universal reason' test - should show that machines, while doing many things as well as human beings, would necessarily fail to do other things, showing that they did not act from knowledge 'but only from the disposition of their organs' (AT VI, 57; CSM I, 140). Reason, for Descartes, is a universal tool that may serve in all kinds of circumstances whereas the mechanical organs need 'some special adaption' for each particular action. He concludes that it is impossible that a machine should contain so many varied arrangements to allow it 'to make it act in all the contingencies of life in the way in which our reason makes us act' (AT VI, 57; CSM I, 141).

Where Descartes speaks of special arrangements or adaptions and of the specialized dispositions of mechanical organs, a modern philosopher would speak of computers running programs. Though Descartes did not, of course, possess a concept of programming or of the distinction between software and hardware - since he was familiar only with mechanical or clockwork machines -

his concept of automaton is sufficiently abstract to cover modern robotic computers, including computers composed of artificial networks which are said to be 'trained' rather than directly programmed. That he was prepared to grant a high degree of sophistication to automata is indicated by his determination to regard animals as kinds of machines. (His conceptual revisionism is, arguably, not so much a demotion of animals to the status of machines as a promotion of machines to the status of animals.) By classifying animals as machines he is perhaps setting himself a more difficult task than a modern philosopher devising thought-experiments with digital computers or with sophisticated robots possessing artificial neural networks. In the form of his *bête machine*, Descartes already has a living equivalent of a 'neural net' robot. He goes so far as to accept that the physical analogies between human and animal bodies are quite close. Some animals, he claims, possess sound-making organs similar to human organs and can utter words like ourselves. The behaviour-patterns of animals sometimes resemble those of human beings in their apparent purposefulness; and there are certain 'calculative' activities which are better performed by machines (e.g., clocks) than by human beings. Descartes' motive for making so many concessions to the mechanistic thesis is to enable him to argue, first, that the real difference between human beings and animals (or automata) is a difference of kind rather than of degree, and, second, that this essential or intrinsic difference will be apparent not in a particular performance but in certain general qualities or styles of behaviour.

Both the language test and the universal reason test are intended to show that automata and animals cannot be described as rational, or as possessing minds at all. Animals and machines - and animals are, after all, a species of Cartesian machine - do not use speech-sounds nor exhibit behavioural responses in the spontaneous, universally apposite way that would indicate a capacity for understanding. Their signals and actions can be explained in terms of the mindless, inbuilt dispositions of their organs. These inbuilt dispositions are designed to deal with specific tasks - measuring time, building a nest - and are not functions of the universal, general, plastic intelligence which is a feature of the human mind. Contrary to the imputations of his critics, Descartes does not always insist on a radical dualism of mind and behaviour. Mind is something that can be 'read off' from speech or behaviour. It produces forms of expression which are characteristically mindful or intelligent. Mindful speech and behaviour display a spontaneity and a creativity that instinctive or mechanical behaviour does not. Mind, in other words, is not reproducible or replaceable by mechanism. The mental is the antithesis of the mechanical; the conscious inner life is not intelligible in mechanical terms, nor can a machine be thought to possess such an inner life. But many contemporary philosophers, especially functionalists and advocates of the Artificial Intelligence thesis, would say otherwise. They would argue that the Cartesian antithesis between the mental and the mechanical must be rejected along with the Cartesian dualism of mind and body, and that informative analogies can be established between the internal mental processes of human beings and the internal logical processes of machines.

A beast-machine for the Chinese room?

It is the Cartesian concept of the universality and plasticity of human reason which Alan Turing appeared to challenge in his 'imitation game' hypothesis (1950), which is the hypothesis that if a team of interrogators are unable to distinguish between the responses of a human intelligence and those of a computer, then we no longer have good grounds for denying the conceivability of an intelligent artifact or machine. It was Turing's own belief that, given a universal machine - i.e., a machine capable of computing anything that can be computed - 'an average interrogator would not have more than a 70 per cent chance of making the right identification after five minutes of questioning' (1950, p. 442). He went on to predict that by the end of the century general opinion would have altered so much that 'one will be able to speak of machines thinking without expecting to be contradicted' (p. 442).

The idea of a machine so universal in its repertoire of responses that it could be considered intelligent represents an important challenge to the notion of an inner life, since it threatens to reduce mental states to the functional states of a system. It prompts the thought that if a machine can be a thinking thing, then all thinking things could turn out to be some kind of machine, or at least some kind of rule-following, symbol-manipulating, data-processing system. Given such a scenario, there would be no conceptual space left over for the kind of subjective interiority we might want to defend. Since a machine is, in a sense, all 'exteriority', it could turn out that other sorts of thinking things, including human beings, are just so much closely-packed, folded-in exteriority. The physically internal workings can be fully exposed at any time. Take away enough components, peel back enough layers, expose enough of the internal workings and you find either another component - or just nothing. Since the notion of a universal Turing machine seems central to the functionalist model of mentality we need to take a close look at it. We need to see how it compares with something like the Cartesian notion of the uniquely plastic human mind.

By all accounts, a universal Turing machine is a device which is designed to perform operations on symbols or data by following instructions or rules. What any Turing machine does is basically to scan, print, erase, and replace discrete symbols, sequentially, as appropriate, according to a rule. At any particular time the machine will be scanning a square on its tape and it will be in some specific internal state relative to its instructions and to the symbol on its tape. This conjunction of symbol, internal state and instruction will determine the next operation in a determinate sequence of operations. The machine must respond 'externally' to the square or symbol being scanned, by printing a symbol, or erasing a symbol, or leaving be the symbol already there. It must also respond 'internally' by remaining in its present internal state or changing its internal state. The machine's operations are always exactly specifiable in the form of a machine table which indicates the rule to be activated, the present internal state, the symbol being scanned, and the move to be made. A universal Turing machine is simply one which operates like any particular Turing machine (as described above) but which is so designed that it can perform any set of operations that any particular machine can perform. Every general purpose digital computer is, in principle, like a universal Turing machine - when it runs a program it behaves like a machine designed to perform whatever specific task the program requires.

The question which the concept of a universal machine raises in this context is whether the machine's putative universality could simulate, even duplicate, the universality of a Cartesian mind. It is likely that Descartes would have rejected the very concept of a universal Turing machine, since it presupposes the conceivability of mechanical universality. A universal Turing machine would be, for Descartes, just a machine capable of a wide and complex range of special adaptions, each special adaption designed to carry out a specific task, perhaps even a task that surpasses human achievement - but this would not mean that it had succeeded in passing his language and rationality tests. No number of special adaptions is going to add up to a mind if no particular adaption is in itself indicative of mind. Descartes, after all, acknowledged the fact that there are certain things that automata and beasts can do better than human beings - but this does not prove that automata or beasts are endowed with minds. If such specialized adaptions *were* instances of intelligence, then it would be the case that the animals or machines possessing them had more intelligence than human beings 'and would excel us in everything' (AT VI, 58; CSM I, 141). But since they clearly do not surpass us in all other things, it can only be because those abilities are not exercises of intelligence or reason but of specially adapted instincts or mindless mechanisms. Just adding on more special adaptions until you get a multi-purpose machine does not magically transmute such a machine into a 'thinking thing'.

But surely if a machine had such a large number of special adaptions that it began to surpass us in a large number of things, should we not then consider the possibility that it is becoming intelligent? Descartes is on less secure ground here but he still does not have to concede much of it. When a being which possesses universal reason - or a mind - performs some task rationally or intelligently, it is because it is capable of performing an indefinite range of tasks with similar rationality or intelligence. A human being or other thinking thing who can calculate or read stories or paint pictures can also do a range of other things reasonably well, sometimes achieving above average, sometimes below; but the performance of any one task, such as writing a letter or a poem, already presupposes a range of other very general abilities, including a capacity for observation, feeling, listening, reading, writing, etc. Intelligent or creative behaviour is an instance of general perceptual and cognitive abilities rather than a realization or expression of some task-specific ability or program, or the exercise of organs which require 'some special adaption' for every particular action.[1] The difference between a universal Turing machine and a Cartesian mind is that the Turing machine is really a package or bundle of discretely task-specific programs, whereas the Cartesian mind is a unitary, singularly plastic entity with an unspecified, non-dedicated range of innate potentials or abilities. These abilities are 'occasioned' and thereby 'individuated' by the tasks that the world presents; but they are not 'added on' or pre-emptively designed to meet particular exigencies, and they are never exhausted in any particular task or operation. The 'universality' of the Turing machine consists not in any inherently native plasticity or 'creativity' but in the fact that there is always room in the machine for another 'special adaption' or another set of instructions. But each adaption need not be internally related to the next, as the ability of human beings to read stories is related to their ability to write a shopping list, listen to a news report, take a phone call, sing a song. We do not even think of these as merely externally related activities - they are just exercises of a general ability to use language and signs in the course of responding appositely or creatively to one's environment.

One of the most thought-provoking criticisms of the Turing test has been Searle's well-known 'argument from semantics' (1984), which has certain affinities with Descartes' language test. Searle's argument is based on a thought-experiment or 'likely story' designed to counteract Turing's hypothesis. Very briefly, it goes like this: You do not understand Chinese; you are placed in a room containing baskets of Chinese symbols and given a rule-book (in English) which contains instructions for manipulating Chinese symbols according to their 'syntax' - shape, location - but not according to their meaning or semantic content. The people outside the room hand in symbols which you manipulate according to the rules. This involves sending out of the room packets of symbols from the baskets. What you don't know is that the incoming symbols are questions, the outgoing symbols answers, and the incoming and outgoing symbols are manipulated in such a way that the answers received by those outside the room are indistinguishable from those of a native Chinese speaker. In effect, in terms of an input-output model - i.e., Turing's model - you are speaking Chinese; in reality, you do not. The symbols are manipulated according to syntax, according to formal rules, but you attach no meaning to them. By virtue of implementing a program - 'following the instructions' - you behave as if he understood Chinese but all the same you do not. Though your 'outputs' are similar to those of a Chinese speaker, you do not *speak* Chinese. And if going through the appropriate computer program for understanding Chinese is not enough to give you an understanding of

105

Chinese, neither, Searle argues, is it enough to give any computer an understanding of the symbolic contents of its manipulations. All that any computer has is a formal program for manipulating uninterpreted symbols. Programs 'are purely formally specifiable - that is, they have no semantic content' (1984, p. 33).

To the question, 'Is instantiating or implementing a program sufficient for, or constitutive of, thinking?' the answer, for Searle, is a definite 'no'. Thinking is more than a matter of manipulating meaningless symbols; it involves having an interpretation, or a meaning, attached to these symbols. Formal syntax is not sufficient for semantics, and programs are entirely defined by their formal or syntactical structure. Minds, by contrast, have semantic or 'mental' contents. Minds by their very nature attach meanings to things; computers by their very nature do not. Searle concludes that (a) no computer program by itself is sufficient to give a system a mind, and (b) the way that brain-functions cause minds cannot solely be in virtue of running a computer program (1984, pp. 39-40).

Searle's inversion of the Turing imitation game is significant in that it shares with Descartes' linguistic criterion of mentality an emphasis on the intimate relationship between mentality and the possession and use of a language. Descartes would have little cause to disagree with Searle's statement that minds have semantic contents. Both Descartes and Searle are saying that language is, in some sense, the mark of the mental. True, Descartes' accounts of the relations between mind and language and between mind and brain are, when set against the background of modern linguistic theory, rather naive and objectionable. But there is one respect in which Searle has something to learn from the Cartesian concept of a *bête machine*. If Descartes lacks a concept of programming, Searle lacks a concept of 'training', especially the kind of non-programmatic training which can produce intelligent-seeming behaviour in an artificial neural network system. One of the weaknesses of Searle's position is that he deals exclusively with classical AI in his formulation of the Chinese room thought-experiment, and does not explicitly take account of the new connectionist or 'artificial neural network' thesis. In an artificial network information is stored not in any form resembling a conventional computer program but structurally, as it is in the natural brain, 'as distributed patterns of excitatory and inhibitory synaptic strengths' (Schwartz, 1988, p. 124). Connectionism is the theory that artificial neural networks, like natural neural networks, actually learn and generate new concepts and skills An exemplary connectionist computer is composed of parallel layers of microprocessors which are said to be neuron-like in their interactions. What happens among the units and the layers of units is going to be as important as what happens within a unit. Writing of one such machine (which he calls 'Exor') Seymour Papert writes:

Each unit in the network receives signals from the others or from sensor units connected to the outside world; at any given time, each unit has a certain level of activation that depends on the weighted sum of the states of activation of the units sending signals to it, and the signals sent out along the unit's 'axon' reflect its state of activation. Learning takes place by a process that adjusts the weights (strengths of connection) between the units; when the weights are different, activation patterns produced by a given input (stimulus) will change. (1988, p. 9)

Insofar as Papert's description of what happens inside Exor is correct, then it is closer to the sorts of description which might be given of neuronal activity in the natural brain than to the sorts of description which might be given of the processes taking place within a classical serial computer. When a connectionist system 'learns' it does so as a result of trial and error, and not in virtue of following a program. Such systems are described as 'parallel' and 'distributed' because the units comprising the system function simultaneously and co-operatively until a desired pattern of activity is 'learnt', and this pattern is represented or distributed throughout the system as a whole.

Paul and Patricia Churchland have given particular emphasis to the fact that connectionist systems do not manipulate symbols according to structure-sensitive rules, and have criticized Searle on that account:

Rather, symbol manipulation appears to be just one of many cognitive skills that a network may or may not learn to display. Rule-governed symbol manipulation is not its basic mode of operation.... Searle's argument is directed against rule-governed SM [symbol manipulating] machines; vector transformers of the kind we describe are therefore not threatened by his Chinese room argument even if it were sound... (1990, p. 30)

In the Churchlands' view, connectionist or parallel network systems really are 'trained' - not programmed - to carry out tasks. The process of 'training up the networks' proceeds by successive adjustments of the network weights until the system performs the input-output transformations desired. They would agree with Rumelhart and McClelland that the currency of parallel distributed processing is not symbols, 'but excitation and inhibition' (1986, p. 132).

Searle's own reply has been to say that, computationally, serial and parallel systems are equivalent. Any computation that can be done in parallel can also be done in serial. The Chinese room argument, he claims, applies to any computational system, regardless of whether it is serial or parallel. You can't, he says, get 'semantically loaded thought contents from formal computations alone' (1990, p. 22). But Searle has not quite taken on board the difference here between 'programming' and 'training up the networks'. The point is not whether a parallel network system can duplicate the computational performance of a serial machine but whether the 'inner processes' of the input-output transformations are the same. It is process rather than product which is of most interest here. If it is possible to design a machine which works, even in a simplified way, like a brain, and if this artificial brain can impressively perform computations or other cognitive operations, then it could make perfect sense to say that it has been trained rather than programmed. And if it makes sense to say that, then the Chinese room argument, as it stands, will not remain a compelling argument against those who believe themselves to be in the business of designing thinking machines.

Little philosophical sideshow: 'learned' animals and neural nets

It is at this point, however, that the Cartesian criteria for demarcating human beings (or 'thinking things') from machines can prove useful to Searle. A *bête machine* in Descartes' sense is certainly something that can be trained even more obviously and with greater facility than any artificial neural system. The term 'training', moreover, is associated conventionally with animals, specifically in getting them to perform useful or amusing actions or acquire habits that are not 'natural' to them, such as carrying riders, leaping fences, standing on their hind legs, responding to whistles or other sounds, jumping through hoops, or raucously uttering phrases like 'Pieces of eight, pieces of eight!' More pertinently, animals can also be trained to carry out actions that have all the appearance of matching or instantiating human intelligence. For centuries, until the early decades of this century, 'learned' animals - pigs, horses, and birds - were a feature of fairs and sideshows throughout Europe. These animals were trained to perform mathematical calculations, to spell, and to answer factual questions by motioning to numbered or lettered cards, or by making sounds or gestures. Milbourne Christopher, an American historian of magic and charlatanry, describes a horse which appeared to work out its own solutions to mathematical problems 'and had a better knowledge of world affairs than most fourteen-year old children' (1970, p. 46). Another wonder-horse, 'The Little Scientific Spanish Poney' (sic), was publicized in England as performing astonishing feats under the poster rubric of 'Philosophical, Mathematical and Mechanical Operations.' A talking horse named Captain was one of the attractions at the San Francisco Exposition of 1915. Captain finished his act by playing popular tunes on a set of chimes linked to a control board. A dog called Munito was so good at answering questions in geography, botany and natural history (by picking up lettered cards between its teeth) that 'fond parents brought lackadaisical youngsters to see the show, hoping that Munito's talents would serve as an object lesson' (Christopher, 1970, p. 51). Leibniz is reputed to have vouched for the existence of a 'learned dog' that had a vocabulary of thirty words, and apparently used his influence to have the dog's achievements recorded by the French Academy. 'Learned pigs' were regular attractions at Bartholomew Fair in London, and in 1789 a 'learned goose' was able to draw an admission fee of two shillings at the Haymarket, in London. Christopher expresses some disappointment that he came upon only one reference to a 'goat of knowledge'.

Although some learned humans were obviously impressed by these feats of animal intelligence, a booklet published in Boston in 1805 by a successful trainer of learned pigs revealed the truth of the matter. In *The Expositer; or Many Mysteries Unravelled*, Willem Frederick Pinchbeck offered a series of lessons instructing the reader how to teach a 'pig of knowledge'. The trainer's basic task is to get his animal accustomed to the cues that will trigger appropriate responses, using a technique that would now be called 'reward and punishment'.[2] It appears that, with practice, quite subtle cues (e.g., the slight movement of a foot or cane) could be used to cause appropriate responses in the animal. A good performer, according to Christopher, remains apparently idle while the animal seems to do all the intelligent work.

The point of this digression into the history of learned animals is to show what training can accomplish. It is clear enough that the animals are not literally programmed to respond to questions, but rather have had their 'networks' trained to respond to environmental cues or triggers. From a Cartesian point of view, these *bête machines* are living equivalents of full-fledged artificial neural network systems, with the trainer occupying a position analogous to the network-trainer whose training program 'nudges' and 'cues' the trainee towards the appropriate input-output transformations. The network-trainer sets the goals and controls the input-output transformations, although he does not directly control the processes by which the goal is achieved, any more than a trainer of learned pigs has direct access to the brain-processes of his trainee. Training, however, resembles programming in that it does not depend for its success on the trainee's possession of meanings, nor on the trainee's possession of the ability to make creative or globally apposite uses of language. It turns out that training is as task-specific, requiring as much 'special adaption', as programming. The learned animal's manipulation of symbols is still purely syntactical and mechanical, devoid of semantic content. Indeed, a learned animal could in principle replace the manipulator in the Chinese room, thereby anticipating some of the objections that have been made against Searle's thought-experiment. One of the problems with the occupant of the Chinese room is that he is too intelligent and understands too much to begin with - he understands the rule-book, for one thing. But if a well-trained 'learned animal' were to replace the human occupant then there would be altogether less understanding in the system as a whole. Moreover, from a Cartesian point of view, that learned, symbol-manipulating animal, considered as a *bête machine*, can be seen as part of the very machinery of the Chinese room. Even if the learned animal needs to be continually cued by its trainer, there is nevertheless a significant sense in which it could be a candidate for the Turing test - or the Chinese room test.

It might be objected at this point that the animal trainer is dealing with an already existing animal intelligence, and that while it may be true that pigs and other animals do not really possess *human* intelligence, they do possess some intelligence. Consequently, it might be argued that since artificial neural networks are capable of 'learning' to perform certain tasks they must also possess some indigenous intelligence. Like learned animals, they may not understand the semantic content of the human symbols they manipulate, but in learning to do them at all they must possess some kind of intelligence. After all, as Gunderson suggests, 'not everything with a mind - and this *could* include machines - will mirror a *human* mind' (p. 170). The difficulty, however, with the notion of indigenous machine intelligence, by contrast with native animal intelligence, is that animals display their primary, native intelligence in coping with their natural environment, while there is no obviously analogous sense in which connectionist systems can be said to do likewise. Until they are integrated into a training programme they have no independent function and cannot therefore be said to have some indigenous intelligence in the sense in which animals have it. Indeed, since training implies the possession of native intelligence, it is only in a figurative sense that we can say that machines are trained at all. In the end, the fact that neural network systems appear intelligent and appear to learn, is no more significant than the fact that the human processor in the Chinese room can answer questions in Chinese, or that 'The Little Scientific Spanish Poney' can learn to perform Philosophical, Mathematical and Mechanical Operations.

Functionalism and the machine analogy

Functionalism, especially that version of it which is based on 'the machine analogy', resembles the Artificial Intelligence hypothesis in its tendency to 'mechanize' the inner life, to explain the mental in terms of functional-causal relations rather than in terms of the properties of either a brain or a Cartesian mind. The identity of a mental state lies in its 'occupying a particular niche within a complex causal network of possible states which mediates, as a whole, the causal relationship between sensory (and other) inputs and behavioural (and other) outputs' (Lockwood, 1989, p. 26). In order to define what a particular mental state is we have to say what kinds of environmental inputs bring it about, what other kinds of (internal) states it is related to or distinguishable from, and what kinds of behavioural output it causes. Thus pain is that mental state which 'characteristically results from some bodily damage or trauma; it causes distress, annoyance, and practical reasoning aimed at relief; and it causes wincing, blanching, and nursing of the traumatized area' (Churchland, 1984, p. 36). This conception of mental states is similar to Armstrong's 'inner cause' theory, but differs from it to the extent that it is articulated within the context of an abstract input-output model.

Functionalism in this abstractly input-output sense has been defended by Hilary Putnam in his early work where he offers it as a synthetic hypothesis about the nature of mental states. The analogy between logical states of a Turing machine and mental states of a human being, on the one hand, and structural states of a Turing machine and physical states of a human being, on the other, is one which he finds 'very suggestive' (1975, p. 373). What is suggestive about the analogy is the fact that the 'behaviour' of, for example, a computer is not explained by the physics and chemistry of the machine but 'by the machine's program'. The fact that the program is realized in and through a particular physical system does not make it a physical property of that system. It is, rather, an abstract property of the machine. Similarly, according to Putnam, the psychological properties of human beings are not physical and chemical properties as such, although they may be realized in or by physical and chemical properties. The relation of the mental to the physical is analogous to that between the functional description of a computer (or Turing Machine) and the physical description of the functioning hardware. Mental states are essentially functional states of a system but are not reducible to any physical feature of any particular system. A computer might be made which was functionally isomorphic to a human being, to the extent of exhibiting mental states, but this functioning could be embodied in a way which was very different from human physiology. This isomorphism of function but variability of embodiment or realization makes Putnam sceptical about both the traditional mind-body problem and the question of whether machines can think. The question of whether or not persons are material or spiritual in nature is not a promising one for Putnam and does not get close to determining what the nature of the mental really is. If we imagine two parallel worlds, in one of which people have old-fashioned souls operating through the pineal gland, and in the other of which people have complex brains, and if we suppose 'that the souls in the soul world are functionally isomorphic to brains in the brain world,' then there is no sense in attaching significance to the difference in 'hardware' (p. 193). What matters is 'the common structure' and not the hardware. The 'etheriality' of the hardware is no more explanatory than its materiality, and the question of how souls think is no less difficult a question than how brains think. To say that something is a soul and that the function of souls is to think is no more helpful than to say that something is a brain and the function of brains is to think. Nothing about the nature of thinking or consciousness can be learnt from studying the ethereal, mechanical or bodily hardware, just as nothing about the nature of dance can be learnt by studying the anatomy and physiology of the dancer.

111

Putnam takes the functionalist analogy quite a distance, and applies it to 'the puzzle of privacy' (p. 362). He begins by observing that the questions 'How do I know I have a pain?' or 'How does anyone know he is in pain?' are logically odd or 'deviant' utterances, whereas the question 'How do I know someone else is in pain?' is not. The difference in status between deviant and non-deviant questions is mirrored, significantly, in the case of Turing machines: if T is a Turing machine, the question 'How does T ascertain that it is in state A?' is also logically odd, although it would not be logically odd to ask 'How does T ascertain that T' is in state A?' where T' is a neighbouring machine. The deviance lies in the assumption that a self-report requires a cognitive method or process similar to the method or process involved in our reports of other human beings - or of other Turing machines if one is a Turing machine! It is assumed that there must be something that one does in order to produce a self-report. But this is not so, according to Putnam, and he invites us to make the following supposition. Suppose that whenever a Turing machine is in one particular state (state A, for example), it prints the words 'I am in state A'. One might say that in this case the machine 'ascertained' that it was in state A, which would be analogous to the case of a human being who has been conditioned to say 'I am in pain' (or Ouch!) whenever he is in pain. The verbal report in both cases issues directly from the state it reports; no computation or additional evidence, no act of introspection, is necessary in order to account for the report. The utterances occur without thinking, without passing through any introspectible mental or computational states other than the state which is the subject of the report. There is no method at work in either case and therefore no answer to the question 'How does T ascertain that it is in state A?' or 'How does Jones know he is in pain?' Instead of inviting such logically odd questions by using such formulations as 'The machine ascertained that it was in state A' or 'Jones knew he was in pain', it is wiser to find alternative formulations which are more semantically acceptable - e.g., 'The machine was in state A, and this caused it to print: "I am in state A" ' or 'Jones was in pain, and this caused him to say "I am in pain".'

Putnam, it ought to be noted, does not have a problem with the concept of privacy. His version of functionalism simply gives an account of first-person psychological statements which is not grounded in a theory of introspection. The limitation of this account consists only in the sort of assumptions he must make in order to establish a telling analogical parity between human beings and Turing machines. The machine is *programmed* to print 'I am in state A' whenever it is in fact in state A, whereas the human being is *conditioned* to say 'I am in pain' whenever he is in fact in pain. The point about human beings, however, is that they have the specific capacity to simulate, suppress, or disguise psychological states and can resist processes of conditioning in a way that Turing machines cannot resist programming. Conditioning presupposes the existence of a mind or self - a thinking thing - in a way in which

112

programming quite simply does not. If a machine does not print 'I am in state A' when it is in state A, we do not readily suppose that it is withholding a self-report or resisting the will of the programmer. If it had been programmed to print such a self-report and failed to do so we should look for a fault in the system. Of course, if we failed to find such a fault we might begin to think that something strange was happening, that the machine had generated a fragment of mind. But it is significant that the very thing which would alert us to the possibility of the emergence of a fragment of mind, or of a burgeoning self, is not the ability of the machine to process information or carry out instructions but, on the contrary, its apparently newfound ability to resist a program-instruction, to develop what Gunderson calls a 'program-resistant' property. We would then have to ask ourselves if it makes any sort of sense to attempt to program a machine to develop program-resistant powers. Could a mind or self emerge through a process of program-resistance in a Turing machine, given that a Turing machine is, by all accounts, a program-driven system? Before giving voice to an intuitive inclination to say 'no', we should dwell awhile on Dennett's attempt to develop an 'intentional system' functionalism in terms of which he proposes to show that persons themselves - minds, inner lives, and all - are analysable into sub-personal parts.

From intentional systems to the tell-tale self

Dennett rejects Turing-machine functionalism because he thinks it claims too much. It supposes that there could be some principled way of describing all believers, pain-sufferers, and dreamers as Turing machines 'so that they would be in the same logical state whenever they shared a mental epithet' (1981, p. xvi), and this is a fond hope, in Dennett's view. In the event of any particular mental state, there is no more reason to believe that two subjects have the 'same program', considering differences of nature and nurture, than there is to believe that they have identical physico-chemical descriptions. To avoid the reductionist claims of both the mind-brain identity theory and Turing-machine functionalism, Dennett proposes a new approach - an 'intentional system' functionalism. What two people have in common when they both believe, for example, that snow is white, is that both can be predictively attributed the belief that snow is white. Symbolically,

(x) (x believes that snow is white = x can be predictively attributed the belief that snow is white) (1981, p. xvii).

While this version of functionalism seems to make minimally revisionist claims, its chief virtue is to move from a reductionist strategy to a linguistic one. Mentality and intentionality will no longer be discussed as intrinsic features of a (physical) system but as features of uses of language, of perspectives, of the ways in which we characterize people and anything else that moves. Anything

113

that moves, that elicits a response from us, that orientates itself towards us, can be regarded as - construed, constituted as - an intentional system. The main point which Dennett makes about intentional systems is that 'a particular thing is an intentional system only in relation to the strategies of someone who is trying to explain and predict its behaviour' (pp. 3-4). Whether or not a thing is an intentional system - a thinking thing, if you like - is a question of stance rather than essence.

Dennett illustrates his position by inviting us to consider the case of a chess-playing computer, and the different stances one might adopt as an opponent trying to predict its moves. There are three stances of interest to us - the design stance, the physical stance, and the intentional stance. We can adopt the design stance when making predictions about the behaviour of mechanical objects. If we know how the computer is designed we can predict its designed response to any move we make by following the computation instructions of the program. The essential feature of the design stance is that we make predictions solely from knowledge of the system's functional design, irrespective of the physical constitution of the 'innards' of the particular object. The physical stance, by contrast, bases its predictions on the actual physical state of that particular object, and predictions are worked out by applying whatever knowledge we have of the laws of nature. The physical stance is generally reserved for instances of breakdown 'where the condition preventing normal operation is generalized and easily locatable, e.g., "Nothing will happen when you type in your questions, because it isn't plugged in"' (p. 5). Neither the design stance nor the physical stance can be usefully applied to modern computers. Attempting to give a physical account or prediction of the chess-playing computer would be a pointless and 'herculean' labour; the best machines are too complex to be accessible to design-based prediction, even by their own designers. A chess-player's best hope of defeating a computer is to predict its responses by figuring out as best he can what the most rational move would be, given the rules and goals of chess. That is, one assumes not only that the machine will function as designed, but that the design is optimal as well - that the machine will 'choose' the most rational move according to the rules and goals of chess. This means assuming the intentional stance towards the computer. One predicts behaviour in such a case by ascribing to the system the possession of certain information and supposing it to be directed by certain goals, and then working out the most reasonable or appropriate action on the basis of these ascriptions. In the measure that the machine responds appropriately to one's moves, to that extent it confirms the intentional stance. The machine functions as an intentional system, effectively:

> Lingering doubts about whether the chess-playing computer really has beliefs and desires are misplaced; for the definition of intentional systems I have given does not say that intentional systems really have beliefs and

114

desires, but that one can explain and predict their behavior by ascribing beliefs and desires to them, and whether one calls what one ascribes to the computer beliefs or belief-analogues or information complexes or intentional whatnots makes no difference to the nature of the calculation one makes on the basis of the ascriptions. One will arrive at the same predictions whether one forthrightly thinks in terms of the computer's beliefs and desires, or in terms of the computer's information-store and goal-specifications. (1981, p. 7)

Although he does not wish to claim that the chess-playing computer is going to provide us with a completely adequate model for the simulation of intelligent human or animal activity, Dennett is prepared to apply the intentional stance to any system that can be perceived to behave rationally, be it purely mechanical or purely creaturely (See Dennett, 1988, p. 122). The assumption that something is an intentional system is the assumption that it is rule-following or rational. There is even a sense in which non-human animals are rational animals after all, i.e., they can be said to believe or to follow the truths of logic. Consider a mouse in a situation where it can see a cat waiting at one mousehole and see a piece of cheese placed at another. We know which way the mouse will go, providing it is not deranged. We suppose the mouse can see the cat and the cheese, and hence has beliefs to the effect that there is a cat to the left, cheese to the right, and we ascribe to the mouse also the desire to eat the cheese and the desire to avoid the cat; so we predict that the mouse will do what is appropriate to such beliefs and desires, and go to the right to get the cheese and avoid the cat. Whether or not the mouse is said to believe the truths of logic, it must be supposed to 'follow' the rules of logic. The mouse, according to Dennett, effectively follows or believes in *modus ponens*, because we can ascribe to it the beliefs: (a) *there is a cat to the left*, and (b) *if there is a cat to the left, I had better not go left*. Our prediction relies on the mouse's ability to get to the appropriate conclusion. We are free, indeed, to ascribe to the mouse 'either a few inference rules and belief in many logical propositions, or many inference rules and few if any logical beliefs' (1981, p. 11).

In ascribing beliefs in this way, Dennett is, significantly, not ascribing either cerebral or other inner processes. Mental talk or intentional talk is not talk about minds or inner selves or even brains. It is talk which makes sense in intentional, rational, purposeful terms of the observed responses of animals and organisms to an environment which includes the acriber. It is an interpretation of (behavioural) output in the light of (environmental) input, but without any attempt to posit an inner event or representation, let alone an inner entity which negotiates these events and representations. Beliefs, desires and pains, considered as things, are not, in Dennett's view, good theoretical things, and it is not in any case the business of a functionalist to postulate theoretical entities. The business of the intentional-system functionalist is simply to apply the categories of rationality, perception and action, without worrying about the stuff of which inner processes are made.

The intentional-system functionalist may, like the behaviourist, deny the existence of inner processes altogether. Dennett's functionalism is in fact open to the same kind of criticism as conventional behaviourism because it is essentially a third-person account of intentional terms. It is an account which thrives on criteria, observation, and predictive strategies. The intentional stance is a stance that one adopts towards *others*, towards anything out there in the field of perception that orientates itself in our regard. But ascribing intentional states to others for strategic purposes, and on observational grounds, is only one use of intentional predicates. What account are we to give of the way we ascribe such terms to ourselves? We normally ascribe mental or intentional states to ourselves non-criterially. How then can we adopt the intentional stance, or the predictive strategy, towards ourselves? It is in fact easier to adopt the intentional stance towards a chess-playing computer, or towards a mouse, or even towards a thermostat, than it is to adopt it towards oneself. For the simple reason that 'adopting a stance' presupposes a predictive, observational, third-person perspective. The more appropriate such a stance is towards others, the less appropriate it is in one's own case. We are back with the problem of 'non-other' minds, the problem of how we ascribe to ourselves, on a non-observational, non-predictive basis, the same terms that we ascribe to others criterially, predictively, on the basis of observation. We are back with Malcolm's critique of behaviourism. To reiterate: (a) if we are to account for a being's status as a subject and a person, we must credit him/her with an autonomous status, with the right and the power of self-testimony; (b) a basic feature of mental concepts is that there is a radical asymmetry between their application by oneself to oneself, and their application by oneself to others; (c) this asymmetry consists in the fact that mental concepts are ascribed to others on a criterial, evidential basis but are not so ascribed to ourselves.

If it is true that we cannot meaningfully ascribe intentional states to ourselves on a criterial, evidential basis ('I am putting on my hat and coat so I must intend to go home'), then it is also true, and for roughly the same reasons, that we cannot normally adopt the intentional stance - a predictive strategy - towards ourselves. Sometimes, of course, we do not know what move to make in the chess-game, or what position to take at the emergency meeting. But we do not arrive at our own personal decisions or resolutions by way of a predictive strategy. We make a decision or arrive at a resolution, but not because we have successfully predicted our own behaviour. The predictive strategy works - but for others, not for oneself. And it works for others just because it does not - cannot - work for oneself. In adopting a predictive strategy one's aim is to render others as predictable as possible, while at the same time rendering oneself as unpredictable as possible. There is no point in my adopting a predictive strategy towards you if I do not enjoy a non-predictive relation with my own psychological states. If my intentions were always transparent to you, then my predictive strategies with regard to you would soon be set at nought.

If we then go on to attempt to describe what it is to make oneself unpredictable, we must have recourse to the language of privacy, the language of thinking (strategically) to oneself. The hiddenness of my thoughts is not, of course, guaranteed in some mythically Cartesian sense. It may have to be worked at, like a poker face or a good feint. But the fact that an inner life can be achieved at all, if only as a result of my making myself unpredictable in a world of predictively strategic thinking, is one of the things that marks the difference between self and other, between the first- and third-person perspectives. Being a self consists in having and sustaining an inner life, an inner life which includes centrally the capacity to *conceal* one's real intentions, feelings, and states of mind, thus obliging others to adopt predictive strategies towards us. If there were no such capacity there would be no need for predictive strategies in the first place. Given that predictive strategies presuppose subjects who enjoy a non-predictive relation with at least some of their own intentional states, then intentional-system functionalism, like behaviourism, tells only half the story, the half that can be told by the third-person narrator, from a predictively strategic third-party perspective.

Unlike a conventional behaviourist, however, Dennett is aware of the problem of constructing a self, 'a first person', with a privileged relation to some set of mental features, out of 'the third-person stuff' of intentional systems. He is aware of the need to take account of 'the ineliminable sense of *intimacy* we feel with the program-resistant side of our mentality' (1981, p. 30). Rather than denying (as the behaviourist does) the existence of the self or the inner life, he proposes to 'construct a full-fledged "I" out of sub-personal parts' by exploiting sub-personal notions of 'access" (1981, p. 154). In doing so he believes himself to be keeping faith with the assumption that functionalist theories are theories of the sub-personal level, without at the same time denying the reality of the person as a unitary subject of experience. Sub-personal theories proceed by analysing a person into an organization of subsystems (organs, routines, nerves, faculties, components - even atoms) 'and attempting to explain the behavior of the whole person as the outcome of the interaction of these subsystems' (p.153). But these theories have sometimes, in Dennett's view, permitted 'instantiations' that obviously are not subjects of experience with an inner, conscious life. His first step towards a more acceptable sub-personal, functionalist theory of mind is to make a sub-personal flow chart composed of interacting units, such as a central processing unit (Control), a short-term memory unit, a problem-solving unit, a perceptual analysis unit, and a print-out faculty. He maintains that the flow-charted system can function intelligently and consciously without a central, privileged, unanalysable unit called 'the self'. Even introspection can be analysed as the specialized information-seeking activity of the Control unit and not as the paradigmatic, instantaneous, infallible activity of a simple, substantial self. The Control unit is programmed to 'introspect' by accessing Memory unit and subsequently interpreting, censoring, and inferring answers, and relaying these answers to the Print-Out unit. The Print-Out unit takes as input 'orders to perform speech acts, or semantic intentions, and executes these orders' (p. 156). The lines of control between Control, Memory (M), and Print-Out (PR), in the case of an episode of that most supposedly self-centred and Cartesian of mental activities, viz. introspection, would be as follows:

(1) [Control] goes into its introspection subroutine, in which
(2) it directs a question to M;
(3) when an answer comes back (and none may) it assesses the answer: it may
    (a) censor the answer
    (b) 'interpret' the answer in the light of other information
    (c) 'draw inferences' from the answer, or
    (d) relay the answer as retrieved direct to PR
(4) The outcome of any of (a-d) can be a speech command to PR. (p. 156)

On this model, introspection is the end-result of a series of processes whereby the higher executive component in the brain, viz. the Control unit, directs questions to the Memory unit, assesses the answers, and passes them on to the speech centre where they may be expressed. Such an inter-modular, functionalist model suggests that introspection does not involve some kind of direct, instantaneous acquaintance with internal events, but is rather a process of internal monitoring, of putting questions to the Memory unit concerning internal computations and relevant bits of system-related information. The processes involved happen so consecutively and so quickly that they create the illusion of immediate and privileged access. It is the force of this illusion which leads to the claim of incorrigibility for introspective reports. According to Dennett's analysis, however, no such incorrigibility can be claimed since various kinds of omissions and errors may occur at any stage in the series of processes, although these may go unnoticed and unrecorded.

By way of collecting evidence for his flow-chart hypothesis and against the 'direct access' theory, he draws our attention to a class of intuition-like mental phenomena which includes presentiments and premonitions. These events are propositional episodes, 'thinkings that p', and they may be expressed to others or kept to oneself. When they occur in us - and this is Dennett's main point in this context - 'we have not the faintest idea what their etiology is' (1981, p. 165). From the introspective point of view, they arrive from we know not where. They are, as it were, generated by the intentional system as a whole and do not have their origins in introspective awareness itself. Other examples include wanting to say something, or actually saying it, without knowing how

118

or why. Witticisms are also significant in that they 'occur to us', but we do not know how we produce them. Dennett cites Karl Lashley's claim that if asked to think a thought in dactylic hexameter we can oblige but have no awareness of how we do it: 'the *result* arrives, and that is the extent of our direct access to the whole business' (1981, p. 165). Lashley's own comment on this example was that no activity of the mind is ever conscious, which Dennett interprets to mean that we have access - conscious access - to the results of mental processes, but not to the processes themselves:

> My contention is that far from being rare and anomalous occurrences, propositional episodes, these thinkings that p, are our normal and continuous avenue to self-knowledge, that they exhaust our immediate awareness, and that the odd varieties, such as the presentiment that someone is looking over one's shoulder, are striking only because of their isolation from the preceding and following sentiments, only because of our inability to follow them up with related propositional episodes about the same topic. (pp. 165-6)

Dennett concludes that it is our propensities to make unstudied utterances that constitute our primary evidence for making self-comments, and not access to the processes which produce the unstudied utterances. Those processes take place at a sub-personal, sub-conscious level to which we have no direct access - which means that we have no direct access to the structure of these contentful events within us. For Dennett, the 'inner eye' model of introspection is best replaced by something like the process-chart model according to which the (illusory) experience of direct, incorrigible access to an intimate inner life is accounted for in terms of interactions among sub-personal, sub-conscious functions, and not as the instantaneous activity of a substantial self. Introspection is explicable as 'a routine by means of which a person gains access to and reports on the contents of his or her buffer memory' (1981, p. 80). In his later work (1991) he prefers to speak of a 'multiple drafts' or 'virtual machine' model which has no place in it for a 'central meaner' or inner spectator, but the point remains the same, namely, that an account can be given of mind and self which does not require the positing of some irreducible entity, such as an immaterial - or, for that matter, a material - Cartesian ego.

The significance of Dennett's approach is not its assertion that machines could have inner lives of a human kind but the converse claim that the inner lives or inner processes of human beings can be understood in machine-like terms. In some respects this really is a greater threat to the Cartesian conception of self than an old-style Turing-machine functionalism. It seems to strike especially hard at the Cartesian notion of the unity of consciousness and at the immediacy of the intuitions which the thinking self is supposed to have of its own existence and nature. It also challenges the identity of mind and self which is central to the Cartesian view. It does so by effectively extending to human beings the very machine analogy that Descartes himself extended originally to animals. The doctrine of the *bête machine* has been superseded by the doctrine of *l'homme machine*. This latter phrase brings to mind the work of an earlier critic of Descartes, La Mettrie (1774). Dennett, for all his efforts to distinguish himself from the Turing-machine functionalists, belongs to the school of La Mettrie. La Mettrie, as Gunderson has shown, used the Cartesian claim that animals are machines to support a mechanistic view of human nature. By emphasizing similarities between animals and human beings, La Mettrie argued that there was no essential difference between their intelligence and ours. Animals, he believed, share to some degree in our intelligence and sentience, while we share fully in their 'machineness'. Hence, as Keith Gunderson puts it, 'the *bête machine* doctrine comes to be extended to man ..., and thought and feelings are "extended" to animals' (1985, p. 27). Sometimes La Mettrie spoke passionately of the virtual humanity of animals: 'The internal senses are no more lacking to animals than the external ones; consequently they are endowed as we are with the same spiritual faculties which depend on them, I mean perception, memory, imagination, judgment, reason ....' (Cited in Gunderson, 1985, p. 26). By 'spiritual' faculties, however, La Mettrie did not mean anything of a Cartesian nature. His intention was not to invest animals or machines with minds or souls. On the contrary, he denied that there is any mental self over and above the complex mechanical clockwork workings of the body. As impressed by clockwork automata as modern philosophers are by computers, La Mettrie described the human body as a large watch constructed with great skill and ingenuity. He added that thought was compatible with organized matter, and was indeed one of its properties, on a par with electricity, the faculty of motion, impenetrability, extension, etc. In Gunderson's view, La Mettrie did not regard reasoning, thought, or the use of language 'as anything more than the output of highly complex machines' (1985, p. 29). It is not too much of an exaggeration to say that this would also serve as a summation of not only the Artificial Intelligence thesis but also of Dennett's sort of intentional stance functionalism.

The point of Dennett's modular model is to show that intentional systems can be composed of sub-personal parts, none of which is identical with an autonomous mind or self. If we must speak in terms of autonomy we will have to say it resides in the system. However, the autonomy of the system does not depend on the presence of some inner metaphysical entity but on the efficiency of integration among the component unit-parts. The most general implication of the functionalist view and of the AI thesis is to analyze away the mental self of Cartesian philosophy and to cast doubt once again on the concept of an inner life of which only first-person accounts can be given. In the Sixth Meditation, having found in himself the power to enjoy certain modes of consciousness such as imagination and sensory perception, Descartes argued that he could clearly and distinctly understand himself as a whole apart from these faculties 'but I cannot, conversely, understand these faculties without me, that is, without an intellectual substance to inhere in' (AT VII, 78; CSM II, 54). Later in the same Meditation, in the course of distinguishing between mind and body, he argues that body of its nature is always divisible, while mind is wholly indivisible:

> For when I consider the mind, or myself in so far as I am merely a thinking thing, I am unable to distinguish any parts within myself; I understand myself to be something quite single and complete. Although the whole mind seems to be united to the whole body, I recognize that if a foot or arm or any other part of the body is cut off, nothing has thereby been taken away from the mind. As for the faculties of willing, of understanding, of sensory perception and so on, these cannot be termed parts of the mind, since it is one and the same mind that wills, and understands and has sensory perceptions. (AT VII, 86; CSM II, 59)

It is the idea of an autonomous, indivisible self which is repugnant to Dennett as it is to most functionalist and materialist philosophers. The same idea has been rejected by social and psychological theorists, especially psychoanalysts. Sherry Turkle, for example, believes that the functionalist AI thesis is effectively carrying forward the 'deconstructionist' enterprise initiated by psychoanalysis. The self is fundamentally divided by the psychoanalyst into conscious and unconscious parts, and it makes decisions and entertains thoughts that are unconsciously motivated while being consciously rationalised. The concept of the unconscious does not merely require us to modify our notion of an autonomous self, it constitutes a conceptual challenge, i.e., it puts into question not only whether the self is free, but whether there is one at all. And as the psychoanalytic subject is fractured and decentred in the processes of the unconscious, so the computational 'subject' is fractured and decentred in the idea of a thinking thing that is a program-driven assemblage of sub-personal functions: 'if mind is program, where is the self?' (Turkle, 1988, p. 245).

Where Dennett used the example of sudden thoughts or presentiments to corroborate his functionalist picture of sub-personal processes, Turkle uses the example of a Freudian slip to show how a computational account could explain the slip in appropriately subrational, subconscious terms. In his *Psychopathology of Everyday Life* Freud discussed the example of a chairman who opens a parliamentary session by declaring it closed. The Freudian interpretation of this slip focuses on the complex feelings or ambivalent wishes that lie behind it. The chairman, for example, may have mixed feelings about the session, and the slip may point to a real but suppressed wish to be elsewhere. The AI theorist, on the other hand, could adopt the classical information-processing view and simply attribute the slip to a bit of information

121

lost or a program derailed - an error of mechanism. Such a view might even be just as plausible as Freud's own analysis. It is interesting to note that for Freud words of opposite meaning are often interchanged because they lie close to each other in linguistic consciousness (Freud, 1960, p. 59). For the computer programmer likewise the two words are also close together, functionally, in the system, since it is natural to code opposite concepts as the same root with a different 'sign bit' attached. Thus, if one thinks of the human brain as storing and processing information, then substituting *closed* for *open* is readily explained as a minor error of mechanism.

Like Dennett, Turkle seems to think that the behaviour of any intelligent or intentional system can be explained in terms of neuron-like entities, sub-minds or mindless 'homuncular' agencies which manage to generate meaning and 'mind' when they are brought into simultaneous interaction with each other. Turkle notes that AI theorist Marvin Minsky has identified a vast array of computational agents - censor agents, recognition agents, emotion agents - and that Minsky recognizes Freud as a colleague in 'society' modelling, i.e., modelling which takes the mind to be a society of interacting simple agents. No agent by itself is intelligent but all the simple (or sub-personal, unconscious agents) working together according to a complex division of labour somehow produce intelligence, consciousness and selfhood. Minsky has even introduced the concept of 'repression' into AI by claiming that there cannot be intelligence, artificial or otherwise, without repression, without censoring agents which can deal systematically with conflicting inputs or messages (See Minsky, 1985, pp. 1-4).

What is most striking about the claims of functionalists and AI theorists alike, from Minsky to Dennett, is their reliance on tendentious, anthropomorphic metaphors. William Lyons has rightly pointed out that Dennett, for example, in describing his Control unit as assessing, directing, censoring, inferring and interpreting, is 'mixing the sub-personal with the personal' (1986, p. 86).[3] That is, a supposedly sub-personal, mechanistic process is described in personalistic, mentalistic terms. Dennett's Control component turns out to be a homunculus with full-blown intentional attitudes, despite the fact that it is supposed to be a stupidly non-intentional mechanistic device. Dennett himself has recognized the difficulty of his 'top-down' reductionist strategy, i.e., a strategy that tries to reduce or analyse the highest levels of mental functioning into sub-mental systems and processes. He argues that a psychology which remains at the level of intentional 'homunculi' is doomed to infinite regress and is impossible as a science. But he admits at the same time that psychology without homunculi is also impossible, and that within AI functionalism itself 'homunculus talk' remains ubiquitous. AI homunculi 'talk' to each other, 'wrest control' from each other, 'volunteer', 'sub-contract', 'supervise', and even 'kill'. He suggests defensively that homunculi are bogeymen 'only if they duplicate entire the talents they are wrung in to explain .... If one can get a team or committee of *relatively* ignorant, narrow-minded, blind homunculi to produce intelligent behaviour on the whole, this is progress' (1981, p. 123). It is not clear, however, where the progress lies. A relatively ignorant, narrow-minded, blind homunculus is also a relatively intelligent, mindful, perceptive homunculus - it is not at all the same thing as a wholly sub-personal device or component. It seems extremely difficult, in other words, to give a wholly non-mentalistic account of higher-level mental representation without employing terms which have residually mental connotations. Dennett suggests positing 'data-structures' or representations which understand themselves but this suggestion makes sense only in relation to (mentalistic) discourses in which the notions of self-understanding or self-knowledge already have a usage. In such an account an 'elementary' mode or level of consciousness is introduced in order to give a reductive gloss on what consciousness is. Higher levels of consciousness are being explained, as it were, in terms of more elementary or lower-level mental mechanisms, but consciousness has not been reduced without remainder to the sub-personal level. Even the notion of unitariness has migrated down from the higher to the lower level. In his most recent work Dennett, still worried about possible charges of homuncular anthropomorphism, suggests that calling the units in different functionalist theories 'homunculi' - or 'demons' or 'agents' or 'sub-minds' - is 'scarcely more contentful than calling them simply ... units' (1991, p. 262). The point of positing such units, homuncular or otherwise, is to show how larger (mental) functions can be accomplished by organizations of units performing smaller (cerebral) functions. But the decision to avoid homuncular talk by adopting unit talk does not necessarily improve matters. After all, if we have a problem about the notion of a unitary self or consciousness - which is really a problem about the very idea of unitariness - why should we not also have a problem about the notion of a unitary homunculus or a (homuncular) unit? On the other hand, if we are going to permit ourselves to talk of unitary homunculi, why not unitary selves or minds?[4]

The fact that one should wish to raise these kinds of questions should not be interpreted as signalling an obscurantist resistance to the explanation of consciousness. Dennett is right when he says that only a theory that explained conscious activities in terms of unconscious events could explain consciousness at all: 'If your model of how pain is a product of brain activity still has a box in it labelled "pain," your haven't yet begun to explain what pain is ...' (1981, pp. 454-5). But likewise if your model of how pain is a product of brain activity has a box in it labelled 'pain-bearing homunculi' or 'pain-bearing units', one still hasn't begun to explain what pain is - it just looks technical and scientific and appropriately explanatory because it's done out in flow-charts and block-diagrams.

The use of metaphoric, anthropomorphic, even spiritualistic phraseology is characteristic of the writing of sub-personalists of all persuasions. For Turkle, for example, natural and artificial minds may be said to be composed of 'subminds' and internal 'agents'; Marvin Minsky writes not only of a 'society of mind' made up of a large number of modules organised like a bureaucracy but pictures each module as behaving like an agent or 'demon' which watches for events 'of interest' to itself and 'acts' only when such events occur. Even the concept of information-processing (which has been accepted by many people, including critics of the AI thesis, as one of the activities which is shared by both natural and artificial brains) is laden with anthropomorphic connotations, trading on the very meanings it is supposed to eliminate. George Reeke and Gerald Edelman point out that the whole enterprise of brain-modelling rests on the assumption that information exists *in* the world, ready-made, just there to be manipulated. The term implies that both organisms and machines move about in an environment of information as receivers rather than creators or finders of information. And once the prior existence of external information is conceded, it is entirely natural to think of programming as simply devising the rules to deal with it, and at the same time to think of both human beings and computers as species of the genus 'information processing system' (1988, p. 145). But computers are not information processors at all, at least not in the sense in which human beings are. In reality it is the programmer/user who does the coding, the categorizing, the defining of procedures, the interpreting, and who creates, generates, gathers and uses information. The computerized storage and processing of information is only a part - and not necessarily an intelligent part - of information-gathering, information-usage, information-creation. Indeed, once all the meanings of the concept of information-processing are unpacked it becomes more apparent that the AI enterprise has much further to go than either its proponents or conventional opponents realize. Information-processing is not something which machines do, even at a very basic level - it is something which human beings do in an information-centred era, using machines which are designed to massively and effectively replace filing cabinets, ledgers and mechanical calculating devices. In practice, the AI project has only seemed plausible because functions have been projected from the programmer on to the machine in a manner which is symptomatic of a modern form of animism.

S. G. Shanker (1989) reminds us that AI scientists speak of a hierarchy of languages involved in computer programming, ranging from the 'machine language' itself to the high-level program language, with the reductions from a higher to a lower-level language performed by 'symbolic assemblers' or 'compilers' which convert the high-level language program into the machine code. The compilers convert the high-level instructions into a binary form, which can in turn be encoded in electrical impulses:

> But the *machine* is not executing the instructions encoded in these electrical impulses; rather, it is still *we* who are executing the instructions, albeit

with the aid of this sophisticated electro-mechanical tool.... What the machine is doing can only be intelligibly described in terms of its electro-mechanical operations (viz. in terms of the computer's 'clock' which generates at a constant rate the electrical pulses which are used to transport the 'bits' around the computer). (Shanker, 1989, p. 82)

Shanker goes on to make the point that it makes little sense to speak of a machine following a rule, even a syntactical rule, since following a rule is a normative action or practice and cannot be a mechanical operation. Following a rule, in other words, implies an understanding and awareness of what one is doing. Practically everything we say about computers reflects what Dennett would call 'the intentional stance'. We talk about computers as if they were in fact intelligent. But it is this very anthropomorphic language which makes it difficult to use the computer as a source-model for the sub-personal components that Dennett and others need in their attempt to explain consciousness or introspection. The model in terms of which they wish to articulate their sub-mental, sub-personal hypothesis is already contaminated by imputations and connotations of the mental and the personal.

Such is the tendentious, mentalistic, question-begging nature of the language of information-processing that it is not yet the major threat to a unitary concept of mind that it is often thought to be. It is, of course, almost universally assumed that self-respecting functionalists or materialists must abandon the notion of a unitary mind or consciousness if they are to maintain any credibility as anti-dualists. But this assumption is the legacy of an anti-Cartesianism which assumes that only dualists can talk anyway about such things as minds, selves and inner lives. It is the point of the next section to suggest that a materialist or functionalist concept of a unified self is in fact defensible without recourse to a Cartesian dualism.

Systems and wholes: the case for a complex yet unified ego

It is not necessary for even the strictest Cartesian egoist to deny that human subjects are divided in some sense. It is certainly not necessary for a post-Cartesian egoist to deny divisions in the human psyche or personality. In the case of the Freudian concept of mind or psyche, the egoist may accept a real division between the conscious and the unconscious levels of mental activity. Such division of processes or functions, however, does not imply some kind of literal or numerical division of consciousness, only a delimiting of the scope and power of consciousness. The unconscious is, by definition, outside of consciousness and therefore not part of consciousness. The division occurs within the psyche or personality but not within consciousness. If there should arise a problem here about the relationship between consciousness and the unconscious it would be no greater a problem for a (post-Freudian) Cartesian egoist than that of the relationship between mind and body. The subconscious could, in fact, be placed among the mechanisms of 'nature' or among the subtler processes of body, brain and nervous system. The post-Freudian, post-Cartesian egoist will have no difficulty in accepting that the *psyche* is divided or in accepting that the ego is a product of the sorts of sub-personal, sub-conscious processes that functionalists love to postulate. The conscious self may be regarded as a part of a divisible or divided psyche and may be understood to have its genesis in the complex mechanics of the brain or in the complex interactions between brain and environment. The fact that consciousness is not divisible does not mean that it cannot itself be a part or unit of a larger whole. We may accept the distinction between *unitary* and *unified* offered by Andrew Collier:

> [T]he psyche is not a *unitary* whole of which the parts merely express a single principle - the 'autonomous' consciousness. It is a unified whole, which has achieved a more or less stable equilibrium under the direction of consciousness, but which has other (unconscious) elements which may obstruct this direction, which may act on and determine consciousness independently of its knowledge or volition, which may in turn be acted upon by consciousness, etc. (1977, p. 27)

What needs to be emphasized is that it makes sense, even from a Cartesian point of view, to say that the psyche is unified in Collier's sense, while consciousness remains unitary in a Cartesian sense. The fact that the material origins of consciousness are complex does not mean that consciousness itself is numerically composite or divided. There is no contradiction in saying that unitariness is an 'emergent' property of consciousness, while accepting that consciousness is 'caused' in the first place by processes that are variously, compositely, systematically related. We may readily accept Mario Bunge's notion of a system as 'a complex object whose components are interrelated, as a consequence of which the system behaves in some respects as a unit or whole' (1981, p. 24). Bunge defends the concept of 'emergent properties' by introducing the notions of *system*, *composition* and *level*. If we divide reality for explanatory purposes into the physical, chemical, biological, social and technical levels, we can begin to allow for the existence of systematically emergent properties. Indeed, we cannot make complete sense of the concepts of composition or evolution unless we *do* allow for the concept of emergent properties. First, every system, insofar as it is a system, possesses at least one emergent property in the trivial sense that every system has a composition and a structure which differs from that of its components. That is, features of integrated systems are different from features of components. Second, given a taxonomy or hierarchy of levels, it will be true to say that systems on every

126

level have emerged or evolved in the course of some 'process of assembly' of lower level entities. Third, every assembly process is accompanied by the emergence of at least one property. The property of 'life' which is a distinctive feature of the biological level - of the cell - is not a feature of the physical and chemical components of the cell but rather 'emerges' when a certain level of complexity is reached by the physical and chemical substances which will compose the cell. Similarly, we may say that mentality or selfhood is an emergent property possessed by organisms endowed with a very complex plastic nervous system. One can hold, according to Bunge, that the mental is emergent, relative to the physical or chemical levels, without reifying the mental after the fashion of Descartes. That is, one can hold that the mind is not a simple spiritual substance, nor an entity composed of lower level things, 'but a collection of functions of certain neural systems' (p. 88). There is nothing mysterious, in Bunge's view, about emergence *if* it is conceived in this evolutionary sense - in terms of an ontology of levels. Emergence only becomes mysterious when it is characterized 'epistemologically', namely as some property of a system which cannot be explained from the low-level components and their relations. Such an obscurantist epistemology is as unacceptable to Bunge as it is to, say, Dennett.

Bunge's emergentism suggests that all systems function as units or wholes, and that complexity of composition is consistent with functional 'wholeness'. Unity is in fact a property which we typically ascribe to complex systems since only systems (as distinct from, say, monads) may be said to lack or possess unity, or possess greater or lesser degrees of unity. Unity is an *emergent* property to the extent that the unity of a whole is not reducible, ontologically, to the sum of its components. Robert Nozick (1981) has emphasized this point by saying that the identity of a whole through time is not specified by the identity through time of its parts. Modally, a whole need not be the sum of its parts in that it is possible that these may diverge over time: 'Something X at time t_1 with parts $p_1, ..., p_n$ is a whole if it is possible that there is a later time t_2 such that X at t_2 does not contain as its exact parts p_1 at t_2, p_2 at t_2, ..., p_n at t_2' (Nozick, 1981, p. 101).

Of course, the divergence, alteration or destruction of parts cannot go on indefinitely. There must be for every emergent whole a threshold beyond which divergence of parts means alteration or loss of identity. Given that the concept of unity is logically interwoven with that of identity, we can say that every whole has a 'divergence-threshold'. We can in fact say this of any object or individual, whether it is a unit of an elementary substance, or a member of a species - or a 'self' or mind. Although an atom of any elementary substance is divisible it is not divisible without loss of elementary identity, i.e., its division implies its disintegration *qua* atom. More complex systems can tolerate more divisions, more removal of components and parts, but no whole or system is indefinitely divisible without loss of identity. Even the most complex or

127

protean system has a threshold beyond which it cannot afford to lose any more components if it is to retain its identity. When that threshold is crossed the system disintegrates, losing its identity *qua* system. This is as true of persons as it is of plants or animals or artifacts, except that persons are in some important respects more 'identity-sensitive', or have a lower divergence-threshold, than some other things.

There is a sense, indeed, in which the mind or self can be said to be indivisible, albeit in a very unCartesian sense. In saying that a self, a person, a mind, is indivisible we are saying that the identity of that self, person, or mind cannot afford the loss of certain of its component faculties or functions and does not survive any such loss. The loss of the faculty of memory, for example, while it does not destroy the biological person, does frequently cause loss of strictly personal or psychological identity. The profoundly amnesiac person is no longer the same to others (or, presumably, to herself, although it is not clear what we should mean here). In that sense, loss of a mental faculty or function can cause such loss of identity that we are entitled to say that mind, relative to certain conditions of identity, is indivisible. Not because the mental self is immutable or immortal or indestructible, but, on the contrary, because all its component faculties are so intrinsically constitutive of, and so integral to, its proper functioning that the removal of one such faculty or function causes immediate alteration, loss, or even disintegration of the pre-trauma identity.

This notion of an identity-relative indivisibility of self does not require us to deny the complexity of mind, or to deny that mind is a product of complex processes in the brain. It may be, as Dennett mischievously reminds us (1981, p. 89), that the verb *cogito* is derived from a Latin idiom which meant *to shake together* - but it nonetheless makes a difference whether the shaking together produces a wholly integrated system (which functions effectively *as if* a unit) or just a collection of externally related 'shakings'. There may be functional complexity of the mind or self that is 'shaken together' out of the brain's components, but it does not follow that the resultant mind bears the traces of its complex genesis. The unitary complexity of mind is of a kind appropriate only to talk about minds or subjects; it is not appropriate to talk about purely 'physical' objects, i.e., objects which are not capable of consciousness or self-awareness. Indeed, if it is the case that we can talk about unity (in the sense of 'unifiedness') only if we can also talk about degrees of complexity and systematic integration, then it begins to look as if cerebral complexity generates a level, a degree and a quality of integration - an exceptional kind of emergent property called *mentality* or *self-awareness* - that has no precedent in the underlying pyramid of nature's evolving levels.

This way of thinking does not commit us to obscurantism. Indeed, towards the end of *Consciousness Explained* Dennett accepts that unified selves are in some sense real. He accepts the reality of the biological self which resides in the nature-given ability to distinguish self from others in order to protect oneself in whatever niche oneself-as-organism occupies. This proclivity towards self-protection is present in all living things, from amoebas to human beings. It expresses itself not merely in self-defensive strategies but also in the instinctive, even mechanical, ability to extend and maintain specific territorial boundaries. Spiders spin webs, albeit without knowing how or why they do it. Beavers, also working instinctively but somewhat more co-operatively than spiders, build dams. Termites, working wholly co-operatively and wholly instinctively, build complex castles of earth. And human beings, working co-operatively in an expansive environment of representations, weave words into self-protective strings of narrative:

> Our fundamental tactic of self-protection, self-control, and self-definition is not spinning webs or building dams, but telling stories, and more particularly concocting and controlling the story we tell others - and ourselves - about who we are. And just as spiders don't have to think, consciously and deliberately, about how to spin their webs, and just as beavers, unlike professional human engineers, do not consciously and deliberately plan the structures they build, we (unlike *professional* human storytellers) do not consciously and deliberately figure out what narratives to tell and how to tell them. Our tales are spun, but for the most part we don't spin them; they spin us. Our human consciousness, and our narrative selfhood, is their product, not their source. (1991, p. 418)

Dennett's self is clearly a constituted self, but it is as real as the unified system of which Bunge writes. Its unity is an 'as-if' unity; it is an abstraction, rather than a thing in the brain - but it is still 'a remarkably robust and almost tangible attractor of properties' (p. 418). Perhaps we would do well to think of systems as essentially self-protective and self-realizing, as essentially striving to maintain a condition of unity and integrity. Selfhood and unity are not therefore incidental by-products of organisms or organic systems but are part of the concept of a living system. The system itself is self-protecting and self-realizing *qua* system. There is no need to think of a self as either an abstract centre or an actual entity which could exist apart from the system. A living system just is an integrated, self-realizing, and, in some cases, self-conscious entity. Perhaps we could say that the felt unity of consciousness in self-conscious systems - in human beings, for instance - is an instantiation of a highly-developed system experiencing from within its own natural proclivity to develop and sustain itself and maintain optimal levels of physical and psychological integrity. A self-conscious system which did not experience itself as unified would not accord well with the logic of evolution, survival, and self-preservation.

Colin McGinn argues that the unity of self is simply the unity conferred by self-consciousness, and that this unity cannot come in grades. Not only does the question of the self arise only when a creature has reflexive awareness, 'it also arises saltatorially' (1982, p. 105). McGinn goes on to argue in defence of the primitiveness and irreducibility of the concept of self, yet without defending a dualistic ontology. From the subjective point of view, the self cannot be divided, although when we think of it objectively or physically, as dependent upon the brain, we seem compelled to suppose that this simplicity is in some way illusory. The truth of the matter for McGinn, as for Nagel, is that we are confronted here with a genuine antinomy: two sets of considerations which are equally compelling even as they lead to contrary conclusions. He suggests that in the absence of powerful arguments or evidence to the contrary, and regardless of whether we are materialists or not, we should learn to live with the despair of our antinomy, and continue to hold provisionally but firmly to the conclusion that the self should be conceived as a simple substance whose identity is primitive and irreducible. Only a theory which explains that simplicity rather than explaining it away should hold our attention for the foreseeable future. The arguments of functionalists and the AI philosophers are still not strong enough to rid us of the antinomy generated by due consideration of both the first-person perspective, within which the self is duly experienced as a unitary centre of awareness, and the third-person perspective, within which the self is duly understood to be a function of the complex processes of the brain. Our first-person conception of the individuality and persistence of a self is simply independent of the nature of the associated brain, regardless of whether the brain is described biologically or in the functionalist terms of artificial intelligence. No amount of further information about the relation between the brain and mental states can compel us to abandon the unitary first-person perspective, although such information may cause us to abandon the idea that the self is a soul in the originally Cartesian sense of an indestructible, independently existing entity. From an informed post-Cartesian point of view it is more plausible to say that the self is indivisible precisely because it is destructible. That is, it is indivisible in the identity-relative sense that a partial or total loss of faculty or function implies a partial or total loss of the pre-traumatic identity. The question of identity, however, is a difficult and complex one and will be discussed again, albeit in a somewhat different context, in Chapter 7.

Notes

1. Cf. Hilary Putnam (1988, pp. 270-271): 'Many years ago I was at a symposium with one of the most "famous names" in AI. The famous name was being duly "modest" about the achievements of AI. He said offhandedly, "We haven't really achieved so much, but I will say that we now have *machines that understand children's stories*." I remarked, "I

know the program you refer to" (it was one of the earliest language-recognition programs). "What you didn't mention is that the program has to be revised for each new children's story." (That is, ... the "program" was a program for answering questions about a specific children's story, not a program for understanding children's stories in general.)'

2. While Pinchbeck seemed to place more emphasis on reward than on punishment, it is commonly believed that the process of 'educating' an animal involves a good deal of punishment, even cruelty, as is suggested in the Circe chapter of James Joyce's *Ulysses*. After Leopold Bloom remarks that 'All tales of circus life are highly demoralising,' a Signor Maffei appears and, with a sinister smile, says: 'Ladies and gentlemen, my educated greyhound. It was I broke in the bucking broncho Ajax with my patent spiked saddle for carnivores. Lash under the belly with a knotted thong. Block tackle and a strangling pully will bring your lion to heel, no matter how fractious, even *Leo ferox* there, the Libyan maneater. A redhot crowbar and some liniment rubbing on the burning part produced Fritz of Amsterdam, the thinking hyena. *(He glares)* I possess the Indian sign. The glint of my eyes does it with these breastsparklers.'

3. The title of this chapter was suggested by the title of Part II of Lyons's *Disappearance of Introspection,* viz., 'The mechanization of introspection' (1986, p. 45).

4. For an interesting discussion of 'the homunculus fallacy' see John Searle (1992, pp. 212-14); see also Gerald Edelman (1994, pp. 79-82) on 'the horror of the homunculus'.

6 The declension of subjectivity

One of the stranger achievements of the anti-Cartesian tendency in contemporary philosophy of mind is to create a problem about the reference of the pronoun 'I'. There is among some philosophers an extraordinary reluctance to accept that 'I' actually refers to anything, lest such acceptance commit one to a belief in the discredited Cartesian ego. If we assume that there is no Cartesian ego or inner self to which the first-person pronoun may unerringly refer then the 'I' becomes, as Amélie Rorty puts it, a simple 'place holder' forced upon us by the structure of declarative sentences (1976, p. 12). The subject of a first-person declarative statement ceases to be the reflective subject of consciousness and becomes instead an effect or figment of grammar, a mere subject of attribution. In place of a dualistic, self-centred psychology we are presented with a reductionist 'grammar of subjectivity' in which there is no space for the Cartesian ego with the capacity to refer unfailingly to itself.

The starting-point for much of the discussion about self-reference is a distinction which Wittgenstein makes between two uses of 'I' - the use of 'I' as object and the use of 'I' as subject (1972, pp. 66-7). One uses 'I' (or 'my') as object in such sentences as 'My arm is broken', 'I have a bump on my forehead', 'The wind blows my hair about.' One uses 'I' as subject in such sentences as 'I see so-and-so', 'I will try to lift my arm', 'I have a toothache'. According to Wittgenstein, one can point to the difference between these two categories of use by saying that the as-object uses involve the identification or recognition of a particular person where there is always, in principle, the possibility of an error. It is possible, for example, that in an accident I should feel pain in my arm, see a broken arm, and think it is mine when in fact it is my neighbour's. On the other hand, there is no question of rightly or wrongly identifying anyone when I say I have toothache. To ask, 'Are you sure that it's you who has a pain?' would be nonsensical: 'it is as impossible that in making the statement "I have toothache" I should have mistaken another person for

132

myself, as it is to moan with pain by mistake, having mistaken someone else for me' (p. 67).

The problem which this passage generates is whether 'I' is a referring expression in each or either of these categories. More particularly, if 'I' refers in its as-subject use, what is the 'subject' it refers to? Is it something like a self, a mind, or - heaven forbid! - a Cartesian ego? G.E.M. Anscombe (1981) denies that 'I' ever refers, either in the as-object or as-subject use. She accepts that the form or character of Descartes' Cogito argument means that each person must administer it to himself in the first person but denies the assumption that 'when one says "I" or "the mind", one is naming something such that the knowledge of its existence, which is a knowledge of itself as thinking in all the various modes, determines what it is that is known to exist' (p. 21). Her short, sharp solution to the problem about the reference of 'I' is that though 'I' functions syntactically as a name, it is neither a name 'nor another kind of expression whose logical role is to mark a reference, *at all'* (P. 32). Her reasoning is that if 'I' is a name, or a demonstrative, or some other kind of referring expression, then there must be some 'conception' that connects 'I' with the object of reference. Because the use of a name for an object is connected with a conception of that object, we are driven to look for something that, for each 'I' user, will be the conception related to the supposed name 'I', as the conception of a city is to the names 'London' and 'Chicago', that of a river to 'Thames' and 'Nile', that of a man to 'John', and 'Pat'. She concludes that such a conception is necessary if 'I' is to function as a name. Nor does it help to insist that 'I' is a demonstrative rather than a name. We still need, according to Anscombe, a conception of the object referred to or indicated: 'For, even though someone may say just "this" or "that", we need to know the answer to the question "this *what*?" if we are to understand him; and he needs to know the answer if he is to be meaning anything' (p. 27).

Norman Malcolm (1986) endorses Anscombe's position. He accepts that we are unable to specify any conception or well-understood general term that corresponds to 'I', and suggests that corresponding terms such as 'self', 'soul', or 'mind' also lack the kind of clear and distinct conception that Anscombe requires. He adds: 'I should hardly know what I was saying if I either asserted or denied that I am a self, soul, or mind' (1986, p. 251). Even in situations where I no longer knew who I was in the sense of knowing my name, my past or my identity, I could still utter 'I' meaningfully:

Suppose that from extreme privation and suffering I no longer knew who I was. Lying on the ground amidst other enfeebled people, and feeling a savage thirst I cry out, 'Water! Water!' An attendant, looking around, says, 'Who wants water?' I might call out 'I', or might instead raise my hand. By uttering 'I', or by holding up my hand, I would equally be drawing attention to myself. But neither the hand gesture nor the utterance

'I', would imply a conception of myself that distinguished me from other persons. My utterance of 'I' in response to the question, would show that I still *retained a mastery of the use of 'I'*, even though I had no conception of who I was. (1986, p. 252)

John Canfield (1991) agrees with Malcolm and Anscombe that if 'I' refers there must be some category associated with it. But he does not accept their argument that there is no such category and that therefore 'I' does not refer. Canfield's own position is that 'I' is not a paradigmatic referring expression, i.e., it does not do the job that paradigmatic referring expressions do. That is, in such uses as 'I think ...' or 'I am in pain' the pronoun does not refer in the way in which referring expressions paradigmatically refer, by picking out or pointing to an individual within a given context or against a background of 'the phenomenally given'. If the function of a singular referring expression in a sentence is to pick out or point to a particular individual, 'the other words in the sentence can then describe the particular, or state a command for that particular to follow, as in "Fido is thirsty" or "Jones, come here!"' (Canfield, 1991, p. 59). But 'I' does not function in this way in many of its most paradigmatic psychological uses, e.g., 'I think ...', 'I am in pain', etc., because there is no room for the identification or recognition of a particular (person) to be made. Where there is no question of identification there is no question of reference, as far as Canfield is concerned. But Canfield, *pace* Malcolm and Anscombe, nonetheless maintains that 'I' sometimes refers. It refers in its 'object' uses, or those uses in which one is a person among other persons and there is a possibility of one's being mistaken about some 'objective' feature of one's body or person. Whereas my learning, when in pain, to express the judgement 'I am in pain' does not involve my observing or identifying any person, my making the judgement 'I have a bump on my head' *does* involve my making observations and attributions which just might be mistaken. In the latter usage 'I' refers like any referring expression but in the former it does not refer at all. The two uses have different 'depth grammars' despite their surface similarity.

If Anscombe, Malcolm, and Canfield are right, then the 'I' in its first-person present-tense psychological or 'subject' uses is reduced to the ceremonial role of filling a grammatical gap in a sentence, like the 'it' in 'it is snowing'. The 'subject' ceases to be the subject of thought and action and becomes the subject of sentential attribution. How acceptable is such a radical attenuation of the subject or self, such a radical shift from ontology to grammar, from self-subsistent ego to pronominal person? Is anyone who acknowledges the constitutive power of language, or who is sympathetic to Wittgenstein's philosophy of language, obliged to reject a post-Cartesian concept of the self and endorse this new reductionist grammar of subjectivity?

Reintroducing the first person

Anscombe, Malcolm, and Canfield attempt to rid the term 'I' of its Cartesian aura by emphasizing its linguistic function in such a way that it need not be understood to refer to anything as elusively metaphysical as a nonphysical self or mind. But does it follow that anyone who argues that 'I' refers is necessarily claiming that it refers to a self in some problematically metaphysical sense? Sidney Shoemaker (1968) does not think so. Shoemaker argues that if we consider the logical powers of first-person statements and the role played by the first-person pronoun in communication, 'nothing seems clearer than that in all first-person statements, including "avowals", the word "I" functions as a ... singular referring expression' (1968, p. 555). The statement 'I feel pain' has it in common with 'He feels pain' and 'Jones feels pain' that they contradict the proposition 'Nobody feels pain' and entail the proposition 'Somebody feels pain.' The statement 'I feel pain' behaves logically as a value of the propositional function 'X feels pain.' In other words, if 'he', 'Jones', and 'X' are referring expressions - and they are, non-controversially, for Shoemaker - then 'I' is also a referring expression.

Shoemaker accepts that first-person statements that are immune to error through misidentification - those in which 'I' is used 'as subject' - could be said to have absolute immunity to error through misidentification. The fact, however, that first-person statements have such immunity does not mean that one's self-reference involves an incorrigible identification. This way of talking is mistaken because it suggests that an identification is made but made incorrigibly: 'My use of the word 'I' as the subject of my statement is not due to my having identified as myself something of which I know, or believe, or wish to say, that the predicate of my statement applies to it' (p. 558). The fact that self-reference does not involve identification does not mean that reference does not occur, nor is reference without identification peculiar to first-person statements. The use of a demonstrative like 'this' in a sentence like 'This one is red', where I can see and point to a red necktie, is an example of reference without identification. In such a case the speaker's intention (in the given context) determines what the reference of his demonstrative pronoun is, and that reference cannot be other than what he intends it to be. The rules governing the use of demonstratives like 'this' do not by themselves determine what the reference is on any particular occasion - that will depend on the speaker's intention, context, and demonstrative gestures. By contrast, the rules governing the use of the personal pronoun 'I' *do* determine once and for all what its reference is to be on any given occasion - its reference is necessarily to the speaker, and leaves no latitude to the speaker's intentions. It is this absence of latitude which is peculiar to the mode of reference of first-person statements. The speaker who utters a first-person present-tense psychological statement cannot successfully intend not to refer to himself.

Another way of highlighting the difference between demonstrative pronouns like 'this' and the personal pronoun 'I' is that while the reference of 'this' cannot be other than that which a speaker intends in a particular context there is always the logical possibility of failure of reference. It may happen in cases of hallucination, for example, that there is no object to which the speaker can actually or effectively refer in saying 'This is red', or in asking 'Is this a dagger I see before me?' But there is, as Descartes' Cogito argument shows, no such possibility of failure of reference in the use of the word 'I'. This is a feature of the first-person character of the Cogito, and also, arguably, of its peculiarly 'performative' character in Hintikka's sense.[1] It is not an implication of saying that self-reference does not involve identification that there can be no such thing as 'finding oneself in the world' or 'being an object to oneself.' It is imaginable that in an environment composed largely of reflective surfaces one might, visually at least, become an object to oneself and frequently come to 'recognize' oneself in a mirror. But the point which Shoemaker wants to stress is that it could not be *on the basis of* such recognition or self-identification that one makes first-person statements in which 'I' is used as subject. The identification of an object as oneself would have to go together with the possibility of misidentification, which is impossible in the case of first-person self-ascriptions.

These first-person self-ascriptions may be regarded as manifestations of self-knowledge or self-awareness but we must be careful how we explicate this sort of self-knowledge. Shoemaker accepts that there is something right about Hume's observation: 'I can never catch myself at any time without a perception, and never can observe anything but the perception' (Hume, 1888, p. 152). There really is no 'experiencing' or perceiving of one's self that can explain one's awareness that one is, for example, in pain in a way analogous to that in which one's perception of John explains one's knowledge that John has a beard. It is erroneous to think of self-awareness as a kind or form of perception, i.e., to think of it on the model of sense-perception: 'In being aware that one feels pain one is, tautologically, aware not simply that the attribute *feel(s) pain* is instantiated, but that it is instantiated *in oneself*' (Shoemaker, 1968, pp. 563-4). Even to put it in these terms - talking of pain as an attribute - is still too close to the model of our perceptual knowledge of objects and their attributes. The way out of the difficulty, for Shoemaker, is to abandon completely the perceptual model of self-knowledge. This will mean at least resisting the temptation to think of psychological predicates as perceptual verbs. Self-ascriptions such as 'I feel pain' must not be equated with 'I feel a bump', as if pains were private, mental objects that one observed - or failed to observe - with one's inner senses. What we must focus on instead is the role that the self-ascription of psychological predicates plays in our language, including the sort of 'logical' relationships that obtain between first- and third-person ascriptions of such terms.

136

The problems that surround the concepts of self, self-knowledge, and self-reference are best understood, then, not as 'metaphysical' problems primarily but as problems arising out of the relationships between speakers, language-uses, and knowledge-claims. The question of how it is possible that there should be self-reference without identification, or self-ascription without self-observation, is equivalent to the question of 'how it is possible that there should be predicates, or attributes, the self-ascription of which is immune to error through misidentification' (1968, p. 565). For Shoemaker this question is at the root of the larger question of how it is possible that there should be an important and central class of psychological predicates which are typically and truthfully ascribed to oneself, by oneself, on a non-observational or noncriterial basis. This question is closely related, as Shoemaker acknowledges, to the important and intriguing questions first introduced into the philosophy of mind by P.F. Strawson (1959): Why are one's states of consciousness ascribed to anything at all? Why are they ascribed to the very same thing as certain corporeal characteristics, a certain physical situation, etc? How is it possible that there should be psychological predicates at all, in the sense of predicates that are ascribed criterially to others but noncriterially to oneself? Before returning to Shoemaker's discussion of self-identity and self-knowledge it is necessary to place his arguments in the wider and more fundamental context established by Strawson's questions.

Bodies, minds, and individuation

Strawson rejects the no-ownership or no-subject doctrine of the self which would argue that the idea of a subject of experience is replaceable by the idea of a body that happens to stand in a certain relationship to experiences. According to the no-ownership theorist, the unique causal position of a certain body in a person's experience is sufficient to give rise to the idea that one's experiences can be ascribed to some particular individual thing. To ascribe a particular psychological state to this body would be to say something contingent, something that might happen to be false. It is not necessary - indeed it is erroneous - to assume that the psychological states are owned in some sense by an ego. The 'having' of experiences by a particular body does not imply their being 'had' by an ego or subject:

> Suppose we call the first type of possession, which is really a certain kind of causal dependence, 'having$_1$,' and the second type of possession, 'having$_2$'; and call the individual of the first type 'B' and the supposed individual of the second type 'E'; Then the difference is that while it is genuinely a contingent matter that all my experiences are had$_1$ by B, it appears as a necessary truth that all my experiences are had$_2$ by E. But the

belief in E and in having$_2$ is an illusion. Only those things whose ownership is logically transferable can be owned at all. So experiences are not owned by anything except in the dubious sense of being causally dependent on the state of a particular body.... (p. 96)

This account of the matter (one ought not say 'This account of the relationship between self and body') is, in Strawson's view, incoherent. It is incoherent because anyone who holds it is forced to make use of that very (non-transferable) sense of possession which he purports to reject. In other words, the no-subject, no-ego theorist cannot begin to present his thesis without assuming his own subjectivity. When he tries to state the contingent fact which he thinks gives rise to the illusion of the 'ego,' the no-subject theorist has to state it in some such form as 'All *my* experiences are had$_1$ by (uniquely dependent on the state of) body B.' Any attempt to eliminate the 'my' would yield something that was scarcely meaningful, and certainly not the contingent fact that the theorist is looking for. The theorist cannot consistently argue that 'all the experiences of person P' means the same thing as 'all the experiences contingently dependent on a certain body B', for then his proposition would be analytic rather than, as he requires, contingent. But if the experiences in question have in fact the defining characteristic that they are *my* experiences then it must be in a sense of possession which is closer to 'having$_2$' than to 'having$_1$.' Insofar as a certain class of experiences are mine, it does not make sense to say, for example, that the identical pain which is in fact one's own might, as a matter of fact, have been another's. Strawson concludes:

> We do not have to seek far in order to understand the place of this logically non-transferable kind of ownership in our general scheme of thought. For if we think of the requirements of identifying reference, in speech, to *particular* states of consciousness, or private experiences, we see that such particulars cannot be thus identifyingly referred to except as the states or experiences of some identified *person*. States, or experiences ... *owe* their identity as particulars to the identity of the person whose states or experiences they are. And from this it follows immediately that if they can be identified as particular states or experiences at all, they must be possessed or ascribable in just that way which the no-ownership theorist ridicules, i.e., in such a way that it is logically impossible that a particular state or experience in fact possessed by someone should have been possessed by anyone else. (p. 97)

The no-subject theorist only takes account of some of the facts about persons and their mental states. One possibility which does not occur to such a theorist, according to Strawson, is the simple but very central thought that 'it is a necessary condition of one's ascribing states of consciousness, experiences, to

138

oneself, in the way one does, that one should also ascribe them (or be prepared to ascribe them) to others who are not oneself' (p. 99). This means that the ascribing phrases should be used in just the same sense when the subject is another, as when the subject is oneself. The 'peculiarity' of psychological predicates is not that they have two or more uses, a first-person use and a second- or third-person use, but that they have one use, albeit a complex use, governed by the condition that they are ascribable to oneself only if they are also ascribable to others. This condition 'saves the self' without at the same time positing the kind of private, solipsistic, transcendental ego which is the *bête noir* of the no-subject theorist. It also 'saves the other' without resorting to a behaviouristic account of self-ascription. Strawson writes:

> If, in identifying the things to which states of consciousness are to be ascribed, private experiences are to be all one has to go on, then, just for the very same reason as that for which there is, from one's own point of view, no question of telling that a private experience is one's own, there is also no question of telling that a private experience is another's. All private experiences will be mine, i.e., no one's. To put it briefly: one can ascribe states of consciousness to oneself only if one can ascribe them to others; one can ascribe them to others only if one can identify other subjects of experience; and one cannot identify other subjects of experience if one can identify them *only* as subjects of experience, possessors of states of consciousness. (p. 100)

What we have to acknowledge, according to Strawson, in order to free ourselves from the difficulties that attend the notion of a private ego, Cartesian or otherwise, is 'the *primitiveness* of the concept of a person' (p. 101). By the concept of a person he means the concept of 'a type of entity such that *both* predicates ascribing states of consciousness *and* predicates ascribing corporeal characteristics, a physical situation, etc. are equally applicable to a single individual of that single type' (p. 102). By saying that this concept is primitive he means that it is a necessary condition of states of consciousness being ascribed at all that they should be ascribed to the very same thing as certain corporeal characteristics. States of consciousness would not be applied at all unless they were ascribed to persons in this sense. A person is not two kinds of subject - a subject of experiences plus a subject of corporeal characteristics - nor a compound of a subject (a pure ego) and a non-subject (a body to which the ego is contingently related). The word 'I' never refers to anything like a pure ego or subject in the mythically Cartesian sense. But this does not mean that it never refers at all. It refers, because I am a person among others. The concept of a person is 'logically prior' to that of an individual consciousness and is not reducible to the concept of either an embodied anima or an animated body, since both of these conceptions allow for the possibility of a self-identifying private subject or ego. On this view, statements about persons are not to be construed as statements about their bodies and their bodily behaviour only (as the behaviourist would say) nor as statements about their minds only (as the dualist would say). Rather, persons are in a strict sense of the term individuals, and as such cannot be separated into personal and non-personal components.

Strawson has so far presented us with two principles or conditions of identification - (a) I am able to identify myself, and ascribe conscious states to myself, only because I am able to differentiate myself from other subjects, i.e., only insofar as I am able to ascribe conscious states to others than myself; and (b) it is a conceptual truth that persons, as one class of identifiable particulars, have bodies, which has the consequence that psychological predicates are necessarily ascribable to the very same thing as certain corporeal characteristics. Both of these conditions are closely related in Strawson's conceptual scheme of things. They provide the bases for a solution to the problems of self-identity, personal identity and the problem of other minds. It is only insofar as persons are embodied, and thereby belong to a stable spatio-temporal frame of reference, that they are literally in a position to identify themselves and others. Matter, in the form of a spatio-temporal framework, is the principle of individuation and differentiation. Without individuation and differentiation there is no identification, and without matter or 'embodiment' there is no individuation. Hence the claim that it is a conceptual truth that persons have bodies. A pure, disembodied ego would not be in a position to identify other such egos and, for that reason, could not identify itself. Having a concept of oneself, or of one's identity, entails being in a position to distinguish oneself from others, and this entails being able, first, to identify others. This, of course, I could not do unless those others belonged to the same stable spatio-temporal frame of reference as oneself, i.e., unless they too were 'embodied'. Thus a pure ego which ascribes conscious states only to itself is an impossible entity engaged in an inconceivable activity. Such an ego would have no grounds for establishing or conceiving its identity or for self-ascribing conscious states.

In this way Strawson reverses the terms of the traditional problem of other minds. What has to be explained and justified is not the fact that we ascribe conscious states to others, but the fact that we ascribe them to ourselves. What is also philosophically significant here is the fact that we ascribe conscious states to ourselves in a *noncriterial* sort of way while ascribing them to others on the basis of behavioural criteria. This becomes another principle of predication for Strawson, viz. that one can ascribe conscious states to oneself on a non-observational basis only because one can ascribe them to others on the basis of the observation of their behaviour. This is, as it were, a conceptual fact about the nature of psychological predicates. First, we do not have to observe our own behaviour and listen to our own avowals in order to ascribe to ourselves conscious states, which we must normally do in the case of others. Second, Strawson holds that when we ascribe conscious states to ourselves, we are not merely engaging in some kind of vocal or verbal behaviour. First-person avowals are nothing more or less than true-or-false ascriptions made on a non-observational basis, while our statements about other people's minds are made on an observational basis. But though there is radical asymmetry between the two modes of ascription, the terms used to make the different ascriptions have necessarily the same meaning in both modes. A difference in the mode of ascription or 'verification' does not imply a difference in the meaning of the ascriptive phrases.

The use of the term 'ascription' may prompt the question: how can it be right to talk of ascribing in the case of oneself? Surely there can only be a question of ascribing if there is or could be a question of identifying that to which the ascription is made? And though there may be a question of identifying the one who is in pain when that one is another, how can there be such a question when that one is oneself? But this kind of objection answers itself, according to Strawson, 'as soon as we remember that we *speak* primarily to others, for the information of others' (p. 100). It remains true that I do not have to 'tell who it is' who is in pain when I am, but it is also true that I may have to 'tell who it is', i.e., to let others know who it is. In order to identify myself in the second sense, i.e., for others, it is not necessary that I should somehow have to 'identify' myself in the first sense.

Just as a question may arise about whether it can be right to talk of 'ascribing' in one's own case, so a similar question can arise about such phrases as 'ascribing conscious states to others on the basis of observation' or 'ascribing conscious states according to behavioural criteria.' Does this not introduce a conceptual distinction, even a dualism, between physical behaviour and mental state? Strawson appears to move closer to such a dualism when he makes an explicit distinction between M-predicates which are properly applied to material bodies, including human bodies, and P-predicates which comprise all the other predicates we apply to persons and which ascribe intentional or conscious states. He moves closer still to a property-dualism when he acknowledges that there is no sense in talking of identifiable individuals of a special type, a type, namely, such that they possess both M-predicates and P-predicates, 'unless there is in principle some way of telling, with regard to any individual of the type, and any P-predicate, whether that individual possesses that P-predicate' (p. 105). He attempts to save himself from the charge of dualism when he argues that in the case of at least some P-predicates the ways of telling must constitute in some sense 'logically adequate' kinds of criteria. The behavioural criteria on the basis of which one ascribes P-predicates to others are not just *signs* of the presence of what is meant by the P-predicate, but are logically adequate criteria for the ascription of the predicate. Strawson would claim that the ascribability of person-predicates on the basis of behavioural criteria is part of the essential meaning of these predicates, not simply a matter of association. Psychological terms are neither univocally mental nor univocally behaviouristic; they refer neither to something scandalously public nor to something surreptitiously private.

We may be inclined to think that feelings or states like depression can be felt, but not observed, and that depressed behaviour can be observed but not felt, and that therefore there must be room here to drive in a logical wedge. But the concept of depression spans the place where one wants to drive the wedge. Strawson suggests, first, that in order for there to be such a concept as that of X's depression, the concept must cover both what is felt, but not observed, by X and what may be observed, but not felt, by others than X:

> But it is perhaps better to say: X's depression *is* something, one and the same thing, which is felt but not observed by X and observed but not felt by others than X. (And, of course, what can be observed can also be faked or disguised.) To refuse to accept this is to refuse to accept the structure of the language in which we talk about depression. (p. 109)

It is essential, in other words, to the character of psychological predicates that they have both first- and third-person ascriptive uses, that they are, moreover, both self-ascribable otherwise than on the basis of observation of the behaviour of the subject of them, and other-ascribable on the basis of just such behaviour criteria. To learn their use is to learn to accept the asymmetry of the grounds on which they are ascribed. In order to have the concept of a particular psychological state, one must be both a self-ascriber and an other-ascriber of such states. If there were no such concepts we should not perhaps have a philosophical problem about the nature of mind or soul, 'but equally we should not have our concept of a person' (p. 108).

By logically adequate criteria Strawson seems to mean, then, criteria that provide sufficient grounds for ascribing predicates to others, but of course this does not mean that there exists a 'necessary' relation between internal state and external behaviour, such that all our ascriptions are going to be true, necessarily, as if an x-feeling always issued in y-behaviour, or y-behaviour always expressed an x-feeling in every particular case. The fact that there is not a necessary relation between behaviour and mental state does not of itself undermine Strawson's thesis. The rules of a game do not guarantee that any particular competitor will win or lose, only that someone will win and someone lose - unless, of course, the rules allow for a draw or stalemate. Analogously, people could not be deceived in particular cases unless it was possible to take advantage of the concepts, understandings, and criteria which people conventionally apply in situations in which psychological predicates are ascribed. The precondition of successfully simulating a state of mind is that the conceptually or logically adequate bases for ascribing that state of mind are

142

present, and that the appropriate ascription has in fact been elicited. Conversely, if someone successfully suppresses a state of mind this means that the conceptually adequate bases for ascribing such a state have been suppressed or disguised in a particular case - and an ascription which would have been appropriate in circumstances of normal candour has not been made. The point is that the presence of logically or conceptually adequate criteria only guarantees the appropriateness or 'validity' of an ascription, not its accuracy or 'truth', such that the grounds I have for ascribing a conscious state in the event of simulation are no less adequate than in cases where there is no simulation.

Although Strawson attempts to give an effectively post-Cartesian account of the person without at the same time eliminating the concepts of self, subject or mind, it is not certain that he is completely successful in shedding the legacy of dualism, much as he would purport to so do. There is a particular difficulty with Strawson's claim that there are two distinct classes of predicates which are properly ascribable to persons, viz., material predicates and person predicates. He even defines persons as the only individuals to whom both types of predicate are ascribable. He is, like the identity theorists, postulating one type of subject for two types of predicate, while at the same time maintaining that persons are more than material bodies. A body alone would not be an appropriate subject for P-predicates. But what does it mean to say here that the person is 'more' than a material body? We are immediately tempted to say that 'more' somehow signifies whatever sets persons apart from material bodies, i.e., conscious or mental states. Yet Strawson will not allow us to say that mental states constitute the 'essence', or definitive characteristic, of personhood in his sense, because he has stressed continually that persons are those individuals to which both conscious states and material characteristics are ascribable. He is adamant that neither mind nor body constitutes the essence of personhood. That is, predicates drawn exclusively from one or other predicate-class are not sufficient to give an account of what persons essentially are. But is it not then inconsistent to proceed to talk of mental predicates as person-predicates? If two types of predicate are necessary to characterize some individuals as persons, is it right to to give preference to one type by calling it the class of *person*-predicates? Strawson should be prepared to say that such predicates as 'tall', 'dark,' and 'handsome,' are as much person-predicates as 'believes in God,' 'understands Greek,' and 'loves Mozart'. If the concept of a person cannot be reduced to that of either a mind or a body, then neither can the concept of a person-predicate be reduced to that of either a material or a mental predicate. One wants to say that the ascribability of material predicates is a necessary condition for the identification of anything, including persons - and that the ascribability of mental predicates is a necessary condition for the identification of persons as persons. Persons then become material beings to whom mental predicates are also ascribable, where mental predicates are those predicates which have the peculiarity in human language that a condition of

143

ascribing them to oneself noncriterially, i.e., on a non-observational basis, is that they are also ascribable to others on the basis of observation, i.e., on the basis of behavioural criteria. It is unlikely that such an attenuated version of his position would be acceptable to Strawson, yet without such a modification his position teeters on the verge of a property dualism which could prove as problematic as the substance dualism it is supposed to replace.

The strength of Shoemaker's position, by contrast with that of Strawson, is that it attempts to resolve questions concerning personal identity and self-knowledge by focussing on the way psychological predicates are used, understood - and 'accepted' - in everyday language-uses. Even when he makes a distinction between criterial and non-criterial ascriptions of psychological predicates Shoemaker does not need to distinguish between those that are ascribed on an observational basis and those that are ascribed on a non-observational basis. Nor does he feel the need to talk about behavioural criteria, logically adequate or otherwise. Shoemaker places more emphasis on the rest of the 'form of life' in which talk about oneself and others takes place. He especially places more emphasis on the fact that we normally or conventionally accept that others are sincere in their avowals, i.e., in the statements they make about themselves in terms of thoughts, feelings, hopes, memories, etc. The sort of observation of behaviour which is central to Strawson's account is only a part of Shoemaker's account. Whereas Strawson's individual remains distant, like a voyeuristic police detective, continually observing behaviour, applying his M- and P-predicates, and seeking reassurance in certain general principles of adequate predication, Shoemaker's language-user is more a participant than an observer, more capable of sharing 'uninferred' kinds of knowledge.

Shoemaker does not accept either the view that the identity of a person is simply the identity of a living body, or the view that the real criteria of personal identity must be purely psychological. The fact that persons can make identity judgements about themselves without using criteria of personal identity, and that such statements are generally true and can be said to express knowledge, itself constitutes an important difference between the identities of persons and the identities of other things. Only about persons can identity judgements be made in this way:

> And the noncriterial knowledge that a person has of his identity, or of his past history, can be shared with, i.e., communicated to, other persons; if a person reports that he remembers doing a certain thing, other persons can accept his reporting this as evidence that he, the very person who reports this, did do the thing in question.... If bodily identity were the sole criterion, then we would have to be making an inductive inference when we accept a person's claim to remember doing a certain thing as evidence that he did do that thing.... But I have maintained that it is a necessary

truth, not a contingent one, that confident and sincere memory statements are generally true. If this is so, inferences of the form 'He claims to remember doing X, so he probably did X' cannot be merely inductive, for they are warranted by a generalisation that is necessarily rather than contingently true. (Shoemaker, 1963, pp. 244-5)

Shoemaker goes on to suggest that it is part of our 'form of life' that we accept what other persons say at face value, without raising or even considering the question whether they understand the meanings of the expressions they utter, or whether their apparent testimony is really testimony. Although we could frequently check the meaning and truth of what people tell us the point is that normally we do not. In accepting the memory-testimony of another person one thinks of oneself, not as inferring something about that person's past from his present behaviour - though one could do that - 'but as *sharing* the *uninferred* knowledge he has of his past; one accepts his memory statements as if they were one's own' (p. 250). Shoemaker agrees with Wittgenstein over certain 'extremely general facts of nature', one of which is the fact that human beings are capable of being so trained in the use of language, or in the making of sounds and gestures, that it is possible for the uttering of certain sounds to be regarded as the making of first-person perceptual and memory statements. If human beings did not have this capacity they could not make perceptual or memory statements at all, and could not be taught to make them. More specifically, what human beings are being taught or trained to do is not simply to utter sounds or make gestures but 'to utter certain expressions, or to make certain sounds, when, or only when, certain conditions are satisfied' (p. 242). The test of whether a human being has been so trained (e.g., has been trained to utter the sounds 'I see' in the circumstances in which it would be correct for him to use the English words 'I see') is whether he utters the sounds only when the appropriate conditions are in fact satisfied; it is not essential that he should have *established* that those conditions are satisfied, or that he should utter the sounds because he has established this. If someone is still inclined to ask how it is possible for us to go on making such statements without regularly grounding them (like a Strawsonian individual) on criteria of adequacy or truth, Shoemaker's only answer is that it is just a fact of nature that human beings can be so trained that they are able to make such statements, and, moreover, that if human beings did not respond to training in this way 'there would be no such things as first-person psychological statements' (1963, p. 243).

The making of first-person statements seems mysterious only because we have (according to Shoemaker) a faulty theory of knowledge to begin with, a faulty conception of how statements in general must be made if we are to be 'entitled' to make them, and not because there is anything inexplicable about what actually happens. Thus general facts about human nature and the nature of language-training and language-use (rather than, say, facts about the nature of an inscrutably introspective ego) are appealed to in order to explain the apparently mysterious nature of first-person psychological statements. At the same time, it has not been found necessary to reject, as some Wittgensteinians have done, the notion of a self-referring 'I', or to resort to a no-subject theory of mental states. Shoemaker's position - which may be described as post-Cartesian in the best sense - seems to be that an adequate theory of the self or subject as language-user can do justice both to our modern understanding of the ubiquity of language in human life and to what Canfield calls our 'gut-level belief' in the self or I.

Lacan and the imaginary ego

There are suggestive affinities between some approaches to the concepts of self and mind in contemporary Anglo-American philosophy and approaches to the 'theory of the subject' among some continental European thinkers. These European theorists are often as much influenced by linguistic, cultural and psychological theories as they are by philosophy, but, like many post-Cartesian philosophers of mind, they are convinced of the primary importance of language and social relations in the formation of subjectivity and self-concepts, and are hostile to the 'Cartesian' conception of ego or subject. Following the theoretical linguistics of Ferdinand de Saussure rather than, say, the linguistic philosophy of Wittgenstein, but nonetheless echoing the latter, they accord to the 'sign' (the basic working unit or 'atom' of semantics) a primacy over the 'referent', and within the sign they grant the 'signifier' a primacy over the 'signified'.[2] The human system of signs is then taken to be an intrinsic and determinant feature of human culture and human subjectivity. Language is seen as the *sine qua non* of not only thought and communication but also of self-reflective consciousness itself. All forms of social, cultural and psychological life, including the unconscious, are perceived as governed by systems of signs which are either linguistic or analogous to those of language.

Jacques Lacan (1977) may be regarded as a leading theorist, even 'grammarian', of the subject. He argues that the identity of the self or subject is achieved within the process of differentiation that is integral to language, through which the inchoate subject progressively and systematically marks out a position for itself within 'the signifying chain' of language and speech. There is a kind of dialectical, mutually constitutive relationship between the speaking or linguistic subject and the signifying practices or discourses which it encounters. Only insofar as language is used by a subject does it become 'discourse' or signifying practice. Without speakers to whom things are present or absent there would be no signs, meanings, 'representations'. Verbal communication presupposes a subject 'who manifests himself as such to the intention of another' (1977, p. 9). Only a subject can understand a meaning, while conversely every phenomenon of meaning implies a subject. This seems to grant a certain autonomy to the subject. Yet Lacan also insists that the subject is in some sense constituted from the beginning. What is really a process of being constituted from without is experienced subjectively and illusively as a process of self-activity. Lacan insists that his conception of 'the mirror stage' as a turning-point in childhood leads him away from any notion of the subject as transcendentally autonomous or self-constituting, and causes him specifically to 'oppose any philosophy directly issuing from the Cogito' (p.1). Language in particular is not reducible to the expressions of an autonomous ego: 'The subject goes well beyond what is expressed "subjectively" by the individual....' (p. 55).

The mirror phase is supposed to occur during the pre-linguistic stage of an infant's life when the infant discovers that a reflected image is its own image over which it has immediate and complete control. The infant sees a relationship between a reflected image and its own body and imagines that in controlling the image it controls its body. It is at this point that the ego begins to be formed, albeit on the basis of an imaginary mastery, of an imaginary relationship between the infantile subject and its body. The infant becomes so focused on the specular image that it proceeds in a 'fictional direction', outward, towards an exterior image, towards a mirage which has all the appearance of integrity, definiteness and stability compared with the turbulent interiority of the inchoate, infantile ego. It is in the course of its alienated relationship with the imaginary, ideal, specular I that the actual ego begins to be formed from without, as it is drawn forward by the image and promise of wholeness. The exterior image serves as a kind of 'final cause' of the burgeoning but 'lacking' ego. Yet in the very process of experiencing and sustaining a sense of its own simplicity, autonomy and mastery, the ego is further entangling itself in the self-spun web of imaginary properties and powers. The important point for Lacan is that the total form of the specular body by which the subject anticipates in a mirage the maturation of his power 'is given to him only as a *Gestalt*, that is to say, in an exteriority in which this form is certainly more constituting than constituted' (p. 55). The significance of the mirror phase is that it suggests that the 'I' is an image-like or imaginary entity, constructed from the outside rather than pre-existent or shaped consciously from within. Its mastery is always an illusory mastery as a result of the way it is formed during the mirror phase, and the continuing quest for ever-deeper degrees of wholeness and unity are futile (See Sarup, 1992, p. 83). Moreover, the 'I' is a function of an unstable subjectivity that is at the mercy of unconscious desires. Even as the 'I' thinks that it speaks univocally, self-consciously and knowingly, the unconscious sends out other signals which may result in desire-revealing figures of speech or Freudian slips. Desire itself is understood to be an effect produced in an organism which is always at the mercy of language, 'an effect in the subject of that condition which is imposed upon him by the existence of the discourse, to make his need pass through the defiles of the signifier' (Lacan, 1977, p. 264). Elizabeth Wright (1982) interprets this to mean that a subject's use of words will thus be open to shifts for which his unconscious is responsible, which are instigated by desire: 'The 'it' of the unconscious - the true discourse - will always subvert the 'I' - the imaginary discourse' (Wright, 1982, p. 122). This imaginary discourse is the discourse of the imaginary ego which originates in that virtually mythic moment which Lacan calls the mirror stage.

The implication of this approach to a theory of the subject is that the source of knowledge and action is the unconscious structured by language rather than the self-knowing, solipsistic consciousness posited, supposedly, Descartes. The sources of self-knowledge are not open to view but lie outside or beneath immediate consciousness and may be more visible to others than to oneself. The process of becoming a subject is determined by 'the Imaginary' at an early stage and subsequently by language and 'the discourse of the Other'. Lacan insists that the conscious Cogito must therefore give way to the unconscious Desidero, which is, in a sense, the Freudian cogito (Lacan, 1979, p. 154). The most revealing source of knowledge about oneself is not any self-conscious 'Cartesian' mental state but the unself-conscious state of dreaming or the verbal slips that one may utter unconsciously or unintentionally. Lacan does not, however, reject the Cogito as completely useless, and even situates both himself and Freud in relation to 'the Cartesian subject'. He dares 'to state as a truth that the Freudian field was possible only a certain time after the emergence of the Cartesian subject, in so far as modern science began only after Descartes made his inaugural step' (1979, p. 47). On this step depends the fact that 'one can call upon the subject to re-enter himself in the unconscious - for, after all, it is important to know *who* one is calling' (p. 47). In other words, in order to set about 'de-centring' the subject one must first of all have a concept of that subject, and, historically, it was Descartes who introduced that concept into philosophy and into theoretical discourse generally.

It must be stressed that while Lacan describes the ego as imaginary he does not seek to abolish the human subject in the sense of the complex totality of mental and physical, conscious and unconscious states that constitute an individual. He asserts the reality of the subject when he acknowledges a necessarily mutual interactive relationship between the speaking subject and a language. He does, however, 'de-centre' the subject by refusing to describe it in terms of stability, autonomy, unity, or self-transparency. Subjectivity cannot be described in terms of the imaginary properties which the ego appropriates to itself. The dependence of self and subject upon language must be given particular emphasis. Language is necessarily produced by subjects, and subjects achieve mature self-reflective identities by positioning themselves within a self-referring, other-acknowledging system of signifiers. Lacan even speaks rather obscurely of the subject being born 'as the signifier emerges in the field of the Other,' and of the subject itself thereby 'solidifying' into a signifier. When he

148

says that the effects of language are always mixed with the fact that the subject is subject 'only from being subjected to the field of the Other,' that the subject proceeds from his 'synchronic subjection in the field of the Other' Lacan's reasoning, if not his terminology, is perhaps reminiscent of the reasoning of Strawson and Shoemaker.

Kaja Silverman (1983) suggests that the term 'subject' designates a quite different 'semantic space' from that indicated by the more familiar terms 'individual', 'man', or 'consciousness'. Together the terms 'individual' and 'man' suggest an entity that is both autonomous and stable. 'Man' presupposes a human essence that predates historical and cultural circumstances and which exhibits its crowning glory in the form of reason or consciousness. The attribution of individuality and privacy to this consciousness 'suggests that man's thinking processes are in no way coerced by the material world or by the thoughts of other men ...' (p. 126). For Descartes especially, according to Silverman, the self or 'I' transcends cultural definition, engaged as it is in a solitary enterprise, always fully conscious, self-knowing and coherent. The term 'subject', however, helps to conceive of human reality very differently, as a construction, as the product of signifying activities which are both culturally specific and generally unconscious:

> The category of the subject thus calls into question the notions both of the private, and of a self synonymous with consciousness. It suggests that even desire is culturally instigated, and hence collective; and it decenters consciousness, relegating it (in distinction from the preconscious, where cognitive activity occurs) to a purely receptive capacity. Finally, by drawing attention to the divisions which separate one area of psychic activity from another, the term 'subject' challenges the value of stability attributed to the individual. (1983, p. 127)

In setting the subject (decentred or otherwise) over against the ego (Cartesian or otherwise) one is not comparing like with like, since both terms do in fact occupy different semantic spaces. The concept of a subject is, as Silverman reminds us, broader, deeper and 'richer' than that of an ego, self or consciousness. This is indicated by the fact that the Lacanian subject can be made, conceptually, to contain an unconscious while the Cartesian ego, conventionally conceived, cannot. There is even a sense in which the Lacanian subject can be made to contain the Cartesian ego, albeit by consigning it to the realm of the Imaginary or by re-defining it as 'that nucleus given to consciousness but opaque to reflexion, marked by all the ambiguities which .... structure the experience of the passions in the human subject' (1977, p. 15). Although the notion of 'decentring' is not very clear, we may take it to mean that the subject, as putative source of thought and action, is, unknown to itself, over-determined in its thoughts and actions by forces outside its immediate

149

consciousness or agency. Thought and agency may, indeed, have their sources outside the subject altogether, in the 'discourse of the Other'. The thinking subject is effectively removed from the centre of its homely, familiar, consciously-constructed Imaginary world; it is theoretically decentred, relative to the field of its own conscious thoughts, projects and actions, much as the planet Earth was theoretically decentred by Galileo, relative to the existing folk-cosmological model of the planetary system. But just as decentring the planet Earth did not mean its elimination from the new model but rather its relegation within a well-established cosmology, so the decentring of the subject does not mean its elimination from the new model of self-understanding but rather its relegation within a well-established folk psychology.

To attribute to Descartes an ego-centred folk psychology is erroneous, since Descartes himself undertook what was in effect a major decentring of the rational ego. As a mechanist, he is responsible for positing a problematic relationship between the self-as-agent and the machinery of the world. Indeed, one of the most serious problems with his dualism is that he is unable to give a satisfactory account of how the mind is able to influence the machinery of the body. This is not simply a problem of how mind can interact with body but also of how the mind can 'move' the body, given that the body is a machine, subject to the mechanistic laws of the rest of the universe. As a methodic doubter and postulator of the all-deceiving malicious demon, Descartes placed severe limits on the intuitive claims of everyday conventional thinking, i.e, the claims of folk epistemology. The possibility that one's thinking might be 'programmed' or that the unconscious might play a determinative role in human thought and behaviour are hypotheses which could be included, in principle, among the sources of a modern Cartesian's hyperbolic doubt. That the malicious demon might even take up residence in the unconscious and send out its signals from there - through the 'defiles of the signifier,' perhaps - is not a thought that a Cartesian need reject. The point is that granting the demon such a residency would not make any difference to the 'truth' of the Cogito.

Of course a modern Cartesian cannot rid himself of all the implications of the unconscious in the way that Descartes rid himself of his hypothetical demon i.e., by positing a non-deceitful God. But it is worth noting that in the same way that Descartes needed to posit a nondeceitful God, so Lacan needs to posit a non-deceitful unconscious. The claims of the conscious mind are open to analytical doubt because it is the unconscious - which iterates the Desidero rather than the Cogito - that really 'knows' and obliquely 'speaks' the truth of the inner life, if only to an analyst trained to decipher it. The Lacanian analyst positing a truth-telling unconscious which is dedicated to preserving the truth of the Desidero has a not-too-distant ancestor in the Cartesian thinker positing a truth-guaranteeing God who is dedicated to the preservation of the truth of the Cogito. What seems to set Lacan at an extreme remove from Descartes or any other kind of philosophical egoist is his claim that the ego is in some sense imaginary, a delusory effect of psychic and interpersonal forces. In other words, Lacan seems to achieve what Descartes' demon could not, i.e., cause the ego to doubt its own existence and nature as a thinking thing. Real thinking is not something which the conscious ego does at all but is an activity of the unconscious: 'I think where I am not, therefore I am where I do not think.... I am not wherever I am the plaything of my thought; I think of what I am where I do not think to think' (1977, p. 166). But if Lacan means that I am imagining myself when I say, in the context of the methodic doubt, 'I think therefore I am' he cannot be taken seriously. He has forgotten that the Cogito itself only makes sense in the context of the methodic doubt, which allows for a methodic deception - a process of deception which might be carried out by an evil demon, or by the unconscious, or by anything else one cares to posit. Lacan, like so many other anti-Cartesians, has forgotten that 'I think' can also be 'I doubt' or 'I am deceived' or 'I am deluded' or 'I imagine' - or 'I am constituted by a series of alienating identifications'. The point, moreover, of all such propositions is to lay the foundations not of a psychology but of an epistemology, by pre-empting the possibility of a universal methodic doubt. Thinking, for Descartes, means that thinking which confirms one's minimal status as a being that must exist in order to doubt, be deceived, be alienated or otherwise put upon. Consciousness is of interest to Descartes, the foundationalist, only to the extent that it provides him with the first proposition of his system. The self, ego, and consciousness are important only because they constitute points of departure in the systematic struggle against the methodic doubt, and not because they are ultimately more intelligible, or more ontologically 'centred', than other things.

If one rejects the whole Cartesian project of a search for secure foundations, and along with it the method of doubt, intuition and deduction, there is no good reason to attack the Cogito as if it were the central tenet of a theory of consciousness or a philosophy of psychology. The Cogito and the Sum res cogitans are the primary propositional data of the Cartesian logic and the Cartesian methodology, and have no significance apart from such a context. To dwell on the Cogito, as Lacan and others have done, while ignoring the method and the project which produced it, is to seriously misread and misuse Descartes, and is likely to lead to the sort of gratuitous and misplaced anti-Cartesianism that is apparent in Lacan's remarkable inversion of the Cogito, viz., 'I think where I am not...'

Foucault and the confessional self

One of the most radical reappraisals of the concept of subjectivity may be found in the work of Michel Foucault (1977; 1980; 1984; 1986). In the course of examining the functions of certain paradigmatic social institutions - medical, penitentiary and psychiatric - he suggests that the concept of an autonomous subject is a product of the ubiquitous efforts by administrations and authorities to control and discipline individuals whose abnormal behaviour threatens the rule of law. Modern authorities do not rely on crude force and terror to maintain law and order but rather use institutions of surveillance and control to create *subjects* in the sense of individuals who 'voluntarily' monitor and police themselves. The process of discipline and control is a process of self-policing, individualization, and 'subjection'. The difference between a feudal society and a modern society is that power in feudal societies tended to be gross, arbitrary and extravagant whereas social and economic changes in modern industrialized societies have made it necessary to ensure 'the circulation of effects of power through progressively finer channels, gaining access to individuals themselves, to their bodies, their gestures, and all their daily actions' (1980, pp. 151-2). This process of subjection and internalized self-policing is captured graphically for Foucault in Bentham's image of the Panopticon - a hypothetical prison which is the antithesis of the medieval dungeon in that it renders the inmate wholly visible rather than obliging him to languish in darkness. It is a prison so designed that one guard in a central watch-tower is able to observe a circular arrangement of cells through which light passes, enabling him to monitor the movements of each isolated prisoner but without any prisoner being in a position to see him. Though the guard cannot monitor all the inmates all the time, the fact that he cannot be perceived from within the cells creates an ethos of constant, omniscient surveillance. The major effect of the Panopticon is 'to induce in the inmate a state of conscious and permanent visibility that assures the automatic functioning of power' (1977, p. 201). The prisoners must be themselves 'on guard' or self-vigilant at all times, constantly policing their own behaviour, since any moment may be the moment that the guard in the tower decides to look in the direction of any particular cell. It is this 'unverifiable' gaze, practised in various modes by different institutions, from hospitals to schools, which creates conscientious, self-monitoring subjects:

> He who is subjected to a field of visibility, and who knows it, assumes responsibility for the constraints of power; he makes them play spontaneously upon himself, he inscribes himself in a power relation in which he simultaneously plays both roles; he becomes the principle of his own subjection. (1977, pp. 202-3)

In short, Foucault's 'genealogy of the soul' leads to the conclusion that the formation of a conscientious, self-reflective, self-monitoring subjectivity is largely the result of modern methods of administrative supervision, constraint and punishment, and is not at all a gift of God or nature.

The idea that the subject is originally the effect of surveillance and the policing process, rather than the natural, autonomous source of freely-chosen actions and projects, is also the theme of Foucault's *History of Sexuality* (1984). While there is a widespread assumption ('the repressive hypothesis') that our modern era, by contrast with, say, Victorian society, is sexually liberated, even sexually permissive, Foucault would insist that there has only been a widening of the discourses about sexuality. The proliferation of discourses about sexuality does not necessarily corroborate the libertarian trend of the repressive hypothesis but rather belongs to society's 'polymorphous technologies of power' (1984, p. 11). Rather than reflecting a new sense of freedom about sexuality these discourses seek to police sexuality by, as Patrick Hutton puts it, 'publicly defining codes of legitimate and illegitimate sexual behaviour' (1988, p. 130). This policing of sexual behaviour is in keeping with the historical trend towards the increasing scrutiny and regulation of all human behaviour. Behaviour ceases to be 'human' in a naturalistic sense and becomes more and more socialized, civilized, monitored, regulated, policed. This expansion and deepening of social regulation proceeds, moreover, in terms of binary oppositions or exclusions - sanity and insanity, health and sickness, lawful and criminal activity, permissible and impermissible forms of intimacy. Individuals are either inside or outside the well-defined boundaries of these practices and institutions.

It is through public, 'scientific' discourse, rather than through censorship, that sexuality has been regulated and policed in our era, especially through confessional discourses. Since the Middle Ages Western societies have established the confession as one of the main rituals on which pastoral authorities rely for the production of truth and for the confirmation of power which knowing the truth gives. In Foucault's view, the evolution of the word 'avowal' (and of the legal function it designated) is emblematic of this development of the relationship between truth and power. In the act of avowal or confession one individual 'owns up' to another, recognizing the power of the other, while at the same time assuming full responsibility for actions which are defined and accepted as wrong: 'The truthful confession was inscribed at the heart of the procedures of individualization of power' (1984, pp. 58-9).

Foucault does not merely refer to pastoral or sacramental confession but to a generalized ethos of confession. We have, he maintains, become a confession society; Western man has become a confession animal, confessing not only in public but also in private. The trend towards confession and avowal is evident also in literature where there has been a transition from epic or heroic narratives to a confessional literature 'ordered according to the infinite task of extracting from the depths of oneself ... a truth which the very form of confession holds out like a shimmering image' (1984, p. 59). The obligation to confess has become so ingrained in us, so much part of an ideology of autonomy and liberation, that we no longer perceive it for what it is, an effect of a power that constrains us. If Foucault is right, then confession is not so much an act of self-expression as an act of self-discipline, of voluntary exposure and subjection to a power that seeks in general to organize society along the lines of Bentham's blueprint for the Panopticon.

Foucault's observations on the formation of subjectivity have implications for any philosophy which places a value on the first-person perspective. Even the most basic grammatical notion of the subject is understood to express or reinforce a power relation. The confession, in Foucault's scheme of things, is a ritual of discourse in which the speaking subject 'is also the subject of the statement', as if to suggest that all first-person statements no matter how banal or informative, are confessions or avowals which presuppose a relation of subjection and power. Confessions can only unfold within a power relationship 'for one does not confess without the presence (or virtual absence) of a partner who is not simply the interlocutor but the authority who requires the confession' (1984, p. 61). The simplest avowal now involves construing the speaker as subject and the listener as authority, as if every avowal somehow reproduces or mirrors in its very grammar the structure of the Panopticon or the interrogation centre. Whereas does this leave our claim, iterated throughout the previous chapters, that we should cherish the right and the freedom to make incorrigible first-person statements - that this right and this freedom are centrally implicated in our concepts of self and subjectivity? Foucault is presenting us with the radical counter-claim that our sense of right and freedom is an illusion - that avowals confirm not one's own power and freedom of utterance but the power and freedom of others acting in their capacity as listeners, confessors, agents of a generalized disciplinary authority.

But how valid are Foucault's arguments? It is difficult to see how the simple avowal 'I am depressed', considered as a statement, can itself be interpreted as a confession in which a power relation unfolds. A great deal depends on the circumstances in which it, or any avowal, is uttered. Despite the close attention which Foucault pays to the practices and institutions which make certain activities and discourses possible and meaningful, he fails in the case of avowals to give due regard to the very practices and institutions within which avowals could be said to reinforce a power relation. In typical confessional relationships involving an imbalance of power, the roles of confessor and confessee are already established and institutionalized. That is, the power relationship is not established by the confessional statement itself but by the roles and positions to which people may be ceremonially assigned and in the context of which certain statements are received as confessions. In the paradigmatic case of pastoral confession within the Roman Catholic Church, the confessor is approached by the penitent because he is recognized as someone who has the power to forgive on God's behalf, and the whole process of confession, penance, and forgiveness is recognized by both parties as a sacrament. A person becomes a penitent only because he is recognized as a full member of the Church who 'qualifies' for the sacrament of Penance. The further removed a first-person statement or avowal is from such a ritualistic

154

context, the less confessional it becomes. If someone cries out in the street, 'I have sinned!', or pleads for forgiveness at a bus stop, his words will hardly count as a confession. For one thing, the person who has the power to listen, to forgive, to administer penance - the confessor - is absent. Of course, Foucault writes of confession in a more generalized sense than this but the point may still be made that an avowal is not a confession in the Foucauldian sense unless or until it is evinced in a practice, ritual or institution in which the roles of confessor and confessee constitute a well-defined, well-established power relation. An avowal evinced outside such ritualized or institutionalized power relations is not a confession.

Avowals presuppose subjectivity in the measure that they presuppose the noncriterial usage of first-person psychological statements like 'I am depressed' or 'I am delighted', along with recountings of dreams and memories. To suggest that the self or subject as such is brought into existence by dint of iteration and reiteration of confessional utterances suggests that the capacity to remember, or the capacity to utter first-person, present-tense sentences, does not exist until this confessional practice is established. But this is absurd. The speaking, self-referring, remembering subject must exist in the first place before it can be 'hailed' as a subject in Foucault's sense. As Peter Dews says, 'if the concept of power is to have any critical import, there must be some principle, force or entity which power "crushes", or "subdues", and whose release from repression is considered desirable' (1987, p. 162). The subject is that over which power is exercised in the first instance, rather than that which is constituted by power.

The same point may be made in relation to the Panopticon model of subject-formation. Only an already existing subject could be disciplined and punished in such an environment, i.e., an environment of visible but unverifiable surveillance. Surveillance has its desired effect only because there already exists a subject who feels and fears, who can anticipate the gaze of the overseer and imagine it directed at him. It is only because the power of the overseer is understood and feared that the prisoner will 'cooperate' by policing his own behaviour. In any case, it is only because a punishing force exists in the vicinity of the prison that the prisoners fear the gaze of the overseer - there is no power in the gaze itself, nor even in the person of the overseer. The overseer's gaze is feared only because his eyes are the eyes of the administrators and guards who have the might and the right to discipline and punish. If a rumour should spread that the overseer is alone, without the support of an armed body of men who have the power to kill or punish, then the overseer's power and menace will be diminished, and the prisoners will soon re-assert their primordially subjective desire for freedom. Foucault misrepresents and effectively mystifies the mechanism of the Panopticon by abstracting it from the total set of institutions and forces of which it is merely a part or function. In particular, he misrepresents the effect of the disciplinary technology on the subjectivities of the prisoners. They police themselves only in order to avoid the punishment of the forces who wait in the background, watching for the signal of the overseer. There may be prisoners who become thoroughly institutionalized but in the measure that they do so they could be said to lose their subjectivity, abrogating their subjectivities by submitting wholly to the will of the overseer. Such prisoners are in a sense 'failed' prisoners because they no longer experience imprisonment as punishment. The prisoner experiences punishment only as long as he experiences the desire for freedom and, continually, its negation. Once he surrenders this desire he ceases to care about freedom - or to care about imprisonment, in which case it is hard to claim that a subject is being constituted. In that case, a subject - a subjectivity - has been disciplined out of existence, virtually. In those cases in which prisoners are not institutionalized, it could be said that their self-policing is a means of survival in the face of systematic repression and therefore a drastic 'going to ground' of a seriously threatened subjectivity. These prisoners realize that there is more dignity and less pain in self-policing than in regular subjection to painful disciplinings and punishments. The very term 'self-policing' implies a self that predates the process of policing.

In the light of Foucault's work on the theme of 'care of the self', it could be argued that even in the context of the most disciplinary technologies there is a kind of care of the self taking place. While Foucault in his institutional histories tended to regard the formation of subjects as a function of various technologies of discipline, including the medical, the psychiatric, and the penal, in the third volume of his *History of Sexuality* and in his seminar essay, 'Technologies of the Self,' he recognizes the existence of techniques and practices of self-discipline which are not simply or necessarily related to the larger social institutions. These techniques and practices - 'technologies' - permit individuals to carry out by their own means or with the help of others 'a certain number of operations on their own bodies and souls, thoughts, conduct, and way of being, so as to transform themselves in order to attain a certain state of happiness, purity, wisdom, perfection, or immortality' (1988, p. 18). These techniques can include such things as letters to friends, diaries, examinations of self and conscience, meditation, confession, rituals of self-disclosure and self-renunciation, rituals of purification or repentance, the interpretation of dreams - in sum, 'a type of work on oneself that implies a decipherment of the soul and a purificatory hermeneutics of the desires' (1986, p. 239).

These techniques presuppose not only a degree of freedom and leisure but also the existence of a self which has the power to set about caring for itself. Foucault suggests that the art of living under the theme of the care of oneself developed slowly during the first two centuries of the imperial epoch: 'a kind of golden age in the cultivation of the self - it being understood, of course, that this phenomenon concerned only the social groups, very limited in number, that were bearers of culture' (1986, p. 45). But it is arguable that techniques of caring for the self are also used in more constrained and repressive circumstances, even in the Panopticon. In the context of the Panopticon, care of the self takes the only form available, viz., self-policing. Self-policing in that case indicates not the successful subjection of the individual but a refusal of punishment other than imprisonment itself. It is not so much that the prisoner polices himself in the name of the prison but guards himself against the punishing regimes of the prison. Self-policing is self-protection, self-stewardship, self-care. Self-policing begins where subjection ends - it represents the ultimate limit rather than the ultimate triumph of the policing process. And that is why the policing process never comes to an end of its own accord. If the process were successful in subjecting individuals then a point could be reached when the authorities ought to decide that an individual had become so effectively institutionalized and 'policed' that he could be safely 'freed'. But this point is never reached because, while self-policing is an effect of the policing process, of the regime of the Panopticon, it does not at the same time represent the success of that process but rather its failure. The work of the overseer is never done, either within the prison or within the prisoner.

The difficulty with Foucault's hypothesis that individuated selves are a product of technologies of subjection is that the process of subjection can only work on individuals who have already been identified as insane or criminal or otherwise unruly. They are already identified as disorderly subjectivities which need to be confined, disciplined, reformed. The function of the disciplinary institution is to circumscribe and reduce these disorderly subjectivities as much as possible by subjecting them to practices of conformity and regularity. If anything, the truth about power, subjectivity and selfhood lies in a direction contrary to Foucault's: the purpose of disciplinary technologies is not to create individualities or to constitute subjectivities but to abolish individuality and to reconstitute subjectivity in the name of society, order and government. We may still accept much of what Foucault says about the self but in terms of the re-formation or re-constitution of the self by the policing process rather than in terms of its original formation or constitution by that process. We can even accept along with Hutton that the self 'is continually being redesigned in an ongoing discourse generated by the imperatives of the policing process' (1988, p. 135). What we cannot accept is the claim that the self is 'an abstract construction'. The point here is really a logical or Cartesian one, viz., that just as one must first of all exist in order to think doubtfully about one's existence, even in order to be deceived by the demon, so also one must first of all exist in order to participate in the processes of self-discipline, self-policing, and self-renunciation. It is unlikely that the concepts of power and technology of power can be fully elucidated without reference to the fact that, as Dews suggests, what has to be crushed is the material, potentially unruly self that predates the implementation of the technologies of power. These technologies do not absolutely constitute the self - rather, they presuppose it, problematize it, even

157

demonize it, and go to great lengths to flush it out and institutionalize it. The reason that societies must go on refining their technologies of power has to do with the fact that selves remain indefinitely unruly, except perhaps in the case of those who have been so thoroughly institutionalized that they identify themselves more or less completely as the agents or subjects of institutions, as the brokers or bearers of power relations. The lesson of the Cogito is applicable here: the more the self is assailed, whether by the method of doubt, or the deceit of the malicious demon, or by the technologies of subjection, the more its very own existence or identity is intimated and confirmed. Foucault acknowledges that there are no relations of power without resistances, that resistances are all the more real and effective because they are formed right at the point where relations of power are exercised: 'resistance to power does not have to come from elsewhere to be real, nor is it inexorably frustrated through being the compatriot of power. It exists all the more by being in the same place as power....' (1980, p. 142). It should prove extremely difficult for Foucault to give an account of this universal resistance to power if it were the case that subjectivities were originally and absolutely the product of the very power relations which they purport to resist.

Notes

1. See Hintikka (1967, pp. 108-39), where he argues that (a) the utterance 'Descartes does not exist' would have been existentially inconsistent or absurd for Descartes to utter, that (b) the inconsistency of an existentially inconsistent statement is of a performatory character since it depends on an act of utterance which logically defeats its own purpose, and that (c) in the same way as existentially inconsistent utterances defeat themselves when they are uttered or thought of, so their negations verify themselves when they are expressly professed. The Cogito belongs to this category of self-verifying statements, though Descartes did not (Hintikka argues) recognize its performatory character.

2. Saussure (1983, Part I) argues that languages are systems constituted by 'signs' that are arbitrary, conventional and differential. A linguistic sign is reducible in principle to two components, a sound-image or its graphic equivalent - the *signifier* - and a concept - the *signified*.. For instance, the word 'tree' which I see on a page of writing or that I hear when spoken is the signifier, to which corresponds a signified concept, *tree*. The sign which is composed of these two elements is arbitrary, first, because the association of a particular signifier ('tree') with a particular concept (*tree*) is established by convention in the sense that there is no natural link between the signifier and the physical marks or sounds that constitute it, or between the signifier and the linguistically posited concept which it

signifies; and, second, because there is also a conventional relationship between the sign as a whole and the particular reality which it designates. As David Robey puts it on Saussure's behalf, 'instead of things determining the meaning of words, words determine the meaning of things' (1982, p. 39). We come to identify or differentiate words not on the basis of their intrinsically representational qualities but by virtue of their difference from one another within the closed system of language itself. Words or signs are useful and meaningful in the measure that they divide up and differentiate within the continuum of experience, in the way that colour-words paradigmatically and arbitrarily divide up the colour spectrum. The more one tried to make words approximate to the continuum of the spectrum the more they would lose their function as dividers and 'differentiators' and subsequently lose their function and meaning. Without these arbitrary and conventional divisions thought would return to an indefinite continuum of inarticulate or jumbled 'ideas,' and language itself would return to a meaningless continuum of sounds or marks. The idea that thoughts or sound-images could exist as pre-linguistic continua is, of course, a mythical rather than a historical possibility, but the suggestion serves to emphasize that the arbitrariness, conventionality and 'modularity' of language does not act as a screen that blocks out reality but as a kind of complex artist's grid which squares off the landscape of reality and renders it intelligible and transcribable. There is blocking out, one might say, but there is also 'blocking in'. The categories of Kant have migrated into language, as it were, where they have increased and multiplied.

7 The self discontinued

It is often assumed that there is something irredeemably Cartesian about the notions of self-unity and self-identity. Talk of self, self-unity and self-identity smacks of soul-talk, as if only an independently existing entity, the self-as-soul, could possess the putatively Cartesian credentials of strict psychological unity. and strict psychological identity through time. In contemporary philosophy the most controversial attempt to subvert conventional belief in psychological identity and unity of mind has come from Derek Parfit (1979; 1984; 1989) who exhorts everyone, including philosophers, to give up not only the notion of a pure Cartesian ego but the language of identity traditionally associated with it. No cogent case can be made for a post-Cartesian conception of selfhood or subjectivity that does not meet the challenge presented by Parfit's new 'bundle' theory of mind and self.

Parfit's bundle theory

Parfit acknowledges that we are naturally inclined to hold a non-reductionist account of personal identity, according to which selves or persons are 'separately existing entities' whose continuity through time is an all-or-nothing affair and does not admit of degrees or phases, strictly speaking. On the non-reductionist view, unity of consciousness is explained in terms of ownership of different experiences by such a separately existing entity or subject; one's identity through time is also explained in terms of the continuing existence of that self-same entity or subject. But while this is what we happen to believe and while such identity-thinking is 'natural', it is not what we ought to believe, according to Parfit. He offers a new reductionist account according to which we are not separately existing entities, and according to which, on the contrary, personal identity consists in facts that can be described 'impersonally,' in terms of causal relations between mental states and bodies, i.e., in terms of degrees of psychological connectedness and continuity. Psychological continuity obtains when a person can be said to remember earlier deeds or experiences; or when there is persistence of psychological traits over time; or where there is, in general, a chain of significantly overlapping connections between one's present and one's past psychological life. There can be continuity in some significant respects rather than identity in all possible respects, and this degree of continuity is all we need to explain the sorts of relations that obtain in our psychological lives, on the basis of which we make memory-claims, accept responsibilities for past actions, look forward to the future, etc. Psychological connectedness can vary to such an extent that we can say that personal identity is in fact indeterminate. Our existence as 'persons' just involves the existence of brains and bodies, the doing of deeds, and the thinking of thoughts, the having of memories, and the occurrence of certain other related physical and mental events. There does not exist another subsistent entity, a person per se, which exists independently of the shifting sum of thoughts, experiences and activities.

There are two unities or identities to be explained: the unity or identity of consciousness at any time (sometimes called 'synchronic' identity or unity-across-space); and the unity, or 'diachronic' identity, or identity-through-time of a whole personal life. These two unities cannot be explained, in Parfit's view, by claiming that different experiences are had by the self-same, subsistent person or ego. In resorting to such notions we are merely committing ourselves to a question-begging Cartesian ontology. If we are to avoid such an ontology we must try to explain the unities or identities in question by describing the relations between experiences, and the relations of these sets of experiences to a particular body or brain. Parfit is confident that we can refer to experiences, and fully describe the relations between them, without claiming that the experiences are had by independently existing ego, person or subject.

Parfit begins by asking us to imagine the hypothetical situation, first devised by David Wiggins (1967), in which one's brain has been divided in such a way that each half is housed in a new body. The identity question which arises is: What happens to 'me'? Three answers suggest themselves: (1) I do not survive; (2) I survive as one of the two people, each of whom shares 'my' brain; (3) I survive as both. Parfit regards (1) and (2) as highly implausible. The trouble with (1) is that people have in fact survived with half their brains destroyed, so it seems to follow that, whatever other complications there might be, I could survive if half my brain were transplanted in another body. The trouble with (2) is that if each half of my brain is similar to start with, then how can I survive as only one of the two people? It seems more plausible to opt for (3), but only if we abandon the assumption that personal survival in this instance implies identity. We can suggest, according to Parfit, that 'I survive as two different people without implying that I am these people' (1979, p. 190).

161

He argues that there is a sense of 'survive' which does not imply identity, that what matters most in survival scenarios (such as the Wiggins scenario) are relations of connectedness which are essentially relations of degree, such that none of these relations needs to be described in a way that presupposes strict identity.

The most important but also most problematic relation in this context is that involved in memory. If it were a logical truth that we can only remember our own experiences, then Parfit would find it difficult to avoid the language of identity in his proposed solution to the Wiggins operation. But he outlines a concept of memory for which it is not a logical truth that we remember only our own experiences. He calls this quasi-memory or 'q-memory'.[1] I can be said to q-remember an experience if (1) I have a belief about a past experience which seems in itself like a memory belief, (2) someone did have such an experience, and (3) my belief is dependent upon this experience in the same way in which an ordinary memory of an experience is dependent upon it. This concept of q-memory embraces memory in the ordinary sense but also allows for the possibility of 'remembering' experiences that one did not have oneself. Either of Wiggins's post-operative people could have q-memories in Parfit's sense, thus indicating survival without strict psychological identity. Identity is, of course, always strict in the sense that there are no degrees of identity, strictly understood - either X at t_1 is identical with X at t_2 or it is not. There can, however, be degrees of connectedness, such that I can claim some degree of continuity with someone in the past without claiming that I am strictly identical with that someone.

Parfit goes on to discuss 'certain imaginary beings' who are like ourselves except that they reproduce themselves by a process of natural division. A diagram of the relationships between 'ancestral' and 'descendant' selves would look like a family tree. An ancestral being 'A' is psychologically close to its immediate descendant 'B+1' as I today am to myself tomorrow. 'A' is as distant from 'B+30' as I am from my great-great-grandson. Such relations are relations of degree of continuity or connectedness, and can be coherently described without requiring recourse to the language of strict, all-or-nothing identity. First, 'A' can think of any individual, anywhere in his 'tree', as 'a descendant self', thus implying psychological continuity without identity. Similarly, any later individual can think of an earlier individual as an ancestral self. Having past and future selves is a way of continuing to exist which does not imply identity through time. Applied to the Wiggins operation, the original person does, to some significant extent, survive the operation: the two resulting people are his later selves, and each can refer to the 'parent' self as 'my past self', and may have certain memories to support such reference. They can share a past self without being, or claiming to be, the same self as each other, or without claiming to be identical with the parent self. Connectedness-thinking thus replaces identity-thinking.

162

On this view, the word 'I' can be used to imply 'the greatest degree of psychological connectedness' (1979, p. 205). When the connections are reduced - by, for example, a marked loss of memory - then it is possible for the self-dividing imaginary beings to truthfully say 'It was not I who did that, but an earlier self.' This is also the way in which we ourselves could begin to think, in Parfit's view, about our own normal lives or 'selves'. He recalls Proust's claim that 'we are incapable, while we are in love, of acting as fit predecessors of the next persons who, when we are in love no longer, we shall presently have become ....' (Proust, 1949, p. 226). While Proust distinguished implicitly between successive selves, he still thought of one person as being these different selves. Parfit on the other hand wants to make the more radical claim that there is no underlying person of which each 'self' is a phase. There will be no identity relation between earlier and later selves. Whether to say 'I', or 'one of my future selves,' or 'a descendant self' is a matter of choice or decision according to certain criteria of connectedness.

Parfit conducts a thought-experiment with a Simple Teletransporter and a New Teletransporter to illustrate his distinction between questions of survival and questions of identity (1984, Ch. 10). On stepping into the Simple Transporter a scanner on Earth destroys my brain and body while recording the exact genetic states of all my cells. It will then transmit this information by radio to a Replicator on Mars. This will then create, out of new matter, a brain and body exactly like mine. It will be in this body that I shall wake up. Or *do* I wake up in this new body? Have I travelled from Earth to Mars, from Teletransporter to Replicator? Or have I been destroyed and only a replica created elsewhere? If there is no numerical identity between the person who entered the Teletransporter and the person who left the Replicator, in what sense can there be a putative psychological identity between the one and the other? Within the language of identity, such questions do not have a clear answer and become even more difficult if the Simple Transporter is replaced by the New Teletransporter. The new machine does not destroy me before it transmits its information; it copies the information and leaves me intact, although - and this is the conceptual snag - it has such a traumatic effect on my heart that I will survive only a short time on Earth. Since I can communicate with my Replica it is clear that he is not me, numerically speaking. Though he is exactly like me, he is one person and I am another. When I die he will continue to live. If there is identity here it is qualitative identity rather than numerical identity. And if criteria of identity are applicable, then we must decide whether they are physical or psychological or both, and whether they are to be applied in a narrow or a wide sense. But rather than simply widen the concept of identity, Parfit argues that what matters is not strict identity but survival in a 'more or less' sense of survival. What matters is connectedness or continuity rather than identity. Travelling at the speed of light, as impulses of information, from Earth to Mars may not preserve one's numerical identity or psychological identity in a narrow

163

sense (i.e., where experiences and memories must have normal causes), but it gives a kind of survival which is virtually as good, or which is at least preferable to complete extinction. The mental life of the replica is, for most intents and purposes, connected with my present mental life in the ways that matter. Survival is more a matter of preserving significant psychological connections, overlaps and partial continuities than it is a matter of preserving strict one-one identity. Being oneself is a relative affair at the best of times, and a person's psychological life may be less deeply integrated than we conventionally assume. Even death, the ultimate threat to the old identity-seeking ego, loses some of its sting if we learn to substitute the concept of connectedness for determinate identity or strictly transitive continuity:

> My death will break the more direct relations between my present experiences and future experiences, but it will not break various other relations. This is all there is to the fact that there will be no one living who will be me .... Instead of saying , 'I shall be dead', I shall say, 'There will be no future experiences that will be related, in certain ways, to these present experiences.' Because it reminds me what this fact involves, the redescription makes this fact less depressing. (1984, p. 281)

Persons without identity

Parfit describes his own view as a bundle theory of the person or self. According to bundle theories of the person we cannot explain 'either the unity of consciousness at any time, or the unity of a whole life, by referring to a person' (1989, p. 20). Instead we must claim that there are long series of mental states and events, each series constituting a 'life'. Each series or 'life' is unified by various kinds of causal relations, such as the relation that holds between experiences and subsequent memories of them. Each series is like a bundle in the sense that there is nothing else other than the bundle which holds the bundle together - the bundle is the only entity we have to deal with, and even in talking about the 'contents' of the bundle we must be careful not to imply a real distinction between the bundle and its constituents. What Parfit offers here is in fact two bundle theories, or a 'bundle-within-a-bundle' theory, of the person and self. First, the person is reduced to a bundle of life-series or selves, and each life-series or self is further reduced to the mental states between which there exist certain causal relations. Some of his arguments are clearly designed to support a reductionist or bundle theory of the person, while others are directed more obviously towards establishing a bundle theory of the self or of consciousness.

As a bundle theorist Parfit denies the existence of persons, subjects of experience, and egos. While he agrees with Thomas Reid that 'I am not thought, I am not action, I am not feeling; I am something that thinks and acts and feels,' he claims that Reid's assertion only reveals 'a fact about grammar' (1989, p. 20). Echoing the views of various 'grammarians of the subject' from Wittgenstein to Lacan, Parfit argues that it is only in this kind of language-dependent way that there exist persons or subjects at all. Persons or subjects have a 'nominal' rather than a real existence. Parfit looks back beyond our latter-day grammarians to the earlier claims of Broad and Russell who also argued that what gives rise to the belief in subjects or pure egos is the use of the word 'I' as a grammatical subject in first-person psychological statements.[2] Russell maintained that the grammatical form of 'I think' is actually misleading because it suggests that there is a subject in the sense of a substantial ego. But while Russell was prepared to define 'I' as a term which one is entitled to use if one has empirical evidence that there exists something that satisfies the description 'the self that is acquainted with this', other empiricists have been more determined to eliminate the unitary ego or self altogether from their analyses of psychological judgements. Parfit finds another mentor in Ayer who writes:

> We do not deny .... that a given sense-content can legitimately be said to be experienced by a particular subject; but we shall see that this relation of being experienced by a particular subject is to be analysed in terms of the relation of sense-contents to one another, and not in terms of a substantival ego and its mysterious acts. (Ayer, 1946, p. 122)

But if this view is applied to first-person experience, it has the consequence, according to Shoemaker, that when one asserts a statement like 'I see an afterimage' one is asserting that a sense-content is only contingently related to other sense-contents. This consequence Shoemaker finds to have been neatly articulated by Ernst Mach who claimed that the primary fact is not the ego, 'but the elements (sensations) .... The elements constitute the I' (1959, p. 23). Having the sensation *green* signifies that the element green occurs in a given 'complex of elements,' i.e., a complex of other sensations or memories. These views of Ayer and Mach are variations on the Humean account of perception and introspection, according to which we can never perceive anything other than perceptions, regardless of whether our attention is directed inwardly or outwardly. When Hume looked inward among his perceptions he could not detect a perceiving self, ego or subject which 'had' the perceptions, and he concluded that 'Tis the composition of these, therefore, which forms the self' (1888, p. 558).

That Parfit's bundle theory of the self can be traced back through Ayer, Russell and Mach to Hume is suggested by his use of Hume's analogy between the concept of a soul and the concept of a nation or commonwealth: 'I cannot compare the soul more properly to anything than to a republic or

165

commonwealth' (1888, §4). Most of us, Parfit points out, are Reductionists or bundle theorists about nations. We would accept the following claims: Nations exist; France, for example, certainly exists, while Ruritania does not. Nations exist, then, but a nation is not an entity that exists separately, apart from its citizens and its territory. We should be prepared to accept as non-controversial the proposition:

(1) A nation's existence just involves the existence of its citizens, living together in certain ways, on its own territory. We might validly extrapolate from this the proposition: (2) A nation just is these citizens and this territory. Others, however, could equally validly make the less obvious claim: (3) A nation is an entity that is distinct from its citizens and its territory. Provided we do not insist that distinctness implies separate existence, we may believe that (1) and (3) are not inconsistent.

Analogously, we may make the following claims: (4) A person's existence just consists in the existence of a brain and a body, and the occurrence of a series of interrelated physical and mental events; (5) A person *just* is a particular brain and body, and such a series of interrelated events (where *is* should be understood as the *is* of composition rather than of identity); (6) A person is an entity that is distinct from a brain and body, and such a series of events. As with nations and citizens (or clubs and members) we may accept that (4) and (6) are not inconsistent. And if we may accept that, then we can also accept the following propositions: (7) The fact of a person's identity over time just consists in the holding of certain more particular facts, and (8) These facts can be described without either presupposing the identity of this person, or explicitly claiming that the experiences in this person's life are had by this person, or even explicitly claiming that this person exists. These facts can be described in an *impersonal* way.

Parfit concludes: (9) Though persons exist, we could give a *complete* description of reality *without* claiming that persons exist.[3]

Clearly, Parfit's bundle theory is a more radical critique of conventional notions of personal identity and of the unity of consciousness than is, for example, Lacan's. While allowing that we are entitled to our concept of a person, just as we are entitled to our concept of a nation, he also wants to say that neither persons nor nations exist apart from the particulars that constitute them. Those whom we conventionally and conveniently designate persons do not necessarily possess a self or ego which remains transitively continuous throughout the course of a personal life. Any particular individual may have more than one psychological life or more than one self, and may even disown past selves and look forward to the emergence of a new self. The individual whose natural history is marked by her dates of birth and death is only contingently related to her psychological life at any particular time.

In speaking of the person as a succession of selves, Parfit increases and multiplies entities for which it is difficult, conceptually, to find a local habitation. How does a past self differ significantly or demonstrably from a past phase of one's present self? What could be the difference between my remembering an experience and my 'remembering' a past self as having had that experience? In both cases the remembered experience is not attributable to anyone else but 'me now', just as a past action, whether performed by a distantly related past self or by myself in an earlier phase of life, is not attributable to anyone else but 'me now'. A detective working according to the usual criteria of personal identity and following clues to a crime committed by, let us say, one of my past selves, will be led to 'me now', whether I like it or not. If the detective is an impressionable reader of the work of Derek Parfit he may decide that 'I now' am not after all punishable for the crime of a past self. But the point is that the particular crime committed in the past can be traced to no other existing person but 'me now'. (For one thing, the fingerprints of my embodied present self are inconveniently identical with those of my identically embodied past self.) If the detective is not a student of Parfit's work, he may still decide that I am not punishable for the crime, albeit on grounds of certain mitigating circumstances endured by me during an earlier phase of my life. There is nothing in the evidence surrounding the circumstances of the crime which the Parfitian detective can point to in order to demonstrate the existence of a past self rather than the existence a self which has gone through a criminal phase, or just committed a criminal act, in the past. From the point of view of others' perception of my identity, there is no materially compelling difference between the actions of my past self and my actions in the past. And if there are no such materially compelling differences then the distinction between a past self and myself in the past becomes effectively untenable. If third parties are intent on punishing me for a past action they need not be impressed by my attempt to dissociate my present (blameless) self from a past (blameworthy) self. If they wish on the other hand to be lenient with me they may make a significant distinction between the early and later phases of my life, and their leniency may be no less grounded than that of someone who accepted a bundle concept of the person. Conversely, Parfitians are not necessarily more lenient than advocates of strict identity. A hard-line Parfitian judge could decide to punish me on the grounds of an appropriately new concept of q-guilt or guilt-by-association, i.e., association with a past self. The judge might want to deter other potential criminals from a too facile use of the ultimate Parfitian alibi or the ultimate Parfitian sell-out, viz., 'I didn't do it but I know a past self who did.'

But there is a more serious and more important objection that can be made against the notion of a series-person. In claiming that there is a relation of connectedness, rather than a relation of identity or transitive continuity, between

167

my present self and a past self, Parfit implies that the relationship between my present self and my memories of certain past experiences is merely contingent. Memory, after all, is the only way I can establish the presence or absence of the relation of connectedness ('Relation R') that Parfit wishes to put in place of the identity relation. But does it make sense to talk of establishing such a relation in the empirical way that Parfit requires? If I could be said to have an empirically contingent relation with my remembered experiences or actions, in what sense could I be said to 'remember' them at all? If a window was broken at some time in the past, could I, conceivably, have a memory of a former self breaking the window but not at the same time admit to *my* breaking it. Could I claim to remember that someone of a certain familiar description broke a window, whence I infer that the window was broken by a former self, but yet not remember my breaking the window, since memories of my breaking the window will only relate to the actions of my present self? This way of putting things does not seem to follow the logic of memory-claims. On the face of it, it is a scarcely coherent way of talking, since it seems to assert and deny the same thing with respect to the same memory-claimant.

Shoemaker argues that the notion of identifying a remembered self as oneself - by making inferences from criteria of identity - is highly problematic, and may be incoherent. I do not remember that someone broke a window and *then* identify that person as myself; I simply remember that I broke the window. There is no question of remembering and identifying - there is simply the question of remembering or not remembering. What I remember is not 'the breaking of the window by someone,' but is simply 'breaking the window': 'And for me to remember breaking the window is to remember *my* breaking the window' (Shoemaker, 1963, p. 142). To depart significantly from this paradigmatic way of reporting remembered experiences and actions is to run the risk of incoherence. To introduce such notions as quasi-memory merely begs the question of whether it is possible to talk intelligibly of having memories of experiences not had, or of actions not performed, by oneself. It makes more sense to argue that if we can remember past events at all there must be some first-person past-tense statements that can be known without their being inferences grounded on criteria of identity. Applying criteria of identity in one's own case implies the possibility of remembering someone having an experience - and then identifying that person as oneself, or not oneself, as the case may be. Applying criteria of identity in such a case, or in any case, implies the possibility that the criteria may not apply *de facto*, that the person who is the object of one's memory is not in fact oneself, not even in the Parfitian sense of a past self. Even the notion of quasi-memory cannot stretch to include the having of memories that might turn out to be memories of experiences had, or of actions performed, not by oneself but by someone yet to be identified.

The scattered self

Parfit's bundle theory of self and consciousness makes a more radical claim than his bundle theory of the person but runs into even more serious difficulties - the same sort of difficulties that attend the reductionist psychologies of Hume, Russell and Ayer. The most obvious and most general objection to a bundle theory of the self is that there cannot be perceptions without a perceiver, or thoughts without a thinker, or experiences without a subject of experience. The *locus classicus* for this line of objection is Bishop Butler's argument against Locke. Against Locke's view that memory constitutes personal identity, Butler argued that it is self-evident that 'consciousness of personal identity presupposes, and therefore cannot constitute personal identity; any more than knowledge in any other case, can constitute truth, which it presupposes' (1886, p. 388). An interesting variation on Butler's argument has been developed by Shoemaker in his *reductio ad absurdum* of the reductionist position, which we may call 'the argument from empirical properties' (1963, pp. 110-119; 1985, pp. 443-53). This argument is simply stated. If the self is 'scattered', i.e., reduced to a succession of thoughts and other mental states between which there exists a certain empirical or causal relationship only, then it should make sense to suppose that I might observe an image - and also observe that it does not stand in that relationship to certain other sense-contents. But if 'my' perceiving an image consists in its standing in a contingently empirical relationship to other sense-contents, then for me to observe an image and observe that it does not have the right sort of relationship to other sense-contents would mean that I could experience an image and determine that it is not mine, i.e., that I am not after all properly causally acquainted with it (1963, p. 110). In other words, the bundle theory makes the relational property of 'being perceived by me' an empirical property that I can observe something to have - or not to have. Which implies, absurdly, that I could observe some experiential datum not to have the property of being my experience, as if experiences and other mental contents were floating phenomena looking for a place to happen. The empiricist or reductionist assumes that perceiving an image, including a memory-image, is like perceiving an object, as if mental events were separately existing entities, like the contents of a bundle which may exist apart from any particular bundle, or which may migrate from one bundle to another. As Shoemaker says, to claim that we could fully declare or describe our thoughts without claiming that they have thinkers who think them 'suggests that the only entities referred to or quantified over in impersonal descriptions are entities that could exist without there being persons ....' (1985, p. 446).

Shoemaker offers a particularly convincing criticism of the mind/nation or mind/club analogy which Parfit borrows from Hume. The implication of this analogy is that mental states or events could exist without there being persons, just as members of clubs or nations can exist as separate individuals without there being clubs or nations. He notes that Parfit at one point proposed to use the word 'event' rather than 'state' in referring to mental entities, because a state must be a state *of* something, whereas this is not true of events. Parfit proposed, in other words, that we might think of mental entities or events as not necessarily requiring subjects who have them. Shoemaker also notes that while Parfit allows that persons are something distinct from their brains, bodies and experiences, and that they are therefore subjects of experiences in some sense, 'he [Parfit] repeatedly says that it is *because of the way we talk* that it is true that persons are subjects' (1985, p. 446). This suggests to Shoemaker that Parfitian persons or subjects are logical constructions out of entities whose existence does not strictly require that they be states of persons. The existence of these impersonal or sub-personal entities is not 'adjectival' on mental subjects, in the way that seeings are adjectival on seers, or deeds on doers.

The problem with such a Humean view of mental events is that there do not seem to be any impersonal mental entities which could conceivably fill the bill. It does not improve matters for Parfit if some sort of causal or functional account is given of the relations that obtain between these entities, since he will then either fall foul of Shoemaker's original *reductio ad absurdum* or will have to accept that there is a necessary ontological dependence of experiences and other mental entities on the existence of persons or other mental subjects:

> If any sort of causal or functional account of the mental is correct, what constitutes a given mental state or event as being of a particular mental kind (for example an experience or belief having a certain content) is its being so related to a larger system to which it belongs as to be apt to play a certain 'causal role' in the workings of that system - and the existence of such a system will be just what Parfit regards as constituting the existence of a person. (Shoemaker, 1985, p. 446)[4]

A 'system' of mental events, however, is too ambiguous or vague to do the job Parfit wants it to do. If the mental events are only extrinsically related to each other, like the contents of a bundle, then it ought to make sense to wonder whether some experience or memory is mine or not, i.e., belongs to the bundle or not. But if Shoemaker's argument from empirical properties is correct, then such wondering makes no sense. On the other hand, if the mental events are related to each other in a more intrinsically integrated sort of way, such that it would not make sense to wonder whether a particular experience or memory was mine or not, then the reductionist project is compromised. From a reductionist point of view there would be no significant difference between a person who subjectively has or 'owns' experiences and a system in which mental events are so causally or functionally, yet so uniquely, related that the 'empirical properties' objection does not apply. For reductionism to succeed it must fall foul of the empirical properties argument; for reductionism to

170

successfully avoid the empirical properties argument it must cease to be a robust reductionism.

Shoemaker discusses in this context a telling analogy between the identity of a hurricane (a weather system) and the putative identity of a bundle self (a psychological system). Meteorologists may have precise 'criteria of identity' for deciding whether or not two successive events - a rainstorm here, a hailstorm there - are parts of one and the same hurricane. On the basis of their criteria - which may be spatial, temporal, and causal - the meteorologists are entitled to decide whether the observed phenomena belong to the hurricane or not. The reason why criteria are *needed* here, if such questions of identification are to be answerable, is that one *can* observe, on different occasions, weather phenomena that do not in fact belong to the same hurricane: 'the point of having criteria is precisely to enable us to distinguish these cases from cases in which the successive events do belong to the same hurricane (1963 p. 150). The crux of the analogy - or, rather, disanalogy - between the identity of a hurricane and the identity of a self is that what is true of a currently observed weather phenomenon and a remembered one, with respect to the notion of 'same hurricane', is not true of a currently 'observed' experience and a remembered one, with respect to the notion of 'same person'. The empirical, contingent aspect of weather phenomena and their component elements does not hold in the case of the sorts of relations that obtain among the data of one's psychological life. One does not have to identify oneself (for oneself) in order to make a memory-statement or a first-person present-tense psychological statement. As has already been well-and-truly argued, criteria of identity are not appealed to at all by individuals making judgements about their current states of mind. Persons (human subjects, speakers) have - to reiterate a point made by Strawson as well as by Shoemaker - a noncriterial knowledge or awareness of their own identity, and their self-ascriptions or first-person statements are, normally, the best evidence that others can have of the thoughts, feelings, and experiences of the speaker. Only about persons, moreover, can identity judgements be made in this way, and this fact points to an important difference between the identities of persons and the identities of other things. Such facts, however, do not imply that ego-possessing persons are nonphysical substances. Such facts are consistent with the view that persons are biological, social and language-using systems with certain remarkable, if not species-specific, capacities. Such facts are facts about persons embodied or positioned within a spatio-temporal world and within cultural forms of life in which certain self-referring, first-person psychological statements, including memory-claims, are normally accepted as true, even as incorrigible, in the sense that if a person sincerely asserts such statements it does not make sense to suppose that she is lying or is mistaken. That a first-person, present-tense, psychological statement or memory-claim is sincere is, according to Shoemaker, 'a logically sufficient condition of its being true' (1963, p. 216), although, of course, other criteria

171

can be used to show that such a statement is not in fact sincere and therefore not acceptable as true in a particular instance. In accepting as sincere the memory statements of others, one thinks of oneself not as inferring something about that person's past from his testimony, 'but as *sharing* the *uninferred* knowledge he has of his past; one accepts his memory statements almost as if they were one's own' (1963, p. 250). This distinctive feature of human interaction is part of the conception of a form of life in which, following Wittgenstein, we regard human beings as persons without requiring 'evidence' that they are persons and, more particularly, without systematically requiring criteria of individual identity to be provided on every occasion on which first-person statements are made.

Memory and the forensic concept of identity

Much of the philosophical literature on personal identity deals with extremely hypothetical or imaginary cases involving transplanted brain-parts, body-swopping consciousnesses, and replica-producing machines. This tradition of outlandish case-studies extends from Parfit's science-fictional technology of Teletransporters back to Locke's simpler wizardry with the minds of princes and the bodies of cobblers. Such thought-experiments are, of course, thought-provoking, and they help us to get clear about some aspects of our conceptions of identity, continuity, consciousness and accountability. But they also tend to take attention away from the more mundane scenarios in which identity questions can and do arise. Most of these scenarios are 'forensic' in the sense that they involve attempts by law-officers and law-courts to establish identities in relation to criminal offences, or attempts by accused parties to disprove incriminating identifications. This feature of identity-questions was recognized expressly by Locke who described the term person as 'a forensic term, appropriating actions and their merit' (1690, Bk. II, Ch. 27, §26). In other words, it is only in virtue of their being currently conscious of past actions that persons are, strictly speaking, 'accountable' for those actions.

According to Locke, personal identity consists in identity of consciousness and not in identity of substance. This conception of identity has the startling consequence that a person who cannot remember having a particular experience or performing a particular action cannot be properly identified as the person who had that experience or performed that action:

> [I]f the same Socrates waking and sleeping do not partake of the same consciousness, Socrates waking and sleeping is not the same person. And to punish Socrates waking for what sleeping Socrates thought, and waking Socrates was never conscious of, would be no more right, than to punish one twin for what his brother twin did, whereof he knew nothing, because their outsides were the same .... (Ch. 27, §19)

172

Locke's view, however, as encapsulated in this passage, reflects a conflation of two senses of identity, viz., 'personal identity proper', in the sense of third-person identity or the identity one has for others, and 'self-identity proper', in the sense of the identity that is presupposed in the making of memory-claims and first-person present-tense psychological statements generally. It is for others to establish personal identity proper, i.e., to establish, on the basis of bodily and other public criteria, that Socrates waking is identical with Socrates sleeping. Those who wish to establish the relation of identity between Socrates waking and Socrates sleeping are entitled and obliged to have recourse to public criteria - that is what third parties do and that is what public criteria are for. One's personal identity is typically and properly established by others on a criterial basis, i.e., on the basis of evidential or observational criteria, while first-person identity or self-identity proper is not established on such a criterial basis at all. I do not, for example, recognize myself every morning on waking, or identify myself (to myself) as the person who went to bed eight hours previously. I simply come to consciousness and resume the business of making decisions, planning, recollecting, keeping appointments, etc. Remembering who I am is a problem that others may have but it is not - perhaps cannot be - a problem for myself. Those cases in which I forget who I am are really cases in which I lose the sense of the identity I have for others. This is true not only of relatively transient instances of self-forgetful behaviour under the influence of passion, drugs, or alcohol but also of the rather more serious long-term cases of self-forgetfulness caused by trauma, disease, or senility. Even in the serious cases the eventual return of memory, accompanies by complete self-recollection, is something which will occur either naturally and spontaneously or as a result of treatment - it will not normally be a case of one's having successfully re-established one's identity by onself, *for oneself*, criterially or evidentially. (It may not make sense to say 'normally' here.)

Locke's conflation of the third- and first-person perspectives is particularly puzzling in the light of his insistence that his concept of the person or self is forensic, belonging only to accountable, intelligent agents, 'capable of a law, and happiness, and misery' (Ch. 27, §26). The personality extends itself beyond present existence to what is past only in virtue of consciousness, 'whereby it becomes concerned and accountable; owns and imputes to itself past actions, just upon the same ground and for the same reason as it does the present' (Ch. 27, §26). But accountability, one wants to protest, is a forensic term just because it is imputable from a third-party perspective - just because *others* can and do hold us accountable for our actions on the basis of evidence and criteria. We may impute actions to ourselves in the sense that we admit responsibility for them; but we do not impute actions to ourselves if this means that we can somehow retrospectively or introspectively accuse ourselves of some offence on the basis of evidence and criteria. We may be unsure of our moral guilt in relation to a particular action, but this will not be because we are unsure about the identity of the agent. Third parties may have problems of tracing actions to agents, of tracing evidence to identifiable sources, but the actual agents of such actions will normally have no such problems as far as questions of *forensic* accountability are concerned. Questions of *moral* accountability are a different matter, and do not involve questions of personal identity or agency. Indeed, questions of one's moral accountability in any particular circumstance are made the more poignant by the fact that one is all too aware of having performed the action in question. In other words, we agonize over our moral accountability only when and just because our forensic accountability is not in doubt.

That Locke's conflation of the two senses of identity can be reduced to absurdity is suggested by Thomas Reid's well-known 'brave officer' argument. Reid asks us to suppose a brave officer (a) to have been flogged as a boy for robbing an orchard, (ii) to have taken a standard from the enemy in his first campaign as a soldier, and (iii) to have been made a general in later life. Suppose also that the young soldier who took the standard was still conscious of having been flogged at school, and that when he was made a general he was still conscious of having taken the standard, but had by now lost consciousness of having been flogged at school:

> These things being supposed, it follows, from Mr. Locke's doctrine, that he who was flogged at school is the same person who took the standard, and he who took the standard is the same person who was made a general. Whence it follows .... that the general is the same person with him who was flogged at school. But the general's consciousness does not reach so far back as his flogging; therefore according to Mr. Locke's doctrine, he is not the same person who was flogged. Therefore the general is, and at the same time is not, the same person with him who was flogged at school. (1785, pp. 357-8)

What Reid's *reductio* does not make explicit, however, is the fact that identity is being used ambiguously in Locke's argument, mainly to attempt a third-person account of self-identity, i.e., an account which looks for (public) criteria of identity among the contents of a person's consciousness.[5] Those who are fully cognizant with the biography of Reid's brave officer have no problem in establishing a continuity between the flogged boy and the forgetful general. When public criteria are used effectively to establish the identity of x, the mere absence of memory or consciousness on the part of x is not sufficient to undermine the force of the criterial evidence against him.

This idea that all talk about identity is talk about public criteria is defended most forcefully by Bernard Williams when he attempts to reduce all identity questions to questions concerning public or bodily criteria. He argues that memory cannot be used as a criterion of identity by others - or by oneself. It

174

cannot be used as a criterion by others because this would require an 'externalized view' of the contents of a person's mind, a view which is not obtainable from any conceivable vantage-point. It is precisely such a vantage-point that is presupposed by Locke in his passage on Socrates waking and Socrates sleeping. But neither can memory be used as a criterion of identity by oneself since memory, as Bishop Butler (1896) observed, presupposes identity.[6] In saying that memory-consciousness is 'what makes a man be himself to himself' Locke implied that a man could use memory as a criterion in deciding whether he is identical with himself. But this, in Williams's view, is absurd:

> Suppose a man to have had previously some set of memories S, and now a different set S_1. This should presumably be the situation in which he should set about using the criterion to decide the question of his identity. But this cannot be so, for when he has memories S, and again when he has memories S_1, he is in no doubt about his identity, and so the question does not even occur to him. For it to occur to him, he would have to have S and S_1 at the same time, and so S would be included in S_1, which is contrary to the hypothesis that they are, in the relevant sense, different. (1964, p. 338)

He concludes that the facts of self-consciousness and memory prove incapable of yielding 'the secret of personal identity,' and we are forced back into the world of public criteria.

Williams assumes too readily, however, that the facts of memory and self-consciousness cannot have a direct bearing on the world of public criteria. His view effectively reduces all questions of identity to the third-person perspective, as if first-person claims never made a contribution to the establishment of identities. There are, however, not uncommon forensic circumstances in which it does make sense to talk of one's establishing one's identity, in the sense of establishing it for others. Talk about criteria of identity in relation to oneself may arise if, for example, there is a question concerning one's having been present or not at the scene of a crime. This is the point of Strawson's observation, albeit in another context, that we *speak* primarily to others, for the information of others: 'In one sense ... I do not have to *tell who it is* who is in pain, when I am. In another sense, however, I may have to *tell who it is*, i.e., to let others know who it is' (1959, p. 100). It is because one has certain well-defined memories that one can begin, as a suspect, to dissociate oneself from a crime under investigation, mainly by being able to remember one's being elsewhere at the time of the action. Memory is not used in that event as a criterion of identity by oneself, self-referringly, but as a means of bearing witness against the identity-claims of others. Without the capacity to remember and confirm one's whereabouts at certain times one might not be able to prevent

175

one's being 'framed', i.e., being falsely identified as the perpetrator of a crime. Insofar as one's verifiable memories have a direct bearing on the establishment of identities, including one's own identity, then to that extent one's memory-claims belong in some sense among the forensic criteria of personal identity.

It might of course be said that in talking about verifiable memory-claims we are still talking about public criteria only. After all, we don't just *believe* suspects or defendants who say they were elsewhere at the time of a crime. We expect corroboration of such a claim, i.e., we expect an alibi. But there is a difference between law-officers attempting to establish the identity of an unknown criminal and a suspect trying to establish his identity as an innocent party. Both the law-officers and the suspect (or defendant) are looking for clues to an identity but not in quite the same way. The law-officers are looking for already-existing clues, i.e., pieces of evidence which are 'lying around'. These constitute the incriminating aftermath of the crime - they are there to be gathered, and are traceable in principle to the agent of the action. An innocent suspect, however, who distinctly remembers having been elsewhere at the time of the crime can only prove his innocence by sheer dint of recollection - by marshalling evidence that is not lying around but which must be abstracted from the flow of events that constitutes his personal history. Incidents, meetings, and transactions that were formerly not clues to anything must now be constituted as clues to an innocent identity. Much will depend on the quality of the innocent suspect's memories - and on the quality of the memories of others whom he identifies and 'constitutes' as witnesses. Memories in that event become the sources of the information that will count as criterial evidence in the establishment of an identity. The evidence itself remains in some important sense memory-laden or memory-dependent. And in the measure that the suspect is the source of such memory-laden information, to that extent he is involved in first-personally *and* criterially establishing his own personal identity, i.e., the identity he has for others.

What has been neglected by Williams is the fact that 'identifying' oneself or making sincere memory-claims is not, in some forensically relevant contexts, a matter of making self-introspective self-identifications but of making appropriately sincere self-defensive first-person utterances. Such forensically relevant self-identifications belong fairly and squarely in the world of public criteria, i.e., in the world in which identity-claims and counter-claims are sometimes an issue, sometimes a matter of imprisonment or liberty, sometimes even a matter of life and death. While it may be true that the facts of self-consciousness and memory *per se* are incapable of yielding the secrets of personal identity *per se*, it is also true that certain kinds of sincerely-made first-person utterances, especially in the form of memory-claims, may provide some clues to the mystery of particular cases.

These considerations remind us of the 'tragic' disparity between the first- and third-person perspectives on identity and accountability, between the public

176

world in which identities are established and the 'private' world in which intentions, actions, memories and selves originate. Where an innocent suspect can establish, by virtue of his verifiable memory-claims, that he is not in fact the perpetrator of a crime, that he was identifiably elsewhere at the time of the crime - that he has, in other words, an 'alibi' - then he stands a reasonable chance of being acquitted of the criminal charge against him, despite the existence of some incriminating forensic or third-party evidence. But where he has no verifiable memory of his whereabouts at the time of the crime; or where he remembers committing the crime but insists that he was then a different person (in a Parfitian sense); or where there is some incriminating evidence but he has suffered profound loss of memory in relation to the period in which the crime was committed, then there is, tragically, little that can be done from the first-person perspective. An acquittal in such cases would depend on extraordinary intervention by third parties - e.g., by witnesses who come forward to contradict the incriminating evidence of other witnesses, or by special pleading of defence counsel who have decided to take a Lockean or Parfitian view of identity, accountability and consciousness. From the strictly third-party perspective, however, there seems to be no overwhelming reason that the special pleading of Lockean or Parfitian counsel should be accepted in such cases. Locke recognized as much when he said that though a drunkard may not be conscious of what he did while drunk, 'yet human judicatures justly punish him; because the fact is proved against him, but want of consciousness cannot be proved for him' (Ch. 27, §22). Locke attempts to console us with the thought that 'in the Great Day, wherein the secrets of the heart be laid open, it may be reasonable to think, no one shall be made to answer for what he knows nothing of ...' (§22). But it is significant that the 'truth' of the first-person perspective can only be revealed in the absolutely extraordinary forensic circumstance of the Day of Judgement in which an absolutely externalized view is taken, *pace* Williams, of the contents of a person's mind, i.e., the circumstance in which the first-person perspective is exposed to the third-person omniscience of God.

If this is the only conceivable circumstance in which the third- and first-person perspectives coincide, we are entitled to assume that the possibility of injustice is implicit in the procedures of 'human judicatures' because it is implicit in the very procedures whereby identities are criterially - that is to say, forensically - established. These procedures can, of course, be improved and all instances of miscarriage of justice should bring about pertinent reforms in police and judicial procedures. But no judicial system can ever claim to be immune to the possibility of wrongful identification and subsequent miscarriage of justice. The 'tyranny' of the world of public criteria is such that in the face of incriminating evidence it cannot yield to the protests of an innocent consciousness unless that consciousness can establish its innocence through third parties, i. e., witnesses or forensic experts. Since one's innocence is thus in the gift of such third parties, and since third parties are themselves not always wholly adequate, morally or technically, to their task, it follows that the possibility of injustice remains immanent in systems of justice as it does in the world of public criteria generally.

'Me. And me now': a *cogitatio* for the modernist self

Those strange creatures, the divided self, the series-person, and the decentred subject which now wander through the pages of contemporary philosophy and which have been generated by an indiscriminate anti-Cartesianism, have been given their warmest, most uncritical welcome in some areas of contemporary literary theory. Drawing on philosophy, on contemporary cultural theory, and on the literary writings of Joyce, Eliot, Woolf and others, Dennis Brown (1989) argues that modernist poetry, fiction, and drama have subverted the notion of a 'stable, integral self' and revealed the self to be complex, discontinuous, decentred, layered, multiplicitous, multi-voiced, heterogeneous, and conflictual. The traditional notion of a unitary self has been severely tested, according to Brown, and now faces, at a theoretical level, dissolution, metamorphosis, and estrangement. Subjective time is represented in modern literature as 'a cabaret of disjunctive self-roles', reflected most poignantly in Leopold Bloom's passing thought, 'Me. And me now,' in which this most modernist of literary characters expresses a poignant sense of the apparent discontinuity between a present and a past self (Joyce, 1960, p. 176). Earlier in the same chapter (the Lestrygonians or 'Lunch' chapter), Bloom had had the thought: 'I was happier then. Or was that I? Or am I now I?' (p. 167).

Brown maintains that modernism, in its cultural, literary, and artistic senses, has been moving towards Parfit's notion of a series-person 'where interest is transferred from continuing identity to the "Relation R" between experience and world' (p. 142).[7] At any given moment, the self reveals itself as 'a collage of dispositions, conflicts, self-deceptions' (p. 42). Modernist literature in particular may be viewed as a struggle against 'the familiar Western conventions of coherence and the myth of Cartesian self-unity' (p. 129). It typically represents the psychological present as 'an archaic continuum where memory, perception, and possibility are co-equal generators of atomistic awareness' (p. 142). In the mind of Bloom, for example, memory, sensation, and passing thoughts erupt randomly into the present, effecting a complex continuum 'which belies the sequential self' (p. 143).

Much of the indiscriminate anti-Cartesianism that shapes contemporary conceptions of self-identity is present in Brown's book. There is little acknowledgement that the notion of a fragmented or discontinuous self is extremely problematic. The flux that Brown attributes to consciousness, for example, has in fact no negative implications for the 'unitary' concept of a self or subject, even where this is understood in a mythically Cartesian sense. It is simply a feature of consciousness that it can register memories, feelings, anticipations and other mental states in 'a complex continuum' without any apparent order, as is implicit in fact in the very phrase 'complex continuum'. Thinking in an orderly or sequential fashion is just one of the things that a conscious self can do, but if *thinking* is understood in the very broad sense in which Descartes used it, then any mental state, regardless of its ratiocinative status, is a mode of consciousness. It is this protean consciousness, moreover, which constitutes not only the self of the post-Cartesians but also the Cartesian self. As long as I exist, Descartes argued, the proposition 'cogito' is true of me, but as Kenny reminds us, 'the particular *cogitationes* that make it true vary from moment to moment, from dim prenatal pleasures to metaphysical speculations' (Kenny, 1968, p. 55). One might even say that there is nothing in the Joycean internal monologues that a Cartesian could not take to be a *cogitatio*. Indeed, substantial phases of the novel consist of the relatively banal and transient *cogitationes* of its central characters. In that respect it contrasts significantly with the pre-modernist, 'behaviouristic' sort of novel which tends to concentrate on dialogue and description.

One thing which is significant in this context is the fact that despite the internal monologuing of *Ulysses*, the reader can still identify the characters from their 'styles' of consciousness or thought. The inner life of Leopold Bloom is distinguishable from that of Stephen Dedalus or Molly Bloom. There may be no precise centre or boundaries to the selves that are Stephen, Leopold, or Molly but they nevertheless remain distinguishable and identifiable as distinctive personalities or consciousnesses, if not as characters in the conventional, well-defined, behaviouristic sense. Brown, indeed, is unable to avoid references to the 'selves' and inner-life styles of these characters, and even seems to contradict himself when he refers approvingly to 'the plenitude of selfhood' which Joyce manages to convey. He also makes the questionable assumption that 'unitary' means *simple* or *monadic* when he suggests that the notion of a unitary self would have as little meaning for Molly as the word 'metempsychosis'. The term 'unitary', however, can apply to any set or system of components, parts or processes, regardless of how diverse the components or the relations between them. All that matters is that the system function holistically or unitarily, i.e., as a unit. Molly's inconsistencies, contradictions and self-deceptions are still the *cogitationes* of Molly, and are only of interest insofar as they are brought together in the form of her voluble subjectivity and her fluent, hectic inner life. Her inconsistencies and contradictions would indeed not reveal themselves as such were it not for the fact that they occur identifiably and, dare one say, synchronically within the context of her particular subjectivity. The fact that her *cogitationes* - affirmations, negations, understandings, imaginings, sensations, desirings, and feelings, but above all affirmations - are presented not in discrete, logically sequential sentences but in

179

an unpunctuated stream of verbalized consciousness actually emphasizes the subjective unity-in-variety of her mental processes. Her monologue is nothing if not unified and integrated in its subjectivity, despite the diversity of inner states which she experiences and 'expresses'.

Given the inclusiveness of the Cartesian *cogitatio* there is no difficulty, in principle, in isolating any one of Molly's or Leopold's thoughts and, given the appropriate context, making it the basis of the Cogito! The assumption that the Cogito can be based only on intellectual or metaphysically speculative thought is erroneous, since doubts, deceptions, imaginings, feelings, sensations, 'being willing and unwilling' are also thoughts in Descartes' scheme of things. But Brown's most questionable assumption lies behind his claim that the changing, protean nature of consciousness must somehow corroborate his hypothesis of a fragmented or discontinuous self. When he takes Bloom's expression 'Me. And me now' as the symptomatic expression of a fragmented or divided self he effectively ignores the continuity of consciousness and memory that enables Bloom to have and articulate his passing thoughts and impressions. What Bloom experiences and expresses in this particular passing thought is not his fragmentation but rather his continuity or identity over a period of time. Bloom's passing thought is in fact reminiscent of Bishop Butler's observations on personal identity. Butler argued that there is no difficulty in ascertaining the idea 'wherein personal identity consists' (1896, p. 387). Just as the comparison of two triangles brings to mind the idea of similitude, 'so likewise, upon comparing the consciousnesses of one's self, or one's own existence, in any two moments, there as immediately arises to the mind the idea of personal identity' (p. 388). This latter comparison shows us the identity of ourselves in those two moments, 'the present, suppose, and the immediately past; or the present, and that a month, a year, or twenty years past' (p. 388). On Bloom's behalf, and against Brown, Butler would have said that, reflecting on the two moments of 'Me. And me now', one discerns that there are not two selves involved 'but one and the same self'.[8]

It should not be assumed that in citing Butler's critique of Locke or in defending Descartes against certain charges made against him that one is committed to the dualistic ontologies of either. Butler's critique of Locke is, simply, as valid as Shoemaker's critique of Parfit. A theme of both critiques is that mental states are not conceivable except as the states of something, in this case the states of a person. It should be added that the reductionist who posits mental states that are not in some sense the states *of* something is no better off than the anti-reductionist who posits a nonphysical ego as the subject of his mental states. Both philosophies present us with entities to which it is difficult, if not impossible, to give a local habitation and a name, conceptually speaking. It has been the motivating assumption of this book that in order to retain the distinction between the mental and the physical (for the sorts of reasons outlined by Rorty), it is not necessary to retain the concept of either a nonphysical ego or

180

of subject-less, detached mental states. A mental state is not necessarily the state of a 'disembodiable' ego in Descartes' sense. Since we possess the language of mental states and know what mental states are and how to ascribe them to ourselves and others, but since we do not possess an unproblematic concept of a disembodied ego, it follows that our continuing to talk about mental states or even minds and egos does not depend on showing whether certain arguments for substance dualism are erroneous or not.

If Nagel is right, a dualistic conception of the person or self does not in any case offer a better account of the nature of subjectivity than does the account offered by conventional physicalism. If Strawson is right, the very peculiar nature of psychological predicates cannot be accounted for by the notional picture of a world of disembodied, anti-social egos but only by the picture of a stable spatio-temporal world in which persons are necessarily embodied. If both Strawson and Shoemaker are right, the most significant fact about human beings is not that they are thinking things (although, of course, they are that) but that they are embodied language-users who have established a remarkable link between certain internal states and certain usages of language in which inner-state predicates are ascribed criterially to others but noncriterially to oneself. None of these facts of language and psychology are better explicated by dualists than by physicalists, although physicalists do not always explicate them very well either. If some materialists - for example, Bunge and Davidson - are right, there is no reason why a commitment to the irreducibility of the mental should imply at the same time a commitment to the notion of a disembodiable ego. The conceivability of such an ego does not have to be ruled out, of course, but the point is that we are not committing ourselves to the existence of such an ego when we argue in favour of the proposition that any conscious human individual has a mind, a self and an inner life. In defending this proposition we are not defending a problematic ontology but rather a way of speaking about and characterizing human individuals. It is only through the language of mind, self, and inner process that we can grant ourselves a basic autonomy and privacy, including the very basic right to make certain kinds of claims about ourselves. It is only through the language of the first-person perspective that we can set fundamental moral and political limits to the objectifying perspectives of third parties. It is only in terms of the language of interiority that people living in a materialist and technocratic era can begin to fully acknowledge the miracle of uniquely individual lives and consciousnesses.

Notes

1.   This term was first used by Sidney Shoemaker (1970, p. 271): 'What we need to consider is whether there could be a kind of knowledge of past events such that someone's having this sort of knowledge of an event does

181

involve there being a correspondence between his present cognitive state and a past cognitive and sensory state that was of the event, but such that this correspondence, although otherwise just like that which exists in memory, does not necessarily involve that past state's having been a state of the very same person who subsequently has the knowledge. Let us speak of such knowledge, supposing for the moment that it is possible, as "quasi-memory knowledge," and let us say that a person who has this sort of knowledge of a past event "quasi-remembers" that past event.' Shoemaker concludes that if our concern is with our present concept of personal identity, rather than with a concept of identity that would obtain in a hypothetical world of psychological fission and fusion, then the notion of quasi-remembering cannot be taken very seriously.

2. See Shoemaker (1963, pp. 48-63) for an important discussion of the attempt by Broad and Russell to re-interpret the terms 'substance', 'subject' and 'ego' as meaning whatever is designated by the grammatical subject of a psychological statement.

3. This is a condensed and re-formatted version of Parfit, 1984, pp. 210-13.

4. For a discussion of the notion of a 'structured' Humean bundle, see Andrew Brennan (1988, p. 290).

5. As Bernard Williams points out, Hume's account of personal identity is the most revealingly mistaken in this respect, especially when he writes as follows: 'Suppose we could see clearly into the breast of another, and observe that succession of perceptions, which constitutes his mind or thinking principle, and suppose that he always preserves the memory of a considerable part of past perceptions ...' (Hume, 1888, Bk. I, Pt. IV, §VI) Thus an externalized view of a person's mind is attempted, but it is, according to Williams, a view obtainable from no conceivable vantage point. (See Williams, 1964, p. 339).

6. See Bishop Butler (1896, pp. 338-9): 'But though consciousness of what is past does thus ascertain our personal identity to ourselves, yet to say that it makes personal identity, or is necessary to our being the same persons, is to say that a person has not existed a single moment, nor done one action, but what he can remember ....

   This wonderful mistake may possibly have arisen from hence; that to be endued with consciousness is inseparable from the idea of a person, or intelligent being.... But though present consciousness of what we at present do and feel is necessary to our being the persons we now are; yet present consciousness of past actions or feelings is not necessary to our being the same persons who performed those actions, or had those feelings.'

7. An interesting dramatization of the problem of personal identity in pre-modern literature is to be found in Robert Louis Stevenson's *Dr Jekyll and Mr Hyde* (1886). In the concluding chapter, Dr Jekyll explains his

preoccupation with 'man's dual nature' and, most interestingly, hazards the guess 'that man will be ultimately known for a mere polity of multifarious, incongruous and independent denizens.'

8.   When Butler synopsizes the views of those whom he regards as confusing consciousness with personality or self, he prophetically anticipates the sort of view that would be expressed a century later by Parfit, Brown, and other bundle theorists. He summarizes the views of the 'hasty followers' of Locke thus: 'That personality is not a permanent, but a transient thing: that it lives and dies, begins and ends continually: that no one can any more remain one and the same person two moments together, than two successive moments can be one and the same moment: that our substance is indeed continually changing; but whether this be so or not, is, it seems, nothing to the purpose; since it is not substance, but consciousness alone, which constitutes personality; which consciousness being successive, cannot be the same in any two moments, nor consequently the personality constituted by it' (1896, p. 392).

Bibliography

Adams, Charles & Tannery, Paul, eds. (1897-1913), *Oeuvres de Descartes*, Paris: Leopold Cerf.

Alexander, Peter (1963), *Sensationalism and Scientific Explanation*, London: Routledge & Kegan Paul.

Anscombe, G.E.M. (1981), *Metaphysics and the Philosophy of Mind*, Oxford: Basil Blackwell.

Armstrong, D.M. (1968), *A Materialist Theory of the Mind*, London: Routledge & Kegan Paul.

Armstrong, D.M. (1970), 'The Nature of Mind,' in Borst, C.V. (ed.), *The Mind/Brain Identity Theory*, London: Macmillan.

Austin, J.L. (1962) *How to do things with Words*, Oxford: Clarendon Press.

Ayer, A.J. (1946), *Language, Truth and Logic*, Harmondsworth: Penguin.

Baier, Kurt (1970), 'Smart on Sensations,' in Borst, C.V. (ed.), *The Mind/Brain Identity Theory*, London: Macmillan.

Baker, G.P. & Hacker, P.M.S. (1984), *Scepticism, Rules and Language*, Oxford: Basil Blackwell.

Bedford, Errol (1967) 'Emotions,' in Gustafson, Donald F. (ed.), *Essays in Philosophical Psychology*, London: Macmillan.

Brennan, Andrew (1988), *Conditions of Identity*, Oxford: Clarendon Press.

Brown, Dennis (1989), *The Modernist Self in Twentieth-Century English Literature*, London: Macmillan.

Buck, R.C. (1986), 'Non-other Minds,' in Canfield, John V. (ed.), *The Private Language Argument*, New York: Praeger.

Bunge, Mario (1981), *Scientific Materialism*, Dordrecht: Reidel Publishing Co.

Butler, Joseph (1896), *The Works of Joseph Butler*, ed. W.E. Gladstone, Oxford: Clarendon Press.

Canfield, John (1991), *The Looking Glass Self*, New York: Praeger.

Christopher, Milbourne (1970), *Seers, Psychics and ESP*, London: Cassell.

Churchland, P.M. (1979), *Scientific Realism and the Plasticity of Mind*, Cambridge: Cambridge University Press.

Churchland, P.M. (1984), *Matter and Consciousness*, Cambridge, Mass: MIT Press.

Churchland, P.M. (1989), *A Neurocomputational Perspective: The Nature of Mind and the Structure of Science*, Cambridge, Mass: MIT Press.

Churchland, P.M. & Churchland, Patricia S. (1990), 'Could a Machine Think?' *Scientific American*, vol. 262, no. 1, Jan., pp. 26-31.

Collier, Andrew (1977), *R.D. Laing: The Philosophy and Politics of Psychotherapy*, Brighton: Harvester Press.

Cottingham, John, Stoothoff, Robert, & Murdoch, Dugald, eds. (1985, 1991), *The Philosophical Writings of Descartes*, Cambridge: Cambridge University Press.

Coward, Rosalind & Ellis, John (1977), *Language and Materialism: Developments in Semiology and the Theory of the Subject*, London: Routledge & Kegan Paul.

Davidson, Donald (1980), *Essays on Actions and Events*, Oxford: Clarendon Press, 1980.

Dennett, Daniel C. (1985), *Brainstorms*, Brighton: Harvester Press.

Dennett, Daniel C. (1988), *The Intentional Stance*, Cambridge, Mass: MIT Press.

Dennett, Daniel C. (1990), 'Quining Qualia,' in Lycan, William G. (ed.), *Mind and Cognition*, Oxford: Basil Blackwell.

Dennett, Daniel C. (1991), *Consciousness Explained*, London: Allen Lane.

Dews, Peter (1987), *The Logics of Disintegration*, London: Verso.

Edelman, Gerald (1994), *Bright Air, Brilliant Fire*, Harmondsworth: Penguin.

Feigl, Herbert (1969), 'Mind-body not a Pseudoproblem,' in Hook, Sidney (ed.), *Dimensions of Mind*, New York: New York University Press.

Feyerabend, Paul (1975), *Against Method*, London: Verso.

Fodor, J. A. (1984), 'Observation Reconsidered,' *Philosophy of Science*, 51, pp. 23-43.

Foucault, Michel (1977), *Discipline and Punish*, trans. Alan Sheridan, Harmondsworth: Penguin.

Foucault, Michel (1980), *Power/Knowledge: Selected Interviews and Other Writings 1972-77*, ed. Colin Gordon, New York: Harvester Wheatsheaf.

Foucault, Michel (1984), *The History of Sexuality*, Harmondsworth: Penguin.

Foucault, Michel (1986), *The Care of the Self*, trans. Robert Hurley, New York: Pantheon Books.

Foucault, Michel (1988), *Technologies of the Self: A Seminar with Michel Foucault*, ed. Luther H. Martin, et al., Amherst: University of Massachussets Press.

Freud, Sigmund (1960), *The Psychopathology of Everyday Life*, trans. James Strachey, London: Hogarth Press.

185

Geach, Peter (1957), *Mental Acts,* London: Routledge & Kegan Paul.

Gunderson, Keith (1985), *Mentality and Machines,* 2nd ed., Minneapolis: Minnesota University Press.

Hacker, P.M.S. (1975), *Insight and Illusion,* Oxford: Oxford University Press.

Hampshire, Stuart (1959), *Thought and Action,* London: Chatto & Windus.

Hampshire, Stuart (1972), *Freedom of Mind,* Oxford: Clarendon Press.

Hannay, Alastair (1990), *Human Consciousness,* London: Routledge.

Hanson, N.R. (1958), *Patterns of Discovery,* Cambridge: Cambridge University Press.

Hempel, C.G. (1966), *Philosophy of Natural Science,* Englewood Cliffs, N.J.: Prentice Hall.

Hintikka, Jaakko (1967), 'Cogito, Ergo Sum: Inference or Performance?' in Doney, Willis (ed.), *Descartes: A Collection of Critical Essays,* New York: Doubleday & Co.

Hume, David (1739), *A Treatise of Human Nature,* ed. L.A. Selby-Bigge (1888), Oxford: Clarendon Press.

Hutton, Patrick H. (1988), 'Foucault, Freud, and the Technologies of the Self, in Luther H. Martin, et al (eds.), *Technologies of the Self: A Seminar with Michel Foucault,* Amherst: University of Massachussets Press.

Jackson, Frank (1990), 'Epiphenomenal Qualia,' in Lycan, William G. (ed.), *Mind and Cognition,* Oxford: Blackwell.

James, William (1950), *The Principles of Psychology,* Vol. 1, New York: Dover.

Joyce, James (1960), *Ulysses,* 2nd ed., Harmondsworth: The Bodley Head & Penguin.

Kenny, Anthony (1966), 'Cartesian Privacy', in Pitcher, George (ed.), *Wittgenstein: The Philosophical Investigations,* London: Macmillan.

Kenny, Anthony (1989), *The Metaphysics of Mind,* Oxford: Clarendon Press.

Kim, Jaegwon (1972), 'Phenomenal Properties, Psychological Laws, and the Identity Theory,' *The Monist* 56, pp. 177-92.

Kripke, Saul (1982), *Wittgenstein On Rules and Private Language,* Oxford: Basil Blackwell.

Lacan, Jacques (1977), *Ecrits: A Selection,* trans. Alan Sheridan, London: Tavistock.

Lacan, Jacques (1979), *The Four Fundamental Concepts of Psycho-Analysis,* trans. Alan Sheridan, Harmondsworth: Penguin.

Locke, John (1690), *An Essay Concerning Human Understanding,* ed. A.C. Fraser (1959), New York: Dover.

Lockwood, Michael (1989), *Mind, Brain and the Quantum,* Oxford: Basil Blackwell.

Lyons, William (1980), *Gilbert Ryle: An Introduction to his Philosophy,* Brighton: Harvester Press, 1980.

Lyons, William (1986), *The Disappearance of Introspection*, Cambridge, Mass.: MIT Press.

Macdonald, Cynthia (1989), *Mind-Body Identity Theories*, London: Routledge.

Mach, Ernst (1959), *Contribution to the Analysis of Sensation*, trans. C. M. Williams, New York.

Malcolm, Norman (1964), 'Behaviourism as a Philosophy of Psychology,' in Wann, T.W. (ed.), *Phenomenology and Behaviourism*, Chicago: Chicago University Press.

Malcolm, Norman (1986), 'Whether "I" is a Referring Expression' in Canfield, John V. (ed.), *The Philosophy of Wittgenstein: Persons*, New York: Garland Publishing, Inc.

Malcolm, Norman (1986), *Nothing is Hidden: Wittgenstein's Criticism of his Early Thought*, Oxford: Basil Blackwell.

Malcolm, Norman (1972), *Problems of Mind*, London: George Allen & Unwin.

Marshall, Sandra E. (1991), 'Public Bodies, Private Selves,' in Almond, Brenda & Hill, Donald (eds.), *Applied Philosophy: Morals and Metaphysics in Contemporary Debate*, London: Routledge.

McGinn, Colin (1982), *The Character of Mind*, Oxford: Clarendon Press.

McGinn, Colin (1983), *The Subjective View*, Oxford: Oxford University Press.

McGinn, Colin (1984), *Wittgenstein on Meaning*, Oxford: Basil Blackwell.

McGinn, Colin (1991), *The Problem of Consciousness*, Oxford: Basil Blackwell.

Minsky, Marvin (1985), *The Society of Mind*, New York: Simon & Schuster.

Nagel, E. (1961), *The Structure of Science*, London: Routledge & Kegan Paul.

Nagel, Thomas (1970), 'Physicalism,' in Borst, C.V. (ed.), *The Mind-Brain Identity Theory*, London: Macmillan.

Nagel, Thomas (1979), *Mortal Questions*, Cambridge: Cambridge University Press.

Nagel, Thomas (1986), *The View from Nowhere*, Oxford: Oxford University Press.

Nozick, Robert (1981), *Philosophical Explanations*, Cambridge, Mass.: Harvard University Press.

Nielsen, Kai (1971), *Reason and Practice*, New York: Harper & Row, 1971.

Papert, Seymour (1988), 'One AI or Many?' in Graubard, Stephen (ed.), *The Artificial Intelligence Debate*, Cambridge, Mass.: MIT Press.

Parfit, Derek (1979), 'Personal Identity,' in Honderich, T. and Burnyeat, M. (eds.), *Philosophy As It Is*, Harmondsworth: Penguin.

Parfit, Derek (1984), *Reasons and Persons*, Oxford: Clarendon Press.

Parfit, Derek (1989), 'Divided Minds and the Nature of Persons,' in Blakemore, Colin and Greenfield, Susan (eds.), *Mindwaves*, Oxford: Basil Blackwell.

Pears, David (1971), *Wittgenstein*, London: Fontana.

Place, U.T. (1962), 'Is Consciousness a Brain Process?' in Chappell, V.C. (ed.), *Philosophy of Mind*, Englewood Cliffs, N. J: Prentice Hall, 1962.

Proust, M., (1949), *Within a Budding Grove*, trans. C.K. Scott-Moncrieff, London: Chatto & Windus.

Putnam, Hilary (1975), *Mind, Language and Reality*, Cambridge: Cambridge University Press.

Putnam, Hilary (1981), *Reason, Truth and History*, Cambridge: Cambridge University Press.

Putnam, Hilary (1988), 'Much Ado About Not Very Much,' in Graubard, Stephen (ed.), *The Artificial Intelligence Debate,* Cambridge, Mass: MIT Press.

Reeke, George N. & Edelman, Gerald M. (1988), 'Real Brains and Artificial Intelligence,' in Graubard, Stephen (ed.), *The Artificial Intelligence Debate*, Cambridge, Mass.: MIT Press.

Reid, Thomas (1785), *Essays on the Intellectual Powers of Man*, ed. Baruch Brody (1969), Cambridge, Mass.: MIT Press.

Robey, David (1982), 'Modern Linguistics and the Language of Literature,' in Jefferson, Ann and Robey, David (eds.), *Modern Literary Theory*, London: Batsford.

Rorty, Amélie O., ed. (1976), *The Identities of Persons,* Berkeley: University of California Press.

Rorty, Richard (1965), 'Mind-body identity, privacy and categories', *Review of Metaphysics*, 29, pp. 24-54; repr. in Borst, C.V. ed., (1970), *The Mind/Brain Identity Theory*, London: Macmillan, pp. 187-213.

Rorty, Richard (1970), 'Incorrigibility as the Mark of the Mental', *The Journal of Philosophy*, vol. 67, pp. 399-424.

Rorty, Richard (1980), *Philosophy and the Mirror of Nature*, Oxford: Basil Blackwell.

Rossi, Paolo (1968), *Francis Bacon: from Magic to Science*, London: Routledge & Kegan Paul.

Rumelhart, D.E. & McClelland, J.L. (1986), *Parallel Distributed Processing*, Cambridge, Mass.: MIT Press.

Ryle, Gilbert (1949), *The Concept of Mind*, New York: Barnes & Noble.

Ryle, Gilbert (1971), *Collected Papers*, London: Hutchinson.

Sarup, Madan 1992), *Jacques Lacan*, New York: Harvester Wheatsheaf.

Saussure, F. de (1983), *Course in General Linguistics*, trans. Roy Harris, London: Duckworth.

Schwartz, Jacob T. (1988), 'The New Connectionism,' in Graubard, Stephen (ed.), *The Artificial Intelligence Debate*, Cambridge, Mass.: MIT Press.

Searle, J.R. (1984), *Minds, Brains and Science*, London: BBC Publications.

Searle, J.R. (1990), 'Is the Brain's Mind a Computer Program?' *Scientific American*, vol. 262, no. 1, Jan., pp. 20-5.

Searle, J.R. (1992), *The Rediscovery of the Mind*, Cambridge, Mass: MIT Press.

Sellars, Wilfrid (1963), *Science, Perception and Reality*, London: Routledge & Kegan Paul.

Shanker, S.G. (1989), 'The Decline and Fall of the Mechanist Metaphor,' in Born, R. (ed.), *Artificial Intelligence: The Case Against*, London: Routledge.

Shoemaker, Sidney (1963), *Self-Knowledge and Self-Identity*, Ithaca: Cornell University Press.

Shoemaker, Sidney (1970), 'Persons and their Pasts,' *American Philosophical Quarterly*, vol. 7, pp. 269-85

Shoemaker, Sidney (1985), 'Critical Notice of *Reasons and Persons*,' *Mind*, 1985, vol. 94, pp. 443-53.

Shoemaker, Sidney, (1968), 'Self-Reference and Self-Awareness', *The Journal of Philosophy*, vol. 65, No 19, pp. 555-67.

Silverman, Kaja (1983), *The Subject of Semiotics*, Oxford: Oxford University Press.

Skinner, B.F. (1964) 'Behaviourism at Fifty,' in Wann, T.W. (ed.), *Phenomenology and Behaviourism*, Chicago: Chicago University Press.

Skinner, B.F. (1965), *Science and Human Behaviour*, New York: Macmillan.

Smart, J.J.C. (1970), 'Sensations and Brain Processes,' in Borst, C.V. (ed.), *The Mind/Brain Identity Theory*, London: Macmillan.

Strawson, P.F. (1959), *Individuals*, London: Methuen.

Thorndike, Lynn (1964), *The History of Magic and Experimental Science*, New York: Columbia University Press.

Thorndike, Lynn (1967), *The Place of Magic in the Intellectual History of Europe*, New York: Columbia University Press.

Turing, A.M. (1950), 'Computing Machinery and Intelligence,' *Mind*, vol. 59, pp. 433-60.

Turkle, Sherry (1988), 'Artificial Intelligence and Psychoanalysis: A New Alliance,' in Graubard, Stephen (ed.), *The Artificial Intelligence Debate*, Cambridge, Mass.: MIT Press.

van Fraassen, Bas C. (1980), *The Scientific Image*, Oxford: Oxford University Press.

Webster, Charles (1980), *From Paracelsus to Newton: the Making of Modern Science*, Cambridge: Cambridge University Press.

Wiggins, David (1967), *Identity and Spatio-temporal Continuity*, Oxford: Oxford University Press.

Williams, Bernard (1978), *Descartes: The Project of Pure Enquiry*, Harmondsworth: Penguin.

Wilson, Margaret Dauler (1978), *Descartes*, London: Routledge and Kegan Paul.

Wisdom, J. (1962), 'The Concept of Mind,' in Chappell, V.C. (ed.), *The Philosophy of Mind*, Englewood Cliffs: Prentice Hall.

Wittgenstein, L. (1963), *Philosophical Investigations*, 3rd ed., trans. G.E.M. Anscombe, Oxford: Blackwell.

Wittgenstein, L. (1969), *On Certainty*, trans. G.E.M. Anscombe, Oxford: Basil Blackwell.

Wittgenstein, L. (1972), *The Blue and Brown Books*, 2nd ed., Oxford: Basil Blackwell.

Wright, Elizabeth (1982), 'Modern Psychoanalytic Criticism,' in Jefferson, Ann and Robey, David (eds.), *Modern Literary Theory*, London: Batsford.

Yolton, John W. (1984), *Perceptual Acquaintance from Descartes to Reid*, Minneapolis: University of Minnesota Press.

Index

125, 141-144, 150

Edelman, G., 74, 124, 131
eliminative materialism, 73, 76, 77
eliminativism, 79, 82, 84
emergentism, 63, 64, 66, 127
emergent properties, 64, 125, 126

Feigl, H., 55
Feyerabend, P., 84
Fodor, J.A., 83
folk psychology, 75, 76, 79, 82,
    85, 150
folk theory, 1, 76-79, 81, 84, 87,
    91
Foucault, M., 2, 151-158
Freud, S., 121, 122, 146, 148
functionalism, 76, 110-113, 116,
    117, 119, 120, 122
    Turing-machine, 113

Gassendi, P., 24
Geach, P., 19
Gunderson, K., 110, 113, 120

Hacker, P.M.S., 5, 6, 8, 9, 21
Hampshire, S., 39, 51
Hannay, A., viii
Hanson, N.R., 88
Hintikka, J., 51, 136, 158
Hume, D., 136, 165, 169, 182
Hutton, P.H., 153, 157

'I'
  as object, 96, 132
  as subject, 96, 132, 135, 136
identity theory, 53, 58-61, 76, 113
  token-token, 61
  type-type, 60
incorrigibility, 13, 24, 56, 69, 71,
    72, 74, 85, 118
indexicals, 94, 95
  indexical expressions, 93

indexical thoughts, 93
inner eye, 17, 22, 119
inner process, 11, 14, 21, 26, 27,
    49, 53-57, 68, 69, 108, 115,
    119, 181
intentional stance, 114, 116, 125
intentional system, 113, 114, 117,
    118, 120, 122
intentionality, 64, 71, 98, 113
interiority, 1, 3, 4, 11, 33, 50, 55,
    61, 62, 91, 103, 147, 181
introspection, 1, 2, 4, 16-18, 24,
    27-29, 32, 42, 43, 46-51, 58,
    59, 60, 65-72, 75, 112, 117,
    119, 125, 131, 165

Jackson, F., 59
James, W., 24, 46
Joyce, J., 131, 178, 179

Kant, I., 69, 159
Kenny, A., 5, 10, 12, 24, 69, 179
Kim, J., 60
Kripke, S., 7-9, 12, 19

La Mettrie, J., 120
Lacan, J., 2, 3, 146-151, 165, 166
Lashley, K., 119
learned animals, 109, 110
  and neural nets, 108
Leibniz's Law, 55-59
Locke, J., 17, 18, 24, 29, 46, 69,
    94, 169, 172-174, 177, 180,
    183
Lockwood, M., 110
Lyons, W., 24, 32, 36, 37, 46-49,
    68, 122, 131

Macdonald, C., 60
Mach, E., 165
magic, 100, 108
Malcolm, N., 40, 48, 50, 58, 64,
    86, 116, 133, 134

192

193